Praise for

3 KINGS

"Millions of words have been written about these titans and their empires, but precious few have been written by business reporters who examine how they actually got where they are. Greenburg brings a business perspective along with just enough context and history so that this book can be appreciated and understood by both hip-hop heads and the financial world."

— Jem Aswad, senior music editor, *Variety*

"Greenburg reveals a blueprint for how billions were made by and for the artists themselves. An excellent read and a valuable education for entrepreneurs, industry insiders and outsiders, and music aficionados.... A uniquely American story of entrepreneurship."

— Josh Davis, author of *Two Awesome Hours:*
Science-Based Strategies to Harness Your Best Time
and Get Your Most Important Work Done

"A vividly clear depiction of the commercial empires built by Diddy, Jay-Z, and Dr Dre. The book documents their humble beginnings and their rise to fame, and illustrates their important connections to the pioneers who paved the way for their success."

— Rocky Bucano, president of the
Universal Hip Hop Museum

"Finance is a central focus in hip-hop, but few writers have the facts and figures to discuss it credibly. Greenburg demystifies three iconic rap artists who these days make most of their money apart from rap. It's a well-constructed analysis that you don't need to be an expert to appreciate."

— Ben Westhoff, author of *Original Gangstas:*
The Untold Story of Dr. Dre, Eazy-E, Ice Cube,
Tupac Shakur, and the Birth of West Coast Rap

"Greenburg has become one of the rare reporters to bring dignified coverage of the hip-hop business into the mainstream."

—Dan Charnas, author of *The Big Payback: The History of the Business of Hip-Hop*

"A pleasingly broad perspective of hip-hop as economic triumph... Greenburg's vivid descriptions—a small sampling includes the 'farty bass lines' of Dre's G-funk period; Suge Knight in his notorious 1995 Source Awards appearance 'looking like a gang-affiliated Kool-Aid Man'; and Diddy dressed like 'a very fashionable porcupine'— make for engaging reporting that will satisfy neophytes and devotees alike. A wide-ranging survey of the first four decades of hip-hop that vividly brings some of the culture's biggest success stories into one place."

—*Kirkus Reviews*

"A veteran music journalist who can successfully draw parallels between street-art culture and multimillion-dollar corporate mergers, Greenburg is the perfect person to take us on a journey through the ascent of hip-hop's greats. He's able to reveal previously hidden sides of rap's 'cash kings' (a term he coined) through deep sourcing, in-depth research, and a true love of and respect for the genre. I came away with a new understanding of hip-hop's trajectory and the significance it bears for general cultural history."

—Hana Alberts, features editor, *New York Post*

"Plain and simple: I'm just a diehard fan."

—Kevin Olusola, Grammy-winning member of Pentatonix

3 KINGS

3 KINGS

DIDDY, DR. DRE, JAY-Z, and HIP-HOP'S MULTIBILLION-DOLLAR RISE

ZACK O'MALLEY GREENBURG

Little, Brown and Company

New York • Boston • London

Little, Brown and Company
Hachette Book Group
1290 Avenue of the Americas, New York, NY 10104
littlebrown.com

First Edition: March 2018

Little, Brown and Company is a division of Hachette Book Group, Inc. The Little, Brown name and logo are trademarks of Hachette Book Group, Inc.

The publisher is not responsible for websites (or their content) that are not owned by the publisher.

The Hachette Speakers Bureau provides a wide range of authors for speaking events. To find out more, go to hachettespeakersbureau.com or call (866) 376-6591.

Crown icon design by Fab 5 Freddy

Library of Congress Cataloging-in-Publication Data
Names: Greenburg, Zack O'Malley.
Title: 3 kings: Diddy, Dr. Dre, Jay-Z, and hip-hop's multibillion-dollar rise / Zack O'Malley Greenburg.
Description: First edition. | New York: Little, Brown and Company, 2018. | Includes bibliographical references and index.
Identifiers: LCCN 2017021046 | ISBN 978-0-316-31653-8
Subjects: LCSH: Rap (Music)—History and criticism. | Rap (Music)—Economic aspects. | Diddy, 1969- | Dr. Dre, 1965– | Jay-Z, 1969–
Classification: LCC ML3531 .G74 2018 | DDC 782.421649092/2—dc23
LC record available at https://lccn.loc.gov/2017021046.

10 9 8 7 6 5 4 3 2 1

LSC-C

Printed in the United States of America

For Danielle, the realest doctor of all

Contents

Foreword xi

Introduction 3

CHAPTER 1: The Originators 13

CHAPTER 2: Writing on the Wall 37

CHAPTER 3: Bad Boys 60

CHAPTER 4: Studio Gangsters 83

CHAPTER 5: Aftermath 105

CHAPTER 6: Fashion Fortunes 125

CHAPTER 7: A Fourth King? 141

CHAPTER 8: The Beats Generation 162

CHAPTER 9: Grape Expectations 180

CHAPTER 10: Sound Investments 199

CHAPTER 11: Ice in the Winter 218

CHAPTER 12: State of the Art 234

AFTERWORD: Kings, Queens, Presidents, and Precedents 249

Acknowledgments 253

Giving Back 256

Cast of Characters 257

Notes 265

Index 298

Foreword

In the old-school world of New York graffiti — starting in the late 1960s when this then-infant form of creative expression, one of the foundational pillars of hip-hop culture, raged across the streets and walls of New York City and its buses, subways, and commercial vehicles — a crown above your name meant you'd designated yourself a king.

Originally, it meant a king of a certain train line — like the A, B, C, or D, or the 1, 2, 3, 4, 5, 6, et cetera. There was no royal court or governing body overseeing these coronations, but in the first decade of the New York graffiti movement, already on the verge of becoming the international street-art movement it is today, graffiti writers who placed a crown over their names felt they earned the right to do so after extensive "tagging" or "bombing," as we called it. If "toys" — graffiti writers with little style and/or minimal saturation of their tag throughout the five boroughs — placed a crown over their tags, other graffiti writers would cross them out or just obliterate them by writing "toy" on top. A wannabe king, humiliated and dethroned.

In the late '70s and early '80s, the crown became a part of the vocabulary of images and embellishments as tagging evolved into spray-painted multicolored mural extravaganzas. Numerous styles of crowns were developed to adorn one's work. My dear deceased friend and cultural comrade Jean-Michel Basquiat developed his own unique graffiti crown. It looked like the letter *V*, multiplied by three and turned upside down, with a straight line across the bottom. Jean's blunt and simple crown became ubiquitous in the downtown areas of Manhattan, where we hung out in the early 1980s, as did his graffiti name, SAMO.

When Jean began to make art, he occasionally drew his crown on his paintings and drawings. His crown has become an iconic symbol to his many fans—including this book's three kings, as I've learned from firsthand conversations. Dre considers Jean to be a kindred artistic spirit; Jay-Z shouts him out in song lyrics and displays his work in his own home; Puffy even has a Basquiat crown tattooed on the back of his neck.

Tattoos today often look to me like physical graffiti of the New York street. Many people have a hodgepodge of images and words done by various tattoo artists on various parts of their bodies, some with deep significance. When Puffy put that Basquiat crown on his neck, he did it to send a clear message. Like Basquiat and New York graffiti writers from decades past, Puffy was rightfully designating himself a king. And like Dre and Jay-Z, the pioneers of graffiti mostly emerged from modest urban means to seize and remix that classic rags-to-riches American Dream story while dominating the zeitgeist of global popular culture.

The crown I made for the cover of this book is a funky fresh Fab 5 Freddy version that hearkens back to old-school crowns that decorated and/or defaced walls, trains, and buses all over New York City back in graffiti's heyday. The interior colorful areas of my crown were sampled from recent paintings I've made, and I digitally placed chunks in the body of the crown's outline. It's a classic graffiti crown remixed for this, my first book cover—a fitting adornment for this insightful look at the three kings and the revolutionary movement driving and driven by them, crowned by one of hip-hop's own.

Fab 5 Freddy
New York, September 2017

3 KINGS

I was flying somewhere over the Atlantic Ocean on a red-eye when word of the biggest deal in hip-hop history to date leaked. Apple had agreed to buy Beats, Andre "Dr. Dre" Young's headphones and music streaming company, for somewhere around $3 billion.

The news started ricocheting around the Internet in early May 2014, after actor Tyrese Gibson released a grainy YouTube video. "They need to update the *Forbes* list," he said, speaking of the magazine's annual accounting of rap's richest acts, while in the midst of a raucous party. "Shit just changed." Then Dre floated into the frame. "The first billionaire in hip-hop," he proclaimed. "Right here from the motherfucking West Coast!"[1]

I discovered all this when I landed, groggy, in Milan and turned on my phone, only to be greeted by casual inquiries from friends, frenzied questions from colleagues, and urgent requests from print, radio, and television producers and reporters for insight into what the news meant for Dre's wealth. Had he become a billionaire? Or at least the richest man in hip-hop? I should know. For the past decade, I've been charting the wealth of the top names for *Forbes*. After the Beats deal went through, I updated Dre's total to $700 million — were it not for the taxman's cut, the deal could have catapulted him to billionaire status then and there. Even so, today Sean "Diddy" Combs, Shawn "Jay-Z" Carter, and Dre are worth around $2.5 billion, per my latest *Forbes* estimates. They are not only the three wealthiest hip-hop acts in the country but the three richest American musicians working in any genre.

These three kings have built their fortunes by creating a 24/7, head-to-toe lifestyle. Because of them, we can start any given day by donning a pair of Jay-Z's Reebok S. Carter sneakers and some Beats headphones, and then heading to a meal at Jay-Z's Spotted Pig restaurant in New York. One might spend the next few hours watching Dez Bryant or Yoenis Céspedes, his sports agency's clients, play an afternoon game, topped off with a glass of his Armand de Brignac champagne or D'Ussé cognac at his 40/40 Club. If the evening goes on to include a few shots of Diddy's Cîroc vodka, it might be necessary to gulp down a bottle of his Aquahydrate alkaline water before slipping under crisp Sean John sheets and dozing off while watching something on his Revolt cable channel, perhaps Dre's film *Straight Outta Compton*.

Just how the trio turned hip-hop into one of the world's most influential and lucrative cultural movements is among the most fascinating business stories of our time. Diddy, Dre, and Jay-Z all grew up effectively fatherless, developed a flair for music, started their own record labels, and released classic albums before moving on to become multifaceted moguls. But despite the basic similarities of their backgrounds and trajectories, the three men aren't so alike. If they all took the Myers-Briggs test, the results would likely be three different personality types. If anyone who knew the trio well had to cast them as Marvel superheroes, or Disney princesses, or Teenage Mutant Ninja Turtles, all three would inevitably end up in disparate roles.[2]

Their traits and paths offer three distinct blueprints for aspiring entrepreneurs. Legendary lyricist Jay-Z plays business like a chess game, plotting moves years—perhaps decades—in advance. Super-producer Dr. Dre is a quiet, intuitive perfectionist prone to social anxiety; he waited to extend his brand until he found something just right, with Beats. Diddy is a charismatic and blustery impresario who has shilled for everything from high-end spirits to acne medication. "I call myself a curator of cool," he told me in a one-on-one keynote interview at South by Southwest in 2014. "I'm not always cool, but that's what I like to call myself when I'm in the zone."[3]

The trio grew up in kingdoms quite different from the ones they later built. Jay-Z's Brooklyn was a gritty, crime-ridden borough unrecognizable from the yuppie utopia it has since become. Dre's Compton, once an oasis that lured midcentury middle-class black families from the rust belt to California, fell victim to racist urban-planning schemes and economic blight. Diddy's Harlem was similarly dangerous during the 1970s and '80s, though it did boast quite a rich heritage. "Harlem became famous when disenfranchised black folks who'd migrated from the Caribbean and the southern states in the beginnings of the twentieth century had a chance to live and feel free for the first time," says Harlem resident and hip-hop pioneer Fred "Fab 5 Freddy" Brathwaite. "This sense of freedom affected every aspect of Harlemites' lives, hence the stylish swagger of folks like Duke Ellington, Count Basie, Bumpy Johnson, and Adam Clayton Powell Jr., [which] all led up to Puff Daddy."[4]

That's the sort of attitude that propelled Diddy to attend prestigious Howard University and then drop out to take a job at Uptown Records in the early 1990s—and, soon after that, start his own label, Bad Boy. Dr. Dre morphed from a teenage disco DJ into one of hip-hop's first superstars as the sonic mastermind of seminal rap group N.W.A. in the late 1980s. Jay-Z's education came from the streets, where he learned the laws of supply and demand while selling cocaine; eventually he plowed those profits into creating his own Roc-A-Fella Records to put out his debut after major labels passed. Indeed, many of hip-hop's most prominent examples of entrepreneurship started out as matters of necessity.

As hip-hop opened the door for a wide range of trends in areas from clothing to cars, mainstream America started taking stylistic cues from rappers. By the 1990s, the genre had attracted not just inner-city fans but massive numbers of Midwestern suburbanites and Hamptons socialites. "They all wanted Rolls-Royces just because hip-hop has got

Rolls-Royces," says Russell Simmons, the founder of Def Jam Recordings and Phat Farm clothing.[5] (As this book was going to press, Simmons was accused of sexual assault and/or rape by several women; he has denied the allegations.) Diddy, Dre, and Jay-Z replicated and improved on Simmons's brand extensions by doing what he couldn't as a behind-the-scenes executive: using their own songs and videos as an opportunity to promote their business ventures.

All three kings are now friends and collaborators—a remarkable feat, given that they found themselves on opposing sides of the deadly rap wars of the mid-1990s, which took the lives of Dr. Dre's labelmate Tupac Shakur and Diddy's close friend Christopher "Notorious B.I.G." Wallace. In the wake of intense conflict, the kings reinvented themselves through business, each developing a different calling card.

Dr. Dre became the most sought-after producer in the industry, a beatmaker who could sell tracks for six-figure sums or use them to boost his label signees, including Eminem, 50 Cent, and Kendrick Lamar. Dre recognized a perfect collaborator in Beats cofounder Jimmy Iovine, whose effectiveness as an executive allowed Dre to focus on tinkering with the sonic side of things. Says Craig Kallman, chief of Atlantic Records: "He's a consummate music man whose actions are all moved by passion and the emotion that he feels for a particular artist or song."[6]

Dre used that energy to build a headphone line that competed not only with Bose and Sennheiser but with fashion and footwear brands for consumer dollars: a $300 pair of Beats became as viable an accessory as a similarly priced pair of Air Jordans. Though Dre functioned as the company's compass for cool and more of an ideas person than an executive (he "wasn't the business guy,"[7] notes Noel Lee, the founder of Monster Cable, which manufactured all of Beats' products for the first half decade of its existence), he displayed an uncanny knack for knowing when to get into and out of financial arrangements. He slipped away from Death Row, the label he cofounded in the early 1990s, months before it came crashing down; Beats fetched billions from Apple less than a year after nearly falling into bankruptcy.

Jay-Z became the most successful recording artist of the bunch. Every album he's released has been certified platinum; he put out a multiplatinum album every single year from 1998 through 2003. Jay-Z has racked up more number one albums than any act in history besides the Beatles; on the business side, he's sprinkled his stardust on companies he started and partnered with, turning investments in middling products into massive gains. Along the way, he's won the respect of figures from Oprah to Obama, Bono to Richard Branson.[8]

One might say that Diddy is hip-hop's Branson. Both are charismatic, outspoken front men for a staggering array of businesses, and though they both started out in the record business, their ability to identify and revolutionize other lucrative sectors truly set them apart. And just as another legendary founder, Steve Jobs, didn't invent MP3 players — but found a way to make them sexy with the iPod — Diddy earned many of his millions by making flavored vodka synonymous with celebration, lifting Diageo's Cîroc from relative obscurity and almost single-handedly making it the number two premium vodka in the world.

"It's like watching Elon Musk today: because he believes in it, he's driven an industry," says Stephen Rust, Diageo's president of new business and reserve brands. "When Sean believes in something and sees it in his head...don't bet against him."[9]

Diddy, Dre, and Jay-Z are modern embodiments of the American dream, but the details of their journeys are surprisingly scant. There have been only two major books on Jay-Z: his lyrics-oriented autobiography, *Decoded,* and my own business-focused *Empire State of Mind.* "That book was horrible!" the rapper once told me.[10] ("He's just messing with you," explained Diddy when I relayed the anecdote. "He's a good cat.")[11] Dre is incredibly private and makes many of those who work with him sign nondisclosure agreements[12]; Diddy, while more open, has never been the subject of a business biography. Despite the three kings' celebrity, their sagas have remained relatively unexplored in an in-depth capacity — and never together — until now.

In the coming pages, I'll work to unravel the layers of mystery surrounding the lives of Dr. Dre and Diddy and add new insights into that of Jay-Z, providing some entrepreneurial lessons along the way. Together, their stories offer a lens through which to view the broader narrative of hip-hop and its journey from local fringes to the global mainstream. I draw on my encounters with all three titular characters, focusing on how their individual paths diverged and converged, each at times directly at odds with at least one of the others, before ultimately coming together.

Scores of others have played major roles in rap's rise, and they make appearances in these pages as well. Among the hundred-plus figures I've interviewed: Kevin "Lovebug Starski" Smith, the rapping DJ arguably responsible for coining the term "hip-hop"; Fab 5 Freddy, the pioneering graffiti artist whose friendships with Keith Haring and Jean-Michel Basquiat helped advance hip-hop's visual sensibility; and Theodore "Grandwizzard Theodore" Livingston — inventor of the scratch technique now used by nearly every DJ on the planet — who believes hip-hop was universal from the outset.

"People around the world were probably pretty much going through the same thing we were going through: single-parent homes, poverty, low income, school, drugs," says Theodore. "This problem was not only here in New York."[13]

While reporting my book, I traveled from the heart of the South Bronx to the fjords of Norway, speaking with pioneering behind-the-scenes operators including aforementioned Def Jam founder Russell Simmons, early artist manager Charles Stettler, and Bronx nightclub owner Sal Abbatiello; new-breed executives like Kevin Liles, Rob Stone, and Troy Carter; and stars of all stripes, including Kasseem "Swizz Beatz" Dean, Kendrick Lamar, and Shaquille O'Neal. I even interviewed Biggie's mom.

Though the three kings have reaped the rewards of the hip-hop economy, the same can't be said for many of the genre's founding fathers. Some of them go as far as to suggest that modern rap should be viewed as an entirely separate category from the genre they invented, despite the fact that rap is widely understood to be a large circle within the Venn diagram of hip-hop; almost all acknowledge that the movement has changed drastically over the decades, for better or worse. "It's really not my hip-hop anymore," says Curtis "Grandmaster Caz" Fisher, a pioneering emcee whose lyrics—cribbed by the Sugarhill Gang—formed the backbone of the genre's first commercial hit, "Rapper's Delight," in 1979.[14]

Caz is one of many who gave or signed away valuable music rights for a pittance decades ago, a showbiz tradition that has become a painful and indelible aspect of the hip-hop psyche, and likely part of the reason financial gain is so often flaunted when it does occur. Unlike rock music, which is in many ways a reaction against wealth, a core element of hip-hop is rejoicing in success.[15] "Hip-hop from the beginning has always been aspirational," Jay-Z told *Forbes* in 2010. "It always broke that notion that an artist can't think about money as well. Just so long as you separate the two and you're not making music with business in mind."[16]

This book offers a peek into both the musical and financial sides of the industry, with a heavy dose of hip-hop history coming in the first few chapters. Most of the myriad characters mentioned in these pages deserve more ink than they're given; to help keep track, I've created a dramatis personae at the back of this book. Throughout the narrative, as the kings ascend to the upper strata of the entertainment and business worlds, their circles grow smaller, and the names become fewer—and more recognizable to the casual reader.

In just a few decades, hip-hop has become deeply and profitably intertwined with mainstream global culture, and emcees born in other countries have gone on to enjoy great success locally and internationally. Take MC Solaar, the French rapper who debuted with the smash single "Bouge de Là" ("move a little") in 1991 and by the 2000s was contributing songs to *The Hills* and *Sex and the City*. Or Tommy Tee, the godfather of Norwegian hip-hop, who took inspiration from the culture coming out of the Bronx in the early 1980s and went on to help launch a similar scene in Scandinavia at around the same time, complete with all the elements of hip-hop. "In the regular newspaper, they had break dance courses — 'How to Break-Dance' — for a whole summer," says Tee, who has released several studio albums and runs his own independent label. "Now we have a generation that's born in the nineties that grew up with hip-hop… *everywhere*."[17]

More recently, the genre has given rise to a film that grossed north of $200 million worldwide (the Dre-produced N.W.A. biopic *Straight Outta Compton*), one of the most popular television shows in the United States (*Empire,* whose lead character is a mélange of the three kings, but particularly Jay-Z and Diddy), and the most-awarded Broadway show in recent memory (*Hamilton,* a hip-hop history written by a New Yorker of Puerto Rican heritage and performed by a cast that brought a much-needed blast of diversity to the Great White Way).

To be sure, Diddy, Dr. Dre, and Jay-Z alone weren't responsible for all of hip-hop's recent triumphs, nor were they on the front lines as the genre's first champions smashed barrier after barrier that stood in the way of its early progress. They weren't always model citizens either — all three had violent episodes, though none did any hard time — yet each man's most serious brushes with the law served as a life lesson and a career turning point.

Hip-hop is now America's most-consumed genre, fronted by a generation of up-and-comers whose trail was blazed by Diddy, Dr. Dre, and Jay-Z. Despite their imperfections, the members of this trio combined to do something vital: transport a mature but evolving movement to places nobody dreamed it could go while providing an incredible set of entrepreneurial blueprints.

"Who thought we were going to be promoting Skittles?" asks former Def Jam president Kevin Liles. "Who thought that we would be in the headphone space? Who thought that we would get bought out? Who thought that we would own a streaming company? Who thought that we would have a five-hundred-million-dollar alcohol? And I don't think we're done."[18]

It may have been Lawrence "KRS-One" Parker, the conscientious old-school "rapper's rapper," who put it best. One day, at a press conference, a writer asked him what he thought about the corporatization of hip-hop.

"I don't look at it as the corporatization of hip-hop," KRS said. "I look at it as the hip-hopitization of corporate America."

The room fell silent.

"You're not changing us," he continued. "We're changing you."[19]

CHAPTER I

The Originators

Lovebug Starski may be best known for getting shouted out by Notorious B.I.G. in "Juicy," a 1994 hit produced by Diddy and later sampled by Jay-Z. The song, however, makes no mention of Starski's chief contribution to hip-hop: though he didn't invent the genre, he may well have been the first to give it a name.

"I would do a rhyme and I would get stuck for a couple of words, and I would just go, 'Then you rock the hip, then you rock the hop, a hip-hop a hippi, da hop hop hippi hippi...'" he explains, recalling his early days as a pioneering rapper-DJ in New York. "And it caught on because I'd be doing it in the rhythm of the record."[1]

He says this sitting at my dining room table, eating takeaway from a five-dollar sushi buffet after declining my offer to take him out for lunch. Starski is nearing age sixty, much older and heavier now than in the faded YouTube videos he shows me on his phone, in which he skips across a pastel stage jovially delivering Dr. Seuss–style rhymes. Today he speaks obliquely about his declining health and tattered finances, wheezing occasionally, but then he'll toss in a detail like the price of his coat: $1,700. Or he'll laugh—a booming, subterranean sort of guffaw that makes it sound as though he just ate a subwoofer—usually while reminiscing about his early days.

Born Kevin Smith in the South Bronx, the aspiring DJ fell in with a gang called the Black Spades. "At first my name was Kool DJ Kev," he says. "Not catchy." While watching a Herbie the Love Bug film with some fellow gang members, his stage name simply erupted from his brain. "I looked up at the screen...I said, 'I'm the l-o-v-e the b-u-g!'" he raps to me. "I just kept doing it and doing it, and got kicked in the head with a fucking army boot by a female Spades member." The second part of his name came to him in rhyme, too: "Like a crippled crab without a crutch, it's Starski without a Hutch."

Following close on the heels of his friend Anthony "DJ Hollywood" Holloway, Starski became one of the first rapping DJs to emerge from the disco scene in the 1970s, and many better-known wordsmiths have gotten rich cribbing his rhymes. As journalists started covering hip-hop, though, the narrative of its origins coalesced around the easily packaged idea of a holy trinity of founders: Afrika Bambaataa, Clive "DJ Kool Herc" Campbell, and Joseph "Grandmaster Flash" Saddler.

All three deserve recognition as much as anyone, but trying to accurately pinpoint three — or even five — originators of a movement with as many diverse influences as hip-hop is tricky. The trinity concept leaves out forerunners like Jalal "Lightnin' Rod" Nuriddin, a member of the civil rights–era group the Last Poets. His 1973 spoken-word album, an underworld Iliad known as *Hustlers Convention,* has caused many to dub him the grandfather of rap. "All the candy rappers got my money," Lightnin' Rod complained when I spoke with him in 2016. (He said that he had known Jay-Z's father. But when I asked if he'd tell me more for the book, he demanded compensation, and I declined per journalistic principle.)[2]

Others with a claim include Brooklyn DJ Grandmaster Flowers, disco group the Fatback Band, jazz poet Gil Scott-Heron, smooth-talking midcentury radio personalities like Frankie Crocker and Jocko Henderson, swaggering rhymester Muhammad Ali, and scatting jazz legend Louis Armstrong. Hip-hop's lineage could even be traced as far back as the troubadours of West Africa, called griots, who've engaged in spoken-word storytelling for ages. For Lightnin' Rod, Starski, and their ilk, there's a palpable bitterness toward the movement they helped create. They feel ignored by the three kings' generation; occasional lip service isn't enough.

"Puffy would never walk up to me and say, 'What up, Lovebug, you all right?'" says Starski, raising his voice as he plays out the hypothetical encounter. "'Hell no, motherfucker! Put a million in my pocket! . . . I don't want no photo op with your ass, 'cause it don't mean nothing. I can't take it down to the subway and get on the train with it.'"[3]

Though the likes of Flash and Fab still earn a comfortable living plying their respective trades, the same can't be said of most of the pioneers, even one of those whose lyrics were used without permission in "Rapper's Delight," the first hip-hop song to crack the pop charts.

"I came up with all those rhymes, you know?" says Starski, his eyes suddenly misty. "It was real good times, Zack, innocent times. We were all innocent. Nobody knew nothing about business."

If Starski, Bambaataa, Flash, Herc, and Hollywood are among hip-hop's founding fathers, you might say that midcentury master builder Robert Moses is the genre's estranged, power-crazed, malevolent granduncle. His policies uprooted scores of New Yorkers and shuffled them into the dysfunctional housing projects where the collective angst of a generation would be channeled into what became hip-hop.

Moses made himself the most influential figure in postwar New York City by amassing appointed positions and political capital, shaping the city's development according to his own imperial worldview. After the 1964 completion of Shea Stadium,[4] he declared,

"When the Emperor Titus opened the Colosseum in eighty A.D. he could have felt no happier." Moses believed the future would be dominated by the automobile, and that he could solve all urban ills by constructing hulking skyscrapers and connecting them by a vast web of thoroughfares. Starting in 1931, he built just about every major highway in the city and all seven bridges leading to and from the Bronx, rigged with enough steel wire to circle the earth.[5]

Though he had his share of triumphs, among them the performance spaces at Lincoln Center, Moses's creations are in many ways overshadowed by what he destroyed. Using highway construction as a pretext for leveling areas deemed blighted, a process that came to be known by the Orwellian name "urban renewal," his minions bulldozed blocks of vibrant minority neighborhoods, uprooting an estimated 250,000 residents. About a quarter of them were evicted from a few square miles of land to clear the way for the Cross Bronx Expressway and resettled into grim housing projects, an operation akin to the forced removals that occurred at around the same time in South African neighborhoods like Cape Town's District Six.[6]

Moses's form of discrimination wasn't codified in the blatant terms of state-sanctioned apartheid, but the destruction wrought by his plans came in concert with new construction bearing a clear message. He "built housing bleak, sterile, cheap — expressive of patronizing condescension in every line," Robert Caro wrote in his Pulitzer-winning book *The Power Broker*. "And he built it in locations that contributed to the ghettoization of the city, dividing up the city by color and income."[7]

On a snowy night in 1967, Clive Campbell and his sister, Cindy, emigrated with their parents from Jamaica to the Bronx. They settled into an apartment at 1520 Sedgwick Ave, a complex almost close enough to the Cross Bronx Expressway to allow them to smell the diesel burning. Six years later, inspired by Cindy's desire to generate cash for back-to-school shopping, the two siblings threw a party in their building's rec room (admission: fifty cents). Clive worked the turntable, selecting the name DJ Kool Herc for himself.

The last part of this moniker aimed to signal his Herculean physical prowess (he earned medals, as well as American friends, for his track-and-field efforts in high school), while "Kool" was inspired by a cigarette commercial. In the spot, a James Bond look-alike drives an Aston Martin, his Kools in a box by the gearshift. When his lady friend reaches for one, he stops the car and tells her to get out. "And the commercial says, 'Nobody touches my silver thin,'" Herc recalled decades later. "I was like, 'Wow, that's Kool!'" Thus, the DJ many consider to be the foremost founding father of hip-hop launched his career with product placement ingrained in his professional name, auguring the multibillion-dollar connection between brands and the genre in the years to come.[8]

In addition to his thick Jamaican accent, Herc possessed something his mostly teenage audience hadn't heard before: a sound system as physically imposing as he was. Borrowed from his father, the speakers became especially important when, after a few parties, Herc outgrew the rec room and started playing outside.[9] He'd crack open streetlamp bases and tap their electric wiring to power his massive system, playing songs with lengthy danceable sections — known as the "break" or the "get-down" — by acts like the Incredible Bongo Band and James Brown. To optimize the experience for what came to be known as break-dancers, he'd pick up his turntable's needle at the end of the break and set it back to the beginning, thereby extending the prime part of the song, or to the break of another song altogether. He called this the "merry-go-round."[10]

The parties, and hip-hop itself, served as an outlet for — and an expression of — the frustrations of life in the Bronx. Local emcee Melvin "Melle Mel" Glover would sum up the harsh realities best in "The Message" several years later: "Broken glass everywhere / People pissin' on the stairs, you know they just don't care," he rapped, going on to bemoan the "rats in the front room, roaches in the back," and the "junkies in the alley with a baseball bat." Crime had indeed surged: from 1965 to 1975, in the wake of Moses's urban renewal, violent offenses tripled across New York.[11]

At 1520 Sedgwick, though, a relatively peaceful atmosphere prevailed, thanks to the presence of hulking Herc himself, with help from his sidekick, an emcee who went by the name Coke La Rock and peppered performances with soon-to-be-ubiquitous ad-libbed phrases like "Ya rock and ya don't stop!" and "To the beat, y'all!" In the mind of many historians, Herc's parties constituted the beginning of hip-hop in 1973. "He's the father," says Caz, who grew up three blocks from 1520 Sedgwick. "He's the guy that everybody aspired to be...Nobody was there when Herc was there in the beginning."[12]

If anyone could match Herc in terms of sheer presence, it was Bambaataa. Even today, the burly DJ explodes out of cars and bursts into restaurants with the bombastic intensity of the Incredible Hulk. Little is known about his origins, and he doesn't offer many clues ("I'm really from the universe...I'm what you call a person of star seed," he said when I first interviewed him in 2009).[13] Working backward, he arrived on this planet—birthed by an Earthly mother, or so he says—in the late 1950s or thereabouts. He grew up in the Bronx River Houses, a Moses monstrosity ten minutes east on the Cross Bronx from Herc's stomping grounds. By the early 1970s, he'd risen to the rank of warlord in the Black Spades.

On a trip to Africa at around this time, he discovered the luscious grooves of Afrobeat legend Fela Kuti; upon his return, Bambaataa created a peaceful organization called the Universal Zulu Nation. He convinced many Black Spades to put down their weapons and pick up his new philosophy, codifying and preaching four pillars: DJing (spinning records), emceeing (rhyming over a beat), graffiti (street art), and b-boying (break dancing). He later added a fifth pillar: knowledge.

"Everybody needs to show respect to each other's ways and culture of life that we get on this planet," Bambaataa told me. "Don't get caught up on, 'I'm black, brown, yellow, red, or white.'" (There are some odious matters that run contrary to this lofty talk: Bambaataa was recently accused of sexually abusing adolescent boys throughout the 1970s, allegations that he has strenuously denied; it appears that he won't face prosecution due to New York's statute of limitations, though the Zulu Nation did remove him from its ranks.)[14]

Bambaataa wasn't the first person to spin records or write graffiti, or to celebrate emceeing or b-boying, but these four core elements of hip-hop coalesced under his aegis when he started throwing parties in the South Bronx. He'd play the unfamiliar music he had found in Africa—from Kuti to Nigerian juju musicians like King Sunny Adé—alongside Sly and the Family Stone, Herbie Hancock, and Kraftwerk. Bambaataa's long grooves enabled a golden age of break dancing.

Meanwhile, a couple of miles south of 1520 Sedgwick, Grandmaster Flash emerged on the scene thanks to even more advanced methods of turntablism. He helped popularize the scratch move invented by his pal Grandwizzard Theodore, who discovered the technique of moving the vinyl back and forth in rhythm in 1975. (While practicing his DJ skills as an adolescent, his mother startled him by bursting into his room and telling him to turn down the volume; he accidentally nudged the vinyl, and the resulting sound went on to become a turntablist staple.) Theodore soon earned a reputation as one of the most dexterous DJs in the neighborhood, as did Flash, who gained an even greater measure of renown for using two turntables at the same time and cutting up the breaks with the precision of a sushi chef.[15]

The technique had been born, but word moved slowly in those days. "Hip-hop is kind of regional in a small sense," Caz explains. "If you from Bronx River, you got your hip-hop from Bambaataa. If you was from the West Side, you got it from Kool Herc. If you was from the South Bronx, you got it from Flash."[16]

Of the three, Bambaataa became the first to draw interest from beyond the Bronx. Tom Silverman was a Colby College geology major who had started a publication called the *Dance Music Report* with other recent grads of the Maine school in 1978. One day, Silverman dropped by Downstairs Records on the seedy fringes of Times Square and found it packed with teenagers from the Bronx. They were scooping up records by the Incredible Bongo Band as well as by rocker Billy Squier and pop-rock quartet the Monkees. When he asked the shoppers why they wanted the records, they replied with an almost religious zeal, "We buy what Afrika Bambaataa plays."[17]

In many ways, the ascendant genre was completely novel. And in others, it seemed strangely familiar.

"Hip-hop was always here, since the beginning of time," says Theodore. "The tribespeople, they sit around the campfire and tell stories to the kids. That's like the emcee right there. Then you got my ancestors, they bang on the drums and that's like the DJ. Then they do the tribal dances to the drums—that's like the b-boys. Then you go to the caves and you see the hieroglyphics...That's like the graffiti artist...Those four elements is hip-hop right there. Basically, what we did, we just reinvented hip-hop."[18]

The beat may have always been there, but the innovators showed up on their own schedules. Closest to the Bronx, geographically, was Sean Combs—alternately known as Puffy, Puff Daddy, P. Diddy, and Diddy—born on November 4, 1969, in Harlem. Roughly three years later, his father, Melvin Combs, was gunned down in a parked car on Central Park West; someone in his circle thought he'd been preparing to talk to the authorities about a sensitive business deal.[19]

As Dan Charnas points out in the first line of his excellent book *The Big Payback,* Harlem was home to Alexander Hamilton—the man who essentially invented American money (and later inspired the most successful Broadway musical in a generation). And over time, the neighborhood has been home to many experts at making and flaunting it. The elder Combs boasted a portfolio of operations that was quite diversified, if not always legal. He made money by driving cabs, owning bars, operating limousine companies, and distributing narcotics. An associate of drug lord Frank Lucas, the titular character played by Denzel Washington in *American Gangster,* Combs would bring his young son to Lucas's home on occasion. (The young Diddy didn't like to share: "My daughter used to push him off the [toys]," Lucas once said.[20]) Though Melvin Combs passed away very early in his child's life, he left a lasting impression.

"I learned early in life that there's only two ways out of that: dead or in jail," explained Diddy in 2013, speaking of his father's lifestyle. "It made me work even harder...I have his hustler's mentality."[21]

Though not quite as conspicuous as Lucas, who famously caught the attention of the feds after showing up at a boxing match between Muhammad Ali and Joe Frazier wearing a $100,000 floor-length chinchilla coat, Combs's flashy fashion preferences earned him the nickname "Pretty Melvin." Says Dillard Morrison Jr., a contemporary of the elder Combs: "You can see him through his son. He was immaculate. Every hair was in place. He stood out among most guys because of the way he carried himself."[22]

Despite the challenges of his early life, the younger Combs came away from his childhood with a certain fondness for the era. "I feel blessed because I was able to be born in nineteen sixty-nine," Diddy told me in 2014. "Then I got to grow up in the seventies as a child, and be trained with that music and that whole vibe around me, and then I got to grow up with hip-hop in the eighties."[23]

As a youngster, he lived in Esplanade Gardens, an affordable-housing complex near the 148th Street subway terminus in Harlem, just a ten-minute drive from Herc's Sedgwick parties. Diddy was raised by his grandmother and mother, Janice, who recognized her son's comfort with being the center of attention. This facilitated his appearance in a Baskin-Robbins television commercial at age two; later, he modeled alongside *The Wiz* star Stephanie Mills in *Essence* magazine. When Diddy reached middle-school age, Janice moved the family to the middle-class Westchester suburb of Mount Vernon. As a teen, Diddy continued to show an interest in fashion, selling shirts and ties at Macy's; he also grew his income by delivering newspapers.[24] ("I didn't settle at one paper route," he explained in a Cîroc commercial. "I went and got four.")

At his new home in Mount Vernon, he became annoyed that his white neighbors didn't invite him over to swim in their pool, so he badgered his mother into installing one of their own — bigger than the one next door — and his house became the place kids of every race wanted to be.[25] He continued to enjoy popularity at Mount Saint Michael Academy, a Catholic high school across the county line in the Bronx, where he starred on the football team. Friends noted that he always walked around with his chest puffed out and gave him a nickname: Puffy. He helped his varsity football team win a division title, but a broken leg during his senior year ended his career prematurely. "That dream got deferred," he says. "God had another plan for me."[26]

The cultural and economic realities of Harlem and the Bronx during the 1970s were separated by a gulf far wider than the narrow river that runs between the two areas. In the Bronx, things got so bad that landlords would pay to have their own apartment buildings burned down, often shelling out as little as fifty dollars to petty criminals in hopes of earning a low-six-figure insurance payout (a fate suffered by Starski's first childhood home).[27] One fire, visible from a 1977 World Series game at Yankee Stadium, prompted commentator Howard Cosell to famously declare, "There it is, ladies and gentlemen: the Bronx is burning."

Harlem, on the other hand, claimed a historic position as the informal capital of black America, home to the Apollo Theater and

Maya Angelou and the Harlem Renaissance. It was also where elite gangsters like Frank Lucas and their midlevel counterparts lived and worked. Money flowed through the streets, not just from drugs, but from an informal — and illegal — citywide lottery known as the numbers game. Players would scrawl three-digit jackpot guesses on slips of paper that they'd hand to their neighborhood runner. (Depending on the neighborhood, the winning number was taken from published horse racing results — the last three digits of the cash taken in at the track on a designated day, for example.) Harlem pulsated as the epicenter of this informal economic engine, which at one point employed an estimated hundred thousand workers and resulted in some eight thousand arrests per year.[28]

All this bustle created an economy that allowed DJ Hollywood to become a celebrity among Harlem's power players, who paid him as much as $5,000 per night to rock glitzy uptown parties. Beyond the traditional DJ patter, he often laid down extended, syncopated rhymes over disco beats.[29] Some therefore consider him one of the first true hip-hop acts, while others strenuously disagree. "When the first school of hip-hop started, we were against what was going on then," says Caz, who grew up near Herc in the Bronx. "All these club and disco DJs...they'd kick us right out of their party."[30]

Hollywood attracted plenty of followers who couldn't make it to his shows. He used an eight-track recorder to create mixtapes of himself rapping over disco rhythms, spreading them through a growing community of listeners in Harlem and the Bronx in the early 1970s. Starski remembers visiting a friend just to sit in his Cadillac, which had an eight-track player capable of broadcasting Hollywood's music.[31] "When I heard [DJ Hollywood] spit that fire, I knew that was what I wanted to do," says Starski. "And nothing in the world was going to stop me."

As a teenager, Starski had gotten his start working as an assistant to a Harlem Globetrotter turned disco DJ by the name of Pete DJ Jones, who would pay him five dollars a night to help carry his equipment—and, rather frequently, to cover for him. "Sometimes he'd overdrink and he'd say, 'Well, Starski, I need you to play this program right here,'" the rapper recalls. "'And don't say nothing on the mic, because I don't want them to know I'm not playing.'" Then the towering Jones would find a quiet corner in which to pass out, waking up hours later to rave reviews of his set. Soon Starski was getting $300 per night for his own gigs, and by 1979 he'd joined Edward "Eddie Cheeba" Sturgis and Hollywood as the top rapping DJs in town.

That same year, the late Sylvia Robinson—a Harlem native who'd reached the top fifteen on the charts in 1957 as soul prodigy Little Sylvia, and later started a small label called Sugar Hill Records with her husband, Joe—was invited to a cousin's birthday party at Harlem World, a club on 116th Street.[32] She and Joe had moved across the river to New Jersey and hadn't even wanted to go to the celebration, but the invitation included a note that Sylvia would be in attendance. "You don't want to upset your fans and not go there," Sylvia's niece, Diane, had told her.[33]

When she arrived at the club, Sylvia immediately saw Starski electrifying the crowd. His audience obeyed his call-and-response orders like army cadets as he rapped over "Good Times" by Chic, tossing out soon-to-be-famous directives such as "Throw your hands in the air, wave 'em like you just don't care." Recalls Starski: "She had never seen anyone like me on the turntables *and* on the microphone."[34]

As Sylvia soaked up the spirit of the club that night, she saw the potential for something even larger: a form of music that could make the jump from parties to vinyl. She suspected that the listeners shaking their hips at Harlem World would pay to get their own copies of such records—and she decided to produce them in her studio. "She was always an entrepreneur," says her son, Leland Robinson. "When everybody else said, 'No,' she said, 'Yes.'"[35]

Sylvia sent Diane up to the DJ booth to tell Starski that she'd like to record him. He thought she was kidding, and jokingly called for security. Undeterred, Sylvia contacted Starski after the show, only to discover that he was under contract with a booking agent who refused to do business with her because he didn't like Joe, a former numbers runner with underworld ties.[36] The Robinsons had launched Sugar Hill with the help of a $20,000 to $25,000 loan from Joe's associate Morris Levy—a music executive notorious for stiffing talent and, eventually, worse. (Levy was convicted of extortion charges alongside a member of the Genovese crime family shortly before his death in 1988.)

But the Robinsons needed a hit to maintain their lifestyle. When Sylvia couldn't get Starski, she went searching for guys in Englewood who could rap. She soon found Henry "Big Bank Hank" Jackson working at a slice joint called Crispy Crust Pizza, along with her sons' intermittently homeless friend Michael "Wonder Mike" Wright. As they talked, Guy "Master Gee" O'Brien walked up and informed them that he could rap, too. Sylvia dubbed them the Sugarhill Gang and hired a band to replicate the rhythm of "Good Times," telling them, "I've got these kids who are going to talk real fast over it; that's the best way I can describe it."[37]

The three youngsters recorded their verses, cribbing most of their lyrics from Starski and Caz. The latter would go on to be a part of the seminal hip-hop act the Cold Crush Brothers; in 1979, though, he mainly focused on his group Mighty Force, for which Hank served as a bouncer-manager hybrid. Before "Rapper's Delight" came out, Hank actually mentioned it to Caz and even borrowed his songwriting notebook. "We didn't discuss any business," Caz told me. "I just figured, if you down with me and you make it, or something happens, then it's going to trickle down to me."[38]

Much like the Reagan-era economics of the same name that promised prosperity to communities like the Bronx, the trickle down never happened. After Wonder Mike opened the song with the classic line, "Now what you hear is not a test, I'm rapping to the beat," Hank delivered the first verse of "Rapper's Delight," and lifted the lyrics of Caz—also known as Casanova Fly—word for word, not even bothering to change his name: "I'm the c-a-s-an, the o-v-a and the rest is f-l-y..."

"They didn't know a lot about rap," says Starski. "They knew just enough to rap sixteen minutes on this record."[39]

The track debuted in September 1979 and became known as the first hip-hop single to crack the Top 40 on the *Billboard* charts, though to this day, many of the genre's founders don't even consider it hip-hop. The song generated $3.5 million in revenues for Sugar Hill[40] and a major lifestyle upgrade for Wonder Mike. ("He bought the classic Lincoln—and went and bought another one the next day," says Leland Robinson.)[41] And that's how a child star from Harlem brought hip-hop's first major cultural moment to life in a New Jersey studio with the help of a trio of teenagers who borrowed their lyrics from the genre's Bronx forefathers.

"Nobody knew about rights or publishing or royalties or anything like that," says Caz.[42] Adds Starski: "There wasn't no lawsuits back in the day. It wasn't like, 'You stole my rhyme, I'm going to sue you.' Niggas didn't know music like that, the politics of it. They weren't business oriented."[43]

A year before the release of "Rapper's Delight," Shawn Carter discovered hip-hop right in his own backyard. On a sweaty summer afternoon in Brooklyn's Marcy Houses, a bleak public-housing project much like the places that had produced Herc and Bambaataa, a nine-year-old boy soon to be known as Jay-Z noticed a group of kids standing in a circle. One of them, a local rapper called Slate, freestyled about everything—anything—that crossed his mind, from the sidewalk to the crowd around him to the quality of his own rhymes. He rapped until dusk fell, spitting lyrics as though possessed.

"*That's some cool shit* was the first thing I thought," Jay-Z wrote in his autobiography. "Then: *I could do that.*" He went home and immediately started filling spiral notebooks with rhymes of his own. (Later, paranoid that rivals would steal his lines, he started stashing songs entirely in his head.)[44]

The Brooklyn of Jay-Z's youth was about as far from its current craft-beer-and-yoga-pants reality as "Rapper's Delight" is from the big-budget singles and videos of today. Jay-Z came into the world on December 4, 1969—exactly a month after Diddy, and barely a decade after the borough lost its beating heart, the Brooklyn Dodgers. The team left Ebbets Field, two and a half miles south of the Marcy Houses, and moved to Los Angeles after the 1957 season. Owner Walter O'Malley had initially wanted to stay in the borough, setting his sights on a downtown location near the Atlantic Yards transit hub. But Robert Moses made it clear that he'd stymie any attempt O'Malley made to stay in Brooklyn, offering only a spot in his planned stadium in Flushing, along with a price tag that would have cost the Dodgers millions more than the package from Los Angeles.[45]

Faced with those choices, O'Malley took his team west. (Ebbets Field would be razed in 1960, replaced with yet another drab housing complex.) Moses managed to deflect the blame for the Dodgers' departure onto the shoulders of O'Malley. (A common Brooklyn question: "If you had a gun with two bullets and walked into a room with Hitler, Stalin, and Walter O'Malley, who would you shoot?" A common Brooklyn answer: "O'Malley—twice!") Others left too—428,000 residents between 1950 and 1980,[46] as tens of thousands of jobs at places like Spalding and the Brooklyn Navy Yard disappeared[47]—and working-class Brooklyn devolved into another urban wasteland. "Outside, in Marcy's courtyards and across the country, teenagers wore automatic weapons like they were sneakers," Jay-Z noted. "Broad daylight shoot-outs had our grandmothers afraid to leave the house."[48]

To make matters worse within his own home, when Jay-Z was ten years old, his father abandoned the family, causing the young rapper to become less trusting and more reclusive.[49] His mother sometimes struggled to put food on the table, and he'd often have to eat at friends' apartments because there wasn't enough at home. To escape his reality, he would listen to his mother's soul records and hone his rap skills, pounding out beats on the kitchen table, often staying inside to scour dictionaries in search of new words while his friends played basketball outside.[50]

Jay-Z's ambitions might not have outgrown Marcy if it hadn't been for a few early mentors. Among them: his sixth grade teacher, who took the class to her house on a field trip, one of his first excursions outside the ghetto. "She had an ice thing on her refrigerator," Jay-Z told Steve Forbes in 2010. "You know: you push it and the ice and the water comes down. I was really amazed by that. I was like, 'I want one of those.' . . . I saw a whole different world that day, and my imagination grew from there."[51]

Then, in 1984, Jay-Z met Jonathan "Jaz-O" Burks. Sensing a potential pupil, the elder rapper instilled in Jay-Z an understanding of metaphor, simile, onomatopoeia, and other crucial concepts. "I basically taught him structure as far as writing songs," says Jaz-O. "I taught him some of the intricacies like vocal projection [and how] convincing people of anything, regardless of what you're saying, is the way you say it."[52]

Shawn Carter soon became Jay-Z, a portmanteau of his childhood nickname (Jazzy) and two of the subway lines that stop near the Marcy Houses (J and Z), as well as, it seems, an homage to his first musical mentor. One of the first songs they recorded together — a track rapped so fast that it seemed someone had simply fast-forwarded an early hip-hop tune — was called "The Originators."

Before hip-hop could become a billion-dollar business, it had to move from housing projects and public parks into its own venues. Starski, Hollywood, and their ilk were practicing an early form of hip-hop in discotheques, to be sure, but disco itself was declining rapidly.

Enter twenty-five-year-old Sal Abbatiello, an Italian American

guy from the Bronx with slicked-back hair, a mustache, and a purple Cadillac. His was one of the few white families that hadn't yet
fled the neighborhood, sticking around to operate lounges and
nightclubs. Sal grew up helping his mother tend bar, and in 1976 he
took charge of the family's newest offering, the Disco Fever. At
167th and Jerome, a twenty-minute walk south from 1520 Sedgwick and just six blocks north of Yankee Stadium, the club was
generally rocked by disco DJs until its 6 a.m. closing time, but
sometimes they'd leave early and put an aspiring turntablist named
Sweet G in charge.

"At the end of the night he would start rhyming and emceeing
on the mic," recalls Abbatiello. "Now, back in the day, in our disco,
nobody spoke on the mic. DJs didn't have a mic in the DJ booth
because there was no business being done on the mic."[53]

But every time Sweet G told the members of the crowd to wave
their hands in the air like they just didn't care, the place erupted.
Abbatiello suspected that he'd stumbled upon something — perhaps
a youth-centric genre that could replace disco. He became friends
with G and asked him to take him to the parks where other DJs of
his type were playing. Flash and his crew of emcees, the Furious
Five, impressed Abbatiello the most.[54]

"I am going to make you a star," he insisted when he finally met
Flash, promising a fifty-dollar-per-night weekly gig.[55]

"Fifty dollars!" replied Flash, outraged.

"What do you want?" said Abbatiello. "We are going to charge
a dollar to get in, a dollar to drink."

Flash eventually agreed to the fee after Abbatiello agreed to
include an additional sum for the Furious Five. But Abbatiello's
father's friends — the older black clientele that filled the family's
other clubs — thought the idea was terrible. A common refrain,
according to the younger Abbatiello: "They talk in the microphone
and they talk over other people's music? What kind of shit is that?"

Abbatiello prevailed upon his father to offer up a weeknight for
the show, and soon he was running around the Bronx handing out

flyers promoting the first performance of Grandmaster Flash and the Furious Five. When the big day finally rolled around, the result was astonishing. "I had about seven hundred people show up the first night," Abbatiello says. "On a Tuesday."

Hip-hop's earliest practitioners caught wind of the parties and found their way to the Disco Fever stage, from Flash to Herc to Starski to Hollywood to Cheeba; young crowds flocked to see them. At the time, the drinking age was eighteen, but plenty of under-age patrons were able to get into what became known simply as the Fever. Abbatiello launched promotions geared to his clientele, offering free admission to students who showed straight A report cards at the door. Sometimes he'd let homeless teenagers sleep in the club overnight or give them money to buy food.

The Fever was far from squeaky-clean, though. Abbatiello rec-ognized that some of his patrons were there for drugs, and instead of trying to root out the practice, he created "get high" rooms in the back. He even built an elaborate system of blinking lights to alert patrons that police were on the way. These sympathetic policies generated a level of loyalty among the revelers, some of whom became stars in their own right. One of them: Harlem emcee Kurt Walker.

"We called him Kurtis Blow for two reasons," says Russell Simmons, the bold, bald Def Jam cofounder who got his start man-aging the aforementioned rapper. "He kept selling fake cocaine... and blow was better than cheeba."[56]

Seemingly overnight, Blow and Simmons went from waiting in line at the Fever to being VIPs after Blow's holiday hit, "Christmas Rappin'," debuted, just weeks after the Sugarhill Gang first put hip-hop on the map. ("When 'Rapper's Delight' came out, we had 'Christmas Rappin'' [ready to go]," explains Simmons. "We felt a little bit as if they had stolen something.") When Blow's song started to explode in clubs, a British executive at PolyGram's Mercury Records tracked him down and inked him to a $10,000 deal, mak-ing him the first rapper to sign with a major label.

By the dawn of the 1980s, hip-hop had established a secure foothold on the East Coast. Out west, things were just getting started.

Andre Romell Young was born on February 18, 1965, making him the oldest of the three kings. The boy who would become Dr. Dre got his middle name as a tribute to the singing group of his seventeen-year-old father, Theodore. Dre's mother, Verna, was just fifteen when her first son arrived; she married Theodore while they were still in high school, but their turbulent union dissolved when Dre was a toddler, as she explained in her memoir, *Long Road Outta Compton*. Verna raised Dre mostly by herself in the Compton section of Los Angeles.

"Andre loved hearing music, even as an infant," she wrote. "When music was playing, he would lie content and look around as if he were searching for the direction from which the sound was coming."[57]

As was the case for Jay-Z, Diddy, and their forerunners, Dre's childhood reverberated with the realities of America's midcentury metropolitan decline. Robert Moses didn't have to unravel the urban fabric of Los Angeles; it was, as novelist Thomas Pynchon wrote, "less an identifiable city than a grouping of concepts—census tracts, special purpose bond-issue districts, shopping nuclei, all overlaid with access roads to its own freeway."[58]

Despite the sprawling randomness of its road map, Los Angeles shared a crucial organizing principle with cities around the country: an insidious, institutionalized brand of racism led by the Federal Housing Administration, which actively recommended that homeowners avoid selling property to unwanted ethnic groups. "If a neighborhood is to retain stability," a 1938 FHA manual explained, "it is necessary that properties shall continue to be occupied by the same social and racial classes."[59] In Los Angeles, civic groups (including one that unabashedly dubbed itself the Anti-African Housing Association) used what were known as restrictive covenants to wall off as much as 95 percent of the city from black and Asian families in the 1920s. The Supreme Court finally ruled against such practices in 1948, but by then, much of the city had been settled along racial lines.[60]

Sandwiched between downtown Los Angeles and the working-class port of Long Beach, Compton emerged as a residential neighborhood less plagued by restrictive covenants than others, drawing midcentury minority middle-class families to California with the promise of a palm tree in every yard — the "black American dream," as a voice-over on Dr. Dre's 2015 album, *Compton,* noted. But the influx caused many prejudiced white families to decamp for new, informally segregated suburban subdivisions.

Capital fled, too. The common midcentury practice known as redlining, wherein banks and other organizations refused to invest in minority-dominated neighborhoods, left Compton's finances in disarray and its infrastructure crumbling. By the 1980s, the number of Los Angeles residents with annual incomes below $15,000 jumped by a third, while individual incomes in excess of $50,000 nearly tripled; the size of the middle-class population in between fell by half.[61] As the crack epidemic took hold (more on this later), Compton became a gang-infested drug center with one of the highest per capita murder rates in the United States.[62]

Dre's personal life also had its share of strife. He had little contact with his father after his parents split up,[63] and his mother remarried, and then divorced again. Dre also lost a baby brother to pneumonia and a half brother to gang violence. He gained a new stepbrother when his mother married William Griffin, the father of Warren "Warren G" Griffin, who would go on to become a successful hip-hop act himself. Dre's mother provided the family with some stability, working a series of clerking jobs — including one at the Compton Police Department's traffic division — before settling in as an operations control analyst at McDonnell Douglas Aircraft Company for thirteen years. That allowed her enough disposable income to accumulate a sizable vinyl collection, much to the delight of little Dre, who would spin records at his mother's social gatherings, often earning a few dollars in tips from her friends.[64]

"Parliament-Funkadelic and James Brown, Isaac Hayes, Marvin Gaye — this is the music I grew up on," Dre told VH1's *Behind the Music* in 1991. "And I love her for that."

Though Dre was a model student in middle school, things changed once he entered high school. He didn't seem to care about doing well in subjects he didn't like, but the faculty still saw signs of brilliance. "I watch him play chess at lunchtime, and he beats everybody," his English instructor said. "Students line up to challenge him, yet he remains undefeated." He excelled in classes that allowed him to flex his creative muscles, such as drafting. One teacher encouraged Dre to apply for an apprenticeship at defense contractor Northrop Aviation, but his grades weren't good enough. The cash would've come in handy, as he fathered the first of his six children at age seventeen (some sources suggest that Dre has closer to a dozen). Schoolwork couldn't compete with Dre's two main interests: music and women.[65]

"Dre would sit in a room sometimes, and you never knew he was there until a woman walked in," says Alonzo Williams, who owned a local nightspot called Eve After Dark. "He was very introverted as a kid. When he got onstage, he would perk up."[66]

Williams learned that firsthand. One night in 1982, after watching Kurtis Blow perform, Dre gathered the courage to get up on the turntables at Williams's club. The audience saw a teenager who had mastered the scratch technique that Blow's DJ had brought from New York; beyond that, he had also figured out how to seamlessly blend two records with different beat-per-minute (BPM) rates. Williams had never seen anything like it and soon invited Dre to be part of his group, a sequin-jumpsuit-wearing disco-soul collective called the World Class Wreckin' Cru. Often anxious beneath his confident exterior, Dre didn't mind taking a back seat to Williams. ("I don't like being in the spotlight," Dre told *Rolling Stone* in 2015. "I made a fucking weird career choice.")[67]

For Christmas in 1984, Dre's mother and her husband bought him a mixer; he attached it to his sound system and two turntables and stayed in his room all day, practicing. After Verna's holiday guests had left the house, she opened Dre's door to say good night. "He was lying on his bed fast asleep, with his headset still on his head and the music blasting," she wrote. "From that day forward, Andre took his place as the music person of our household."[68]

"I always get emotional when I talk about them days," says Starski. "Because those were the happiest days of my career."

We've been talking for over an hour now, and his eyes are getting misty again.

"To this day, I can call Herc, and he'll pick up."[69]

As if to prove a point, he whips out his cell, finds "DJ Kool Herc" in his address book, hits dial, and puts the phone on speaker mode. Sure enough, Herc answers almost immediately.

"Hello?"

"Hey Herc, what's happening, brother?"

"Who's this?"

"Lovebug."

"Who?"

"Lovebug."

"Oh, what up, Lovebug? How you been?"[70]

"The question always comes up about me, you, and Bambaataa," Starski continues. "And I always tell the story of how I met you through Pete DJ Jones when you and Pete used to battle. Do you remember those days, Herc?"

"Of course, son!"

"Pete and Herc used to battle, Pete used to get drunk and have me DJ against Herc," he says to me, as though suddenly forgetting that the DJ is on the phone. "I would hold my own, but I would get my ass kicked every now and then. It was really good times, them days, with me, Herc, Bam, Flash..."

Then Starski stops himself.

"I was just calling you up because I was catching a moment, Herc."

"Yeah."

"You understand."

Starski proceeds to say he's glad Herc got some money for his participation in an upcoming documentary involving Grandmaster Flash; Herc seems less than thrilled, and Starski tries to soothe him.

"Our time is coming, Herc."

But the DJ on the other end of the phone isn't having it, and starts to rattle off a long list of his grievances with other musicians and journalists, his Jamaican accent getting thicker and faster with each passing moment.

"He didn't do shit," Herc says of one figure. "He never mentioned my fucking name once...I got the article, our first fucking write-up, got it in 1976. When he see me, he run."

It's not entirely clear who he's talking about; it's just another name on Herc's decades-old shit list. And just as suddenly as he heated up, the DJ has cooled down.

"Yo, Lovebug, I gotta go."

"Okay, baby. I'll talk to you in a minute."

The line goes dead.

"He's bitter," says Starski, exhaling. "Herc has good days, he'll call me up. Today, evidently, is a bad day."[71]

It's not entirely clear if it's a good day or a bad day for Starski himself. Since the late 1970s, there have been plenty of both. Starski signed with Epic Records in 1986 — brought on by the same executive who signed the Jacksons, he says — and received a $100,000 deal. He filled up his passport playing shows overseas and lived in London for a spell; his spooky "Thriller"-esque single, "Amityville (the House on the Hill)," reached number twelve on the UK charts. But the lighthearted brand of rap practiced by Starski and his peers was fading stateside, where, by the late 1980s, a more aggressive sound was starting to emanate from southern California. Over the years, Starski struggled with substance abuse and at one point landed in jail.

"I feel bad for Herc. I feel bad for me and Hollywood," he says, looking at a copy of my Jay-Z biography, *Empire State of Mind,* which I've just given him. "I don't fault anyone for being a business-man. If I was more business oriented and had the right people around me at the time that I needed them, instead of motherfuck-ers that was trying to shove coke up my nose..."

Starski sighs.

"Sometimes your luck can be so good," he says. "And sometimes it can be like, if it's raining pussy, you get hit with a dick all the time."

For many of Starski's peers, though, the forecast appeared much brighter.

CHAPTER 2

Writing on the Wall

When Fred "Fab 5 Freddy" Brathwaite strolls up to meet me on a bright January afternoon in front of his Harlem studio, he's already embroiled in a cell phone conversation with Tony Shafrazi, a septuagenarian art dealer best known for spray-painting the words "KILL LIES ALL" onto Picasso's *Guernica* at the Museum of Modern Art in 1974.

Fab also made his name by spray-painting, often turning the New York subway's 5 line into his own fabulous canvas in the 1970s. He went on to direct the groundbreaking hip-hop film *Wild Style* and host the hit TV show *Yo! MTV Raps*. Perhaps most importantly, the Brooklyn native served as the connective tissue between Bronx graffiti artists and downtown creatives like Andy Warhol, Keith Haring, and Jean-Michel Basquiat. The latter embodied the essence of hip-hop perhaps better than anyone in the art world, getting his start as the graffiti artist SAMO and evolving into a neo-Expressionist painter whose work now sells for prices on par with Picasso's. (Basquiat died of a heroin overdose in 1988, at age twenty-seven.)

Still on the phone with Shafrazi, Fab leads me into a gated alleyway, empty except for a discarded church pew and a pair of lonely bathtubs. As we walk through a door and down some steps, Fab spots a circular mirror and, for some reason, hands it to me before opening yet another door. Behind it is a large room filled with fluorescent light—and dozens of Fab's latest works, most exhibiting colorful shapes painted over images of stacked subway cars. He directs me to place the mirror next to a red-and-black poster featuring the silhouettes of a woman and a beaver (the heading: "ZOMBEAVERS"). Then he puts Shafrazi, now talking about Basquiat's work, on speakerphone.

"It was so raw . . . so original," the art dealer says. "That's why I miss the motherfucker."

"He's still with us," says Fab, adding a Swarovski crystal to the forehead of a life-size portrait of boxer Jack Johnson on an easel in the middle of the room.

Eventually he bids Shafrazi adieu, and we start talking about Fab's first experiences with hip-hop. When he joined the budding scene during the 1970s, he saw something with the makings of a full-fledged cultural movement, complete with its own music, dance, and visual art. Its name took longer to catch.

"You would be like, 'Well, it was one of them parties where they say that hippety hop thing,'" he says. "It was Lovebug who popularized that word, between him and Hollywood."[1]

Fab goes on to credit Herc, Bambaataa, and Flash with helping to form the movement; his sentences are occasionally punctuated by the loud clang of pedestrians stepping on the part of his basement studio's ceiling that's a metal trapdoor to the sidewalk above. He's careful to point to the earliest of hip-hop's forebears as well, calling out Lightnin' Rod and Grandmaster Flowers, before acknowledging his own contribution.

"I think Herc did important stuff, playing the breakbeats, and setting up a structure and a format that then rapping would become a part of," he says. "But none of this . . . was [widely] called hip-hop at the time. I get a little bit of credit for helping brand it as such."

Fab discovered hip-hop before the genre's first song was recorded— legally, at least. He and his cohort started to hear rap music at parties hosted by mobile DJs in Brooklyn during the mid-1970s, and through bootleg recordings distributed through a booming black market.

"There was a kid named Tapemaster," says Bronx-born photographer Joe Conzo, dubbed "the man who took hip-hop's baby pictures" by the *New York Times*. "He used to record all the shows on cassettes and sell them the next week."[2]

One day, Fab heard a recording of a set performed in the Bronx by Grandmaster Flash and the Furious Five. *I've got to hear these guys with this amazing rhyming,* Fab thought to himself. "The tape, it must have been sixth generation," he recalls. "It was pretty much static and distortion, but I could hear enough to go, 'What the fuck is *this*? This is a whole other thing.'"[3]

As he roamed farther from his native borough, the din of a new movement grew louder. He went to a party in a housing project on Manhattan's Lower East Side and found some six hundred young revelers gyrating to hip-hop beats. At each gathering he attended, he'd learn the location of the next one; there were no cell phones, no social media—only paper flyers advertising exotic names like the Cold Crush Brothers (Grandmaster Caz's group) and the Funky Four Plus One More (the latter featured Sha Rock, considered by many to be the first female rapper).

Fab also began to notice a change in the style of graffiti sprouting across the city's public spaces. The monochromatic tagging that dates back at least to the "Kilroy was here" drawings by U.S. servicemen during the first half of the twentieth century was exploding into a riot of bright colors, bubbly fonts, and bold expressions of urban life, signed by mysterious artists who went by names like "Taki 183" and "Futura 2000."

"Something clicked in my head from cutting school and going to museums and browsing through art books," says Fab. "This stuff, to me, was very similar to what was going on with pop art."

Inspired by Warhol, Lichtenstein, and Rauschenberg, Fab started to experiment with his own graffiti in New York's subway system.

In those days, as he recalls, a single master key unlocked doors to all the city's stations, tunnels, yards, and layups, where trains are parked at night. A plucky graffiti artist had somehow procured a copy of the key and allowed it to be duplicated by other members of the community; Fab managed to get his hands on one.

As he honed his graffiti skills in the yards of the Bronx, using the tag "FRED FAB 5," Fab spent more time downtown. There, at clubs like Danceteria and the Roxy, musicians from Talking Heads and Blondie listened to early hip-hop music alongside up-and-coming artists like Basquiat, whom Fab quickly befriended. As his involvement in pop art and street art grew, Fab yearned for a way to unite them, and then it dawned on him: what if he painted an entire train with Campbell's soup cans as an homage to Warhol?

"The purpose was to disrupt kind of the consciousness of people painting trains, to do something totally out of the box," says Fab. "Also, if anybody [not] aware of our history sees it, to make them think, *Wait: these guys are not just these crazy vandals that they're depicted to be. Some of them — one of them; who knows how many of them? — are familiar with modern art!*"

On a frigid night in 1980, Fab and fellow graffiti artist Lee Quiñones made the trek to Baychester in the north Bronx, armed with spray paint and keys not only to the layup but to the actual subway cars. They targeted the 5 train, a heavily trafficked line that travels south through the heart of Manhattan before continuing on to Brooklyn. Fab and Quiñones slipped into the yard, unlocked a train car, and switched on the heat; it was so cold out that they had to keep their paint inside the car to prevent it from coagulating. Fab painted through the night, creating Campbell's soup cans with his own twist: under the iconic red label, he called the flavors "Da-Da Soup," "Pop Soup," "Fabulous Soup," and "Fred Soup." He rushed off before he was completely finished. "The sun started coming up," he recalls. "So it was time to go."

The reaction to Fab's mobile installation came swiftly as passengers at crowded stops from Grand Central Terminal to Wall Street discovered his handiwork. The notoriety earned Fab an introduction to Warhol himself. "Oh my God, this is so incredible," Fab remembers Warhol exclaiming upon seeing a Polaroid of the mural. "I have to sign this." The two artists soon became friends; Fab had found his fifteen minutes of fame, and then some. (Warhol would often say, "Fred, you're so famous!") The subway in question didn't get "buffed," or cleaned, for several years thereafter — an unofficial arrangement with the Metropolitan Transportation Authority to preserve Fab's art. Graffiti was becoming the visual representation of a rebellion against the dreary uniformity that Robert Moses stood for, carried out by the very people who'd been hemmed in by his midcentury machinations.

Warhol wasn't the only member of the downtown intelligentsia impressed by Fab's work. His new friends in Blondie — especially lead singer Debbie Harry and guitarist Chris Stein — decided to record a tribute to the movement to which he'd introduced them. "Fab 5 Freddy told me everybody's fly," Harry rapped on "Rapture." "DJ spinning, I said, 'My, my.' Flash is fast, Flash is cool..." The band flattered Fab by playing him the song one day. A month later, he was sitting in a cab in Paris with members of Talking Heads when the song came on the radio.

"I never thought it was a real record that was supposed to come out," says Fab. "I just thought they were showing me, 'Look, we got everything you were telling us. We think it's cool, too.' I thought they were just fooling around in the studio."

The band was completely serious. Upon its release in 1980, the song rocketed to number one on the charts, the first track with a rap verse to accomplish that feat.[4] Stein and Harry invited Fab to appear in the music video and asked him to bring along someone to play the role of DJ. Fab invited Flash, but when the scheduled date arrived, he was nowhere to be found. So Basquiat stepped in and pretended to be a DJ. Says Fab: "Jean was like, 'Fuck, man, I'm just going to stand here and look cool. Whatever.'"[5]

With the help of writer-director Charlie Ahearn, Fab parlayed the success of the video into *Wild Style,* a thinly veiled 1983 biopic of hip-hop's origins. This time, Flash did show up, acting in the film alongside Grandmaster Caz, Grandwizzard Theodore, Quiñones, Fab, and others. Reviews of the movie provided some of the first printed references to hip-hop and rap as art forms. Even the *New York Times* weighed in, describing the film as "a partly improvised piece of fiction, about the cheeky, high-spirited art of the South Bronx, that is, subway graffiti, also known as 'writing,' and about rapping and breaking."[6]

Hip-hop had, within a span of less than five years, gone from being a nameless genre whose music had never been recorded to a "Rapper's Delight" novelty to a new form of music cited in mainstream publications—and charts. In 1980, Kurtis Blow's "The Breaks" reached number eighty-seven on *Billboard*'s Hot 100 and sold more than five hundred thousand units. The song broke big in the Netherlands, prompting a trip by Blow and Simmons to Amsterdam; they knew they'd officially made it when the head of PolyGram met them at the airport.[7]

"What would you like, Mr. Simmons?" he asked.

The young mogul didn't hesitate: "Cocaine and pussy."

"Absolutely," the executive replied.[8]

Blow and Simmons had company. By 1981, Tom Silverman had turned his obsession with the nascent genre into the record label Tommy Boy; one of his first signees was Afrika Bambaataa and the Soulsonic Force. Drawing on Bambaataa's burgeoning brand of hip-hop-infused electrofunk, the group released "Planet Rock" in 1982, and the song made it all the way to number forty-eight on the charts while selling over half a million copies in the United States. Yet music industry bigwigs overseas didn't always give hip-hop acts the same treatment Blow and Simmons received in Amsterdam. Silverman still remembers trying to sell British radio DJs on early rap songs. "They were like, 'I love you, Tommy, I'd love to play this record, but they're talking on the record,'" Silverman recalls. "I did the same thing when I took Bambaataa to England. They didn't understand it. They said he was a disgrace to his race."[9]

But the hits kept coming. In 1982, Sylvia Robinson was still working her formula: hiring a house band to back rap tracks, which enabled her to produce songs at a cost of $3,000 to $4,000 apiece and entire albums for less than $50,000.[10] (Today, big-budget videos alone often soar well into the six figures.) She graduated from scouting rappers in New Jersey pizza joints and started signing big-name acts like Grandmaster Flash and the Furious Five. Robinson overcame being a one-hit wonder as a hip-hop producer by releasing the act's aforementioned smash "The Message," despite a heavy dose of skepticism from the members of the group itself. When they first heard the track, one of them threw the cassette into the bushes.[11]

"We hated the song. It was just so different from what we were used to doing…the natural party songs and dance songs," recalls Eddie "Scorpio" Morris, another member of the group. But bandmate Melle Mel believed in Robinson. "Mel said, 'Well, if you like it that much, Ms. Rob, then I'll do it.'"[12]

The song peaked at number sixty-two on the Hot 100, with Melle Mel doing most of the lyrical lifting. At around that time, Grandmaster Flash sued Sugar Hill for $5 million in unpaid royalties (he lost), and the group disbanded in 1983.[13] They reunited intermittently—most notably for their induction into the Rock and Roll Hall of Fame in 2007, becoming the first hip-hop act to earn that honor. It was no doubt a matter of pride for the man who introduced them at the ceremony: Jay-Z.

As far as Fab is concerned, the DJ and his group were sensible choices as the genre's first representatives. "It was all good," he says. "Flash's position and legacy is solid."[14] Other hip-hop acts would go on to be inducted: Run-D.M.C., Public Enemy, the Beastie Boys, N.W.A., and Tupac Shakur, to name a few. But forefathers such as Starski, Caz, Bambaataa, and Herc remain excluded.

Just as hip-hop made its move from the streets to the clubs to the mainstream charts, America's social fabric was upended in a completely different and destructive way by another addictive phenomenon: crack cocaine. The high-grade powdered stuff had been around for ages, fueling the glitzy disco scene in New York and beyond. But the degraded, smokable form — which can be created from pure cocaine with little more than baking soda and a hot plate — was far cheaper and faster-acting.

Cocaine poured into the United States from Latin America in the 1980s, and the glut of supply sent its price tumbling from $50,000 per kilo in 1980 to $35,000 in 1984 to $12,000 in 1992; by the mid-1980s, single doses were available for as little as two dollars a pop. Within a few years, the number of people employed in the distribution of the drug had swelled to 150,000 in New York City alone.[15] "No one hired a skywriter and announced crack's arrival," noted Jay-Z. "But when it landed in your hood, it was a total takeover. Sudden and complete. Like losing your man to gunshots. Or your father walking out the front door for good."[16]

Jay-Z's adolescence was marked by all of the above, but the advent of crack influenced his path perhaps most of all. According to his mentor, Jaz-O, Jay-Z's brother struggled with drug addiction; when Jay-Z was seventeen, he even shot his brother in the shoulder for stealing his jewelry (he'd initially intended to startle him with a near-miss).[17] Still, the young rapper himself entered the trade after childhood friend DeHaven Irby, who lived across the hall from Jay-Z in the Marcy Houses, showed him the ropes.

"If you're a person that's studying and focused on what you do, and you become crafty at it, I begin to mimic what you do," says Irby, explaining Jay-Z's thought process. "Because it works for you. I'm going to put my own twist to it, my own originality."[18]

When Irby moved to Trenton, New Jersey, a teenage Jay-Z would go down on weekends to visit him — alternately impressing

Irby's friends with his spitfire flow and honing his hustling skills. He started out small, selling quantities of crack for as little as ten dollars. As Irby told me for my book *Empire State of Mind,* Jay-Z would never cut the price to nine dollars. Like an airline executive refusing to slash fares on unsold seats two hours before takeoff, Jay-Z didn't want to condition his customers to expect discounts, a philosophy that would follow him into the music business. He was also unflappable: not even the gruesome murder of his trusted supplier — shot in the head, execution-style, with his own testicles stuffed in his mouth — could convince him (or Irby) to leave the drug trade.[19]

The only thing that ever pulled Jay-Z off the streets was music. In 1988, Jaz-O became the first rapper to land a deal with UK-based label EMI, one of the major record companies at the time, and he invited his apprentice to come to London for two months. Shortly after turning nineteen, Jay-Z got his first taste of foreign travel, not to mention luxury: Jaz's entourage motored to his New Year's Eve release party in a Cadillac limo.[20]

Jay-Z returned to the United States in 1989 and tried to break into the stateside hip-hop scene, landing a spot on a tour headlined by Antonio "Big Daddy Kane" Hardy, one of the most successful rappers of hip-hop's late-1980s golden age. They were joined on the road by a host of burgeoning stars, including Tupac Shakur, Queen Latifah, and Michael "MC Serch" Berrin of seminal hip-hop group 3rd Bass. Jay-Z would go onstage and rap during Kane's wardrobe changes, receiving only room and board for his troubles. Despite his subsequent lyrical claims that he was still spending money from 1988, his drug-dealing profits hadn't lasted into the new year: Serch remembers Jay-Z having to beg Kane for cash just so that he could grab fast food for dinner.[21] "He doesn't exaggerate the amount of hustling," adds Jaz. "He exaggerates the magnitude."[22]

Disillusioned with the lack of financial opportunity afforded by hip-hop, Jay-Z turned back to the drug trade in the early 1990s. With connections in New York — the main entry point for illegal drugs in the northeastern United States—and across the river in New Jersey, he reunited with Irby and started testing the laws of supply and demand. Though the per-kilo price of cocaine had plummeted, it was still harder to find, and therefore more expensive, beyond New York. So they expanded their enterprise into new markets like Virginia and Maryland. Jay-Z raked in more cash than he'd ever dreamed possible—and grew even richer in subject matter.

"I stood on cold corners far from home in the middle of the night serving crack fiends and then balled ridiculously in Vegas; I went dead broke and got hood rich," he wrote in his autobiography. "I hated it. I was addicted to it. It nearly killed me. But...I was part of a generation of kids who saw something special about what it means to be human—something bloody and dramatic and scandalous that happened right here in America—and hip-hop was our way of reporting that story."[23]

Charlie Stettler does not look like someone who played an instrumental role in laying the earliest foundation of the business of hip-hop. But that's exactly what the ice-blue-eyed, bald-headed Swiss entrepreneur did after leaving his homeland in 1971, landing in New York with $300 in his pocket and no English in his vocabulary.

Stettler slept in Central Park his first night in the city—after trying marijuana for the first time and blacking out—and woke up to find himself robbed of everything but his underwear. Instead of turning around and going home, he stayed. By 1978 he had learned English, worked a string of nightlife jobs, and gotten so accustomed to New York (and the noise from living next to a fire station) that when he went to Barbados for a vacation with his girlfriend, a coconut falling on the roof in the middle of the night startled him out of his wits.

"I get up the next morning, I tell her I'm going to go back to

New York," recalls Stettler. "I'm going to record the sounds of New York City for people who can't sleep in the country."[24]

Stettler started his own label, Tin Pan Apple, releasing the noise cassettes in 1982. He took to walking around New York in a gorilla costume to promote his product, which soon landed him a TV interview — and helped him sell over a quarter of a million copies of his tape. Flush with cash, he went out to the Roxy one Friday night. He was surprised to find the club full of black teenagers "spinning on their heads," whipped into a frenzy by a sturdy turntablist dressed in African regalia. Imagine Stettler's surprise when the jock walked up to him after the show.

"I saw you, crazy motherfucker, on TV yesterday," the DJ said, having immediately recognized Stettler and his marketing prowess. "You have what we need."

"What *is* this?" said Stettler, gesturing to the scene around him.

"It's called hip-hop."

"Who are you, man?"

"My name is Afrika Bambaataa."

After Bambaataa educated Stettler about the movement, the Swiss entrepreneur hatched a plan: to host a massive hip-hop talent show at Radio City Music Hall, with the idea of further establishing the genre in the mainstream consciousness — and making some more cash for himself. Stettler went to the Fever and met Sal Abbatiello, who put him in touch with the general manager of R & B radio station WBLS. Many outlets had instituted "No rap" policies by this point, even urban stations. ("The African Americans who were working the record business didn't like these voices," says Simmons. "They're very harsh voices. These guys had escaped that.")[25]

WBLS's manager told Stettler he'd put the contest on the radio if it came with advertising; Stettler managed to convince Coca-Cola to pay $300,000 to be associated with the contest. On May 23, 1983, Stettler and Simmons joined the six thousand people who descended upon Radio City for the show. Judges included Abbatiello, Robinson,

Silverman, and agent Cara Lewis, who would go on to represent Tupac Shakur, Kanye West, and others. Kurtis Blow and Whodini performed as guest artists, but a relatively unknown trio of beefy teenagers called the Disco 3 won the crowd—and the grand prize: a record deal with Stettler, who took them to Switzerland to celebrate. Shortly after their return, Simmons appeared at Stettler's office.[26]

"Look," said Simmons. "We don't know who the fuck you are, but we're putting together something called Fresh Fest. Since you got money from Coca-Cola, can you help us get money again?"

Stettler agreed, with two conditions: first, he'd get 10 percent of the proceeds of the proposed tour, and second, his new group would be the opening act. "I just came back from Switzerland and they ate so much food that I got a bill for three hundred and fifty dollars, so I renamed them the Fat Boys," he explained. Simmons laughed. The 10 percent was fine, but he didn't want a bunch of no-names opening for the acts on the roster of his new company, Rush Management. In addition to Blow, he was managing Run-D.M.C., a trio featuring Simmons's brother Joseph "Run" Simmons, alongside bandmates Jason "Jam Master Jay" Mizell and Darryl "D.M.C." McDaniels. The group's first single, "It's Like That / Sucker MCs," had peaked at number fifteen on *Billboard*'s R & B charts.

After Simmons left, Stettler walked down to the Tower Records on Broadway, where he convinced the store's brass to host a cringe-worthy contest revolving around the Fat Boys. Stettler had the trio stand on a meat scale in the window; anyone who could guess the group's combined weight (nearly half a ton) would receive a can of Diet Pepsi for every pound—donated, of course, by the cola company (remarkable, given Stettler's recent tie-up with its top rival). Then Stettler had his girlfriend print up a fake press release saying that the Fat Boys had been selected to open for Michael Jackson and his brothers on their upcoming tour. The attention earned Stettler a spot on *Good Morning America* touting his group. Then he called Simmons.

"Did you see that shit?" asked Stettler.

"All right," Simmons replied. "You're the opening act."

Stettler's next trick: leveraging his European connections to get a $360,000 deal for the Fat Boys with Swatch, the first of its kind for hip-hop, allowing the group to fund a spate of live shows and recording sessions. Their self-titled debut, which featured production from Blow, reached number six on the R & B charts and cracked the top 50 on *Billboard's* broader album rankings. Their association with Simmons also earned them a spot in the film *Krush Groove* in 1985, which chronicles the rise of hip-hop—as well as Simmons's latest venture, Def Jam Recordings.

As hip-hop's first great institutions rose in New York, the West Coast scene was still disentangling itself from disco. That didn't stop the nascent genre's teenage prince from giving himself a moniker reminiscent of his Bronx forerunners: "Dr. Dre, the Master of Mixology." The stage name, which he quickly shortened, was a portmanteau of his given name and the nickname of his favorite basketball player, the soaring dunkmaster Julius "Dr. J" Erving. After cashing in on a steady fifty-dollar-per-night DJ gig at Eve After Dark, Dre did some flying of his own—in an orange Mazda RX-3 coupe purchased secondhand for $3,500 from his boss, Alonzo Williams.[27]

The World Class Wreckin' Cru kept cashing in at Los Angeles–area nightclubs, and Dre's renown grew as a DJ,[28] but his ability to lug around sound equipment—and the moneymaking opportunities that went along with it—was limited by the size of his car. He didn't make it easy for friends to lend him a larger vehicle either. "I would never give Dre my van," says Williams. "Dre would stop and have sex with somebody. He never would make it to the gig."[29]

But Williams put up with the young producer's antics because of his considerable talent. Thanks in part to Dre's beats, Williams landed a $100,000 deal for the Cru with CBS's Epic Records. He spent about $13,000 on the first album, *Rapped in Romance,* and gave each of the group's other members $15,000. The Cru drew on influences coming out of New York: Bambaataa, Run-D.M.C., and Flash, to name a few.

But the record never took off, and Williams soon grew tired of Dre's immaturity. The producer racked up moving violations; he'd leave them unpaid and ignore each summons he received. When he didn't show up in court, the summonses turned into warrants, and Williams had to bail him out of jail repeatedly. The first two times, he had an incentive: the Cru had a show to play, and then studio time booked. When it happened again, the group's schedule was clear, so Williams decided to teach Dre a lesson. Fortunately for Dre, his acquaintance Eric "Eazy-E" Wright, a small-time drug dealer of similarly tiny physical stature, offered to bail him out if he'd make some beats for Eazy's new label.

Eazy had founded Ruthless Records with help from veteran manager Jerry Heller, who'd met Eazy through Williams, another one of his clients. Many rappers (Jay-Z included) would later use drug-dealing profits to start a record company; in an era when many major labels were still squeamish about hard-edged hip-hop, that was often the only way to put their music on wax. At first, Dre's involvement with Eazy only involved producing records to pay back his bail debt, and he remained part of the Cru. Then, one night at Eve After Dark, he saw Run-D.M.C. perform. "That was just it for me," Dre later said.[30]

Dre's contract with the Cru expired in 1986, the same year Ice-T released "6 in the Mornin'," considered by many to be the first example of West Coast gangsta rap (Philadelphia lyricist Schoolly D gets pioneering credit on the East Coast). For Dre, the notion of donning sequined jumpsuits to perform with the Cru no longer seemed tenable. One day, he simply stopped showing up at rehearsals. Along with fellow group member Antoine "DJ Yella" Carraby, he teamed up with Eazy and teenage rapper O'Shea "Ice Cube" Jackson (as well as, briefly, the performer Kim "Arabian Prince"

Nazel and, later, the rapper Lorenzo "MC Ren" Patterson) to form a group of their own: N.W.A. (Niggaz with Attitudes).[31]

Their first production together was Eazy's "Boyz-n-the-Hood," a song with a protagonist who wakes up at noon, immediately gets drunk, and encounters the stereotypical hallmarks of the era's Los Angeles urban experience: guns, drugs, domestic violence. As depicted in the blockbuster biopic *Straight Outta Compton,* Ice Cube wrote the lyrics and Dr. Dre provided the beat, coaching the novice rapper Eazy as he recorded verses line by line over a period of days. The latter went to Macola, a local distributor run by Canadian former tugboat captain Don Macmillan, and had the recording pressed up as a single under Ruthless.

Eazy named himself sole proprietor of Ruthless, with Heller serving as general manager and taking 20 percent of every incoming dollar. Though Eazy offered him a fifty-fifty ownership split, Heller says he proposed the general manager agreement because he "wanted to bend over backward to do what was right." (The setup also left Heller better off in the event of an asset seizure by the authorities, a not-insignificant backstop given Eazy's past.)[32]

Heller found Dre particularly impressive. The producer spoke softly and sparsely, parceling out directives of just a few words at a time, but would sometimes spend eight hours polishing a single line with an artist.[33] Heller helped N.W.A. land a distribution deal with Priority Records, and the other group members eagerly signed the contracts placed in front of them. But their financial savvy lagged behind their musical chops. As Dre put it, "We were just a bunch of creative guys who got together and did something amazing but were clueless about business."[34]

There was soon quite a bit more business to know about. In 1988, N.W.A. launched its debut studio album, *Straight Outta Compton,* which eventually climbed to number thirty-seven on the *Billboard* charts and sold more than three million copies, despite virtually no initial airplay. More impressive than its sales total was the album's polarizing impact on American culture. Many mainstream outlets

lauded its honesty: *Newsweek* dubbed it "some of the most gro-
tesquely exciting music ever made."[35]

Dre himself soon scoffed at the effort, which in hindsight he
viewed as crude. "To this day, I can't stand that album," he said in
1993. "I threw that thing together in six weeks so we could have
something to sell out of the trunk."[36] Yet even traditionally white-
rock-focused publications like *Rolling Stone* have since ranked
Straight Outta Compton among the best albums of all time. That's
no accident: while making the record, Dre would sometimes pull
aside one Caucasian member of the Ruthless staff and ask, "You
think white kids would like this?"[37] The fact that they did was
what made N.W.A. so dangerous for many observers. As Ice-T said
on Oprah Winfrey's show in 1990, "If only my friends were hearing these records, nobody'd care. [But] the white kids from suburbia are listening to N.W.A., and the parents don't know what to do
about it."

Though the members of N.W.A. were essentially nihilist mon-
eymakers who never intended to be political — "Fuck that black
power shit," Eazy once said. "We don't give a fuck"[38] — the record
touched off a political earthquake whose aftershocks made it all
the way to Washington, DC. Officials started to take wary notice
of hip-hop, and they didn't like what they saw, particularly the song
"Fuck tha Police." It didn't matter that the track had been recorded
by a group of kids fresh out of high school with a rap sheet by that
point mostly limited to traffic violations, or that it represented the
unrestrained outcry of a voiceless community against racial profil-
ing and downright brutality. Nor did it seem to matter that the
local authorities often issued similarly violent missives: at around
the same time, Los Angeles police chief Daryl Gates told a Senate
hearing that casual drug users "ought to be taken out and shot."[39]

As N.W.A. embarked upon its first major tour, government
forces began to hound the group. FBI assistant director Milt Ahlerich sent a letter to Priority Records in August 1989, saying that
"recordings such as the one from N.W.A. are both discouraging

and degrading to these brave, dedicated officers." Then he added, somewhat ominously, "Music plays a significant role in society, and I wanted you to be aware of the FBI's position relative to this song and its message."[40]

Under pressure from law enforcement, N.W.A. initially agreed to refrain from playing "Fuck tha Police" at a September show in Detroit—but then launched into a rendition anyway. Officers stormed the stage and escorted the group back to its hotel; one officer reportedly said, "We just wanted to show the kids that you can't say 'Fuck the police' in Detroit."[41] Members of the group were detained at their hotel, but no arrests were made; the FBI never took any action against the group, and the drama turned out to be something of a gift to N.W.A.[42] "I have to say thanks to that FBI agent that wrote us that letter," Dre said on VH1's *Behind the Music*. "You did a big service to us and . . . you made us a lot of money."

Indeed, the group's tour grossed $650,000 in a single year. But $130,000 of that went to Heller, while Ice Cube took home just $23,000, plus another $32,000 for writing or cowriting half of the group's songs. Cube seethed: he was living at home and driving a Suzuki Sidekick as Heller cruised L.A. in a Mercedes. So the rapper retained a lawyer who examined the case and said that Ruthless owed Cube at least $120,000. The two sides couldn't come to an agreement, and the rapper eventually ditched N.W.A. in protest. Heller, who declined to comment for this book and passed away before it was finished, blamed the departure on what he described as Cube's jealousy of Eazy. For his part, the latter didn't seem fazed by losing his chief songwriter, simply saying, "It means we get more money."[43]

But just about everybody else in N.W.A.'s orbit knew that Ice Cube functioned as its lyrical spark plug and Dre its sonic pistons. Heller provided the industry experience and Eazy brought capital, both of which Dre was beginning to amass on his own. And yet Heller and Eazy received the largest checks from Ruthless. Dre soon realized that he wasn't in a terrific situation—and that he might be better off starting his own company. Of course, he was still contractually obligated to Ruthless.

"I know Dre," says Williams. "If he thinks he's being taken advantage of, he'll walk. He has no problem. If he don't like a situation...he'll find a way out."[44]

In 1986, Run-D.M.C. released its third album, *Raising Hell,* which earned triple-platinum certification and peaked at number six on *Billboard*'s mainstream album charts. With Aerosmith's help on its cover of the rock giant's "Walk This Way," the Queens group had made perhaps the most compelling case of any hip-hop act so far that the genre was more than a fad.

The buzz carried over to the group's show at Madison Square Garden later that year. After Jam Master Jay and D.M.C. walked out to a standing ovation, D.M.C. gazed out at the crowd imperiously. "Run is backstage, and he said he's not coming out tonight," he told the audience. "Until you make some motherfucking noise." The crowd started chanting Run's name. When he finally appeared, he opened the show with a line that exemplified hip-hop's unapologetic swagger: "This is my motherfucking Garden."[45]

Having suspected that the group would elicit such a response, Russell Simmons had invited a team of executives from German shoemaker Adidas to the show and prepared a surprise. Before Run-D.M.C. played its song "My Adidas," an ode to shell-toed shoes, the rappers asked everyone to take off their kicks and hoist them in the air. Thousands of pairs of Adidas floated toward the rafters. Thanks to such displays, Simmons brokered an endorsement deal with Adidas for Run-D.M.C. worth $1 million.[46] At the time, he says, "it was easier to sell Adidas by loving them than by making your own."[47]

Hip-hop's first seven-figure branding pact served as a precursor to the even bigger bonanzas that came as the corporate world grew more comfortable with the genre. Many of those deals originated with Simmons, as both a manager and label founder. Starting in the 1980s, he discovered and developed some of hip-hop's brightest behind-the-scenes players. He launched Def Jam with a hard-rocking NYU student named Rick Rubin, now one of music's most respected producers. ("I just realized he was the talented one," says Simmons. "I chose to stay with him.")[48] With the help of lieutenants like Lyor Cohen, a six foot five dynamo of Israeli descent who started as Run-D.M.C.'s road manager, and Harlem-born general manager Andre Harrell, Def Jam went on to add iconic acts like James "LL Cool J" Smith,[49] the Beastie Boys, and Public Enemy.

If the early days of hip-hop were the Wild West, Def Jam operated as the freewheeling frontier capital. MC Serch, whose group 3rd Bass signed for a paltry $5,000 per member, recalls hanging out in the fledgling company's early offices and answering fan mail for Slayer, the thrash metal band brought in by Rubin. "I would call fans and pretend like I was [frontman] Tom Araya," he says, chuckling. "[Def Jam] was this machine...There was a great energy."[50]

As it amassed an increasingly diverse and powerful roster, Def Jam became a force in the world of radio, where one of the only reliable ways to get a hip-hop record played was through the rampant practice of payola, or bribing influential jocks to play a song. Tom Silverman estimates that some DJs were making $50,000 per year on the side.[51] "I think that's probably an understatement," says Serch. "I knew guys in tertiary markets [who] worked less than twenty hours a week [and] had million-dollar condos."[52]

Meanwhile, another promotional medium was providing an alternative to radio: television, in the form of recently desegregated MTV. The channel almost exclusively played videos by white rock and pop acts from its founding in 1981 until 1984, when Michael Jackson's "Billie Jean" broke through with a little help from Walter Yetnikoff, the head of CBS Records. He called MTV chief Bob Pittman and threatened to hold back future videos from all his artists, including Bruce Springsteen and Billy Joel, if Pittman didn't play Jackson's. MTV conceded and started playing rap videos, too.[53]

Soon songs like 1986's "Walk This Way" and LL Cool J's "I'm Bad," from 1987, amped up the demand for hip-hop videos so much that MTV completed its 180-degree turn, tapping Fab to host a new show called *Yo! MTV Raps* in 1988. The two-hour program featured a mix of music videos and interviews with rap stars from Salt-N-Pepa to N.W.A. (When the latter group appeared on the show to promote its second album, Dr. Dre told Fab he wanted to become a billionaire: "We out to take Donald Trump out!")[54]

The following year, when the Grammys created the first award for rap—but chose not to air its presentation—Fab hosted a boycott party on Sunset Boulevard in Los Angeles and filmed an episode of *Yo! MTV Raps* with Ice-T and New York rapper Slick Rick, who'd been nominated alongside DJ Jazzy Jeff and the Fresh Prince (now better known as Will Smith). It turned out to be one of the year's best-attended parties, drawing visitors as unlikely as *Forbes* magazine chief Malcolm Forbes, who rolled in on a motorcycle.

"So, Malcolm, how do you feel about rap?" asked Fab.

"I'm ready to rock!" he said.

To this day, Fab remains amazed.

"We were in the heart of the zeitgeist," says Fab. "Malcolm Forbes confirmed my show, *Yo! MTV Raps*—and hip-hop culture—had truly arrived."[55]

Diddy was similarly ready to rock. Intrigued by the idea of becoming both a performer and an entrepreneur, he applied to college and was accepted at Howard University, the historically black college based in Washington, DC. He spent the summer before his freshman year working as rapper-beatboxer Doug E. Fresh's personal valet, shuttling Fresh's clothes to and from the dry cleaner in his Volkswagen Rabbit convertible.[56]

At Howard, Diddy majored in business but found that he preferred extracurriculars: namely, promoting parties in Washington,

DC, and going back home to do the same on weekends and school breaks. Diddy inserted himself into New York's hip-hop scene, popping up in one of Fresh's videos as a backup dancer and ingratiating himself with influential figures at his events. "Everybody's starting from the bottom," Diddy once told me. "I think that people believed in me because...I had a certain swagger."[57]

His combination of confidence and eagerness helped him land an internship at Uptown Records. Andre Harrell had left Def Jam to found the label in 1986, and Diddy got himself an introduction from the late rapper Dwight "Heavy D" Myers, an acquaintance from Mount Vernon. Diddy made an early impression: one day, Harrell asked Diddy to gas up his car—and when the intern returned, he'd also washed and vacuumed it.[58] Soon Diddy was getting up at dawn every Thursday to take the train from DC to New York, where he'd work two full days for Harrell before returning to Howard, often spending much of the ride in the Amtrak bathroom to avoid having to buy a ticket.

In 1989, Harrell hired party promoter Jessica Rosenblum to throw a platinum-album celebration for Heavy D. "I have a new intern and he's going to call you," Harrell told her. "He'll run errands for you or help you if you need anything." When the youngster phoned, Rosenblum was confused. "I literally couldn't understand what the guy was saying," she recalls. "So in my mind, I had had a phone call with 'Tuffy,' who was Andre's new intern."[59]

She soon came to know Puffy quite well, and when they weren't working, she obliged his requests to take him to all the "freaky" nightspots on the Lower East Side.[60] Rosenblum introduced Diddy to her friends on the scene, and he soaked up their knowledge and style. "I always remember with Puffy, he wore sunglasses that I thought were tacky, and I'm like, 'You gotta get your sunglass game up,'" says Rosenblum. "All I know is he owns dope sunglasses now."[61]

While still at Howard, Diddy heard that Uptown Records' head of artists and repertoire (A&R) — the label's chief talent scout — had left the company. Harrell had publicly stated that, with Uptown, he wanted to create a label with "that Harlem kind of cool hustler cachet to it." Diddy knew he had what Harrell wanted, through both his lineage and his can't-stop-won't-stop attitude, and he took his boss to lunch to ask for the job. It wasn't long before he dropped out of Howard and moved back to New York to work at Uptown full-time.[62]

"Sometimes people become successful and famous because one thing leads to another and they blow up," says Rosenblum. "But there are other people who are like, no matter what, they're going to end up [on top]. And to me, he was one of those people."[63]

Clang!

"I'm going to really talk to them about figuring out a way to secure that so it doesn't just make such abrupt noise," says Fab, after his latest thought gets interrupted by another pedestrian stomping on the metal trapdoor to his studio. "I was in here last night working, and it felt like somebody is going to just end up falling in this motherfucker."[64]

We've been talking for two hours, and in that span we've covered the first two decades of hip-hop and polished off a couple of sandwiches. As we finish by touching on the rise of gangsta rap, Fab's briefly derailed train of thought gets back on track.

"Fascination with the gangsta genre is a part of American culture," he muses. "America, to me, is based on a gangsta concept: 'We're going to come over here, take the land from indigenous peoples, bring black people here to work for free, a.k.a. slavery, and build this great capitalist economy.' Is that not gangsta?"

Fab pauses.

"I guess the only thing I could add in closing this session is the most interesting thing about hip-hop musical culture…It's become the first kind of business, postsegregation, where black men have been able to have a significant business role in the entire process," he says. "Versus prior, based on the way America was constructed, when there were black businessmen during the times of segregation, but we couldn't reach other segments of the American populace."

And that's where the three kings really come in.

"These individuals, particularly, have been able to benefit in that true American capitalist paradigm," he says. "It's kind of cool, because it never happened [before]... They're getting a bigger piece of the pie."

CHAPTER 3

Bad Boys

"I heard something on the radio today," says Branson Belchie, seated at a dimly lit bar on Manhattan's 109th Street and Columbus. "I was trying to really interpret it and trying to decipher and figure out sort of what it meant. I mean, *understand* the music. It usually has a certain feeling…It would move you…A lot of what I hear today is, like, these kids aren't saying nothing…They make sounds."[1]

He swirls his glass of Malbec. The atmosphere, along with his champagne-colored puffy jacket, is fitting: better known as Branson B, he is hip-hop's unofficial sommelier. The dreadlocked Harlem native grew up around hip-hop forefathers like Kurtis Blow and gangsters such as Frank Lucas. (Branson also served as a consultant on the film *American Gangster*.) And he was among the first to bring certain high-life hallmarks—Dom Pérignon and Cristal, along with other goodies—to Jay-Z, Diddy, and Notorious B.I.G.

Back in the early 1980s, he would host parties in Sugar Hill that extended five blocks through the city streets. Neatly arranged rows of empty Veuve Clicquot and Nicolas Feuillatte bottles would stretch along St. Nicholas Place from 151st to 152nd Street as the evenings wore on. Today, he runs a nearby shop called Branson Got Juice and has his own Guy Charlemagne–backed champagne line. But right now, he's uncorking on the state of hip-hop.

"Who's the artist now, got a song out, he's just humming or something?" asks Branson. "Came from Brooklyn. What's his name?"

I tell him I can't remember.

"He's humming the whole song," he continues. "He's not rapping, he's not singing, he's just humming...Where does that come from? Then you got other people, other youth, they identify with that. How are they connected to that?"

The waiter brings me a plate of cheesy garlic bread.

"A lot of the things that go on today, I don't understand it. But the youth of America, they understand it," he says. "It's just completely different."

I offer Branson some garlic bread.

"What kind of cheese is that?"

"Parmesan."

"It's Parmesan?"

"I don't like grated Parmesan," I explain. "But I like the melted Parmesan."

At this moment, the absurdity of our conversation strikes me like a bottle of champagne over the head. Things have changed quite a bit in Harlem and its environs. Just a few decades ago, Diddy's father was gunned down four blocks from where we are now, sitting in a trendy bar co-owned by a handful of local entrepreneurs (including one of Jay-Z's business partners), drinking wine and debating the merits of grated cheese.

Things have changed similarly for Diddy. Branson remembers going to clubs around the city in the early 1990s and, on multiple occasions, finding the aspiring mogul waiting in line with everyone else. "I told the gentleman at the door to let him in, because he's family," Branson recalls. "At that time, he was nobody."

Kenny Meiselas, Diddy's longtime lawyer, first met his client in the early 1990s—after a rapper named Father MC hired him to get the brash young A&R guy away from his second album at

Uptown. Though Diddy, in one of his first tasks at Uptown, had helped the artist create a well-received debut, complete with a gold-certified single, Father MC wanted full creative control over his follow-up.

"Father was never heard from again," says Meiselas. "But Puff was so impressed on how I handled myself in the room representing Father and getting him thrown off the project that he came to me...and basically was like, 'I like how you did that. Will you represent me?'"[2]

An astonished Meiselas agreed, and watched as Diddy assiduously applied his brand of urban panache to acts on Uptown's roster, starting with Mary J. Blige. "This A&R comes in with a cape on, like Superman...understands who this girl is from the hood, puts me in a hat turned backwards, baggy pants, Timb[erland]s," Blige explained between songs at a recent concert. "Now, I'm the queen of hip-hop soul, because of this dude."[3]

Diddy took the same sartorial approach with Jodeci, a God-fearing gospel turned R & B quartet out of Charlotte that Harrell had signed. "They were from North Carolina, and they looked like they were from North Carolina," says Meiselas. "By the time Puff was done with them, they all looked like him...He merged hip-hop culture and music and style and fashion into R & B."[4]

Meanwhile, Diddy expanded his party promotion sideline with Jessica Rosenblum, quickly graduating from errand boy to equal partner. The two started throwing weekly parties at a popular nightspot called Red Zone, drawing a diverse crowd that ranged from Diddy's Harlem cohort to Rosenblum's downtown crew and beyond. Diddy put himself front and center at the events, morphing his childhood nickname, Puffy, into the more commanding Puff Daddy—and giving the parties he promoted with Rosenblum a new label: Daddy's House. He had those words printed on T-shirts that he passed out to friends and colleagues.[5]

"He's always felt like he was bigger than life," says Branson's goddaughter, Chenise Wilson, who became friends with Diddy in the late 1980s on the New York party circuit. "It was one of them things that you could admire, but the person looking from afar who didn't know him would probably hate it."[6]

Diddy's party promotion career continued its upward trajectory until December 28, 1991. That night, he and Rosenblum were hosting what they dubbed the Heavy D and Puff Daddy Celebrity Charity Basketball Game at City College's Nat Holman Gymnasium, with proceeds set to benefit AIDS charities. Big Daddy Kane, Jodeci, and members of Run-D.M.C. were listed among the headliners. The lineup attracted a sold-out crowd north of twenty-five hundred—and thousands more gathered outside, even when it became clear that there wouldn't be enough room for everyone.[7]

Wilson, who was working the event, remembers going with Diddy to ask a police officer to put up a barricade as the crowd grew unruly. But before anything could be done, the multitude began to push frantically toward the entrance, fearing that they wouldn't get in. Within minutes, the crowd surged into the building and down the stairs, right into the closed gym doors, which could open only into the packed stairwell. The stampede slammed dozens of people against the doors, and nine were crushed to death.

"Puff was on the floor, trying to resuscitate people," says Wilson. "I grew up in the crack era...yet I never seen nothing like that in my life. Nine people taking their last breaths."[8]

Because Diddy's name appeared on the flyer, he drew much of the public blame, along with Rosenblum. Both of them stopped working for a spell and lay low, haunted by the images of that night, wondering if they'd be found legally or financially responsible for the tragedy.

"It was just an overwhelming kind of situation—some of those people that passed, Puff knew [them]," says Fab. "I said, 'Listen, man, what he's going through right now, if he can survive this, there's nothing that will ever stop him.'"[9]

While Diddy found himself thrust into the spotlight for reasons planned and unplanned, Jay-Z squeezed vast financial rewards from his expanded role in the drug trade as he ventured south along the Interstate 95 corridor. One source estimates that, in the early 1990s, Jay-Z and his business partner were moving about a kilo of cocaine—which would have translated into tens of thousands of dollars in cash—per week.

Jay-Z had nearly given up on music, but there were some who still believed in him. Shortly after Brooklyn native Rodolfo "DJ Clark Kent" Franklin landed a job at Atlantic Records, he remembered an encounter he'd had with a teenage Jay-Z in the Marcy Houses years earlier, and tracked him down with the goal of convincing him to turn his focus back to rap. But Jay-Z was making so much money that he had little interest in revisiting the world that, only a few years before, had barely allowed him to survive on the road. Kent eventually convinced him to appear on a few tracks, including a 1993 cut called "Can I Get Open" with the group Original Flavor, and another with the middling rapper Sauce Money.[10]

But Jay-Z's early work simply failed to catch. Branson, who dabbled in the music business, remembers putting together a mixtape with Todd "Too Short" Shaw at around this time; the Oakland rapper had recorded a few tracks with Jay-Z, and offered up a handful to Branson, who declined to release any of them. "I could've had a record with Jay-Z on it," he says. "But I didn't see him as a major talent at the time."[11] The young rapper seemed more focused on being a hustler than a musician. Too Short remembers the high-rolling vibe that accompanied Jay-Z and his crew as they sat in the studio playing cards: "They showed you the money."[12]

Jay-Z didn't seem like a good pick to become a fashion magnate either, at least not until Kent introduced him to his future business partner Damon Dash, a flashy Harlem party promoter, in the mid-

1990s. Wilson remembers meeting Jay-Z through Kent at around the same time — "He's going to be the greatest rapper ever," the DJ told her — but she couldn't get past his outfit: brown suede hat, brown suede shirt, black pants, and white Timberland boots. "Don't ever come outside with them on," she remembers telling him. "That matching hat and shirt? Nah, We don't really do that." ("[Damon] gave him his style," she adds.)[13]

Meanwhile, Jay-Z's future nemesis was having much better luck establishing himself. Queens-born Nasir "Nas" Jones scored a healthy five-figure advance and a $250,000 album budget from Columbia Records.[14] The silky flows of his 1994 debut, *Illmatic,* cause many even to this day to consider it one of the best hip-hop records of all time. Nas released his first album, boosted by Columbia's cash and seal of approval, before Jay-Z and Diddy launched theirs. Perhaps because of this, he spent most of his early career focused on music rather than on building a label or lifestyle brand of his own (he opened his opus with an uncompensated nod to Hennessy) before diversifying in recent years to paid endorsement deals and startup investments with the help of a forward-thinking young manager (more on this in chapter 10).

Those early days were a good time to put music first, even from a commercial standpoint. From 1984 to 1987, an average of 2.5 hip-hop albums achieved platinum status each year; from 1988 to 1993, that number quadrupled.[15] Hits by the likes of MC Hammer and Vanilla Ice strengthened rap's hold on the mainstream map, while N.W.A. and Public Enemy continued to develop hip-hop's sociopolitical reach. Def Jam benefited handsomely: PolyGram, the Dutch company whose chief had given Simmons a decadent welcome on his first trip to Amsterdam a decade earlier, purchased half of the label for $33 million in 1994.[16]

In the early days, the recording business brought more money to hip-hop acts than did touring, which today is usually the largest piece of a musician's financial pie. Hip-hop shows developed a reputation as security risks, thanks to reports of fights breaking out in crowds and unruly artist entourages acting up backstage. Of course, this sort of activity happened in other genres as well.

"In the earliest days of rock and roll, [the music] was considered dangerous," says Gary Bongiovanni, chief of live-music publication and touring data outfit Pollstar, noting that Alice Cooper and similar acts were once viewed as a threat to society. "If you're an arena manager, there's very little downside to bringing Ringling Brothers into your building. However, if you're hosting N.W.A., there's a host of things that probably pop into your mind that could happen that aren't good."[17]

A complex stew of risk aversion, racism, and soaring security costs caused many major venues to shy away from booking hip-hop acts well into the 1990s. As a result, the rap shows that did happen were often handled by second-rate promoters, or by entrepreneurs who had little experience with live music. "Nobody else really wanted to step up and do it," says Kevin Morrow, a Los Angeles concert promoter who remembers going to a Public Enemy show at the Palace—and seeing a SWAT team perched on the roof of Capitol Records across the street. "They were afraid of it, you know?"[18]

An unfortunate feedback loop developed: inexperienced promoters put on shows that weren't properly planned, the concerts went poorly, and top promoters felt justified in their initial stance. Morrow was one of the first to get the hip-hop touring paradigm right, booking shows at the now-defunct House of Blues on Sunset Boulevard in Los Angeles. He took a professional approach: he beefed up security and made sure he and his artists were on the same page. Soon he was doing forty hip-hop shows per year with some of the biggest acts in the genre—mostly musicians who could exert control over their crowds, like Chuck D of Public Enemy.

"I don't want any of this gang shit in here," the rapper would say, defusing potential conflicts at the very beginning of his shows. "We're all human beings that got to deal with a lot of problems, some of us more than others because of the color of our skin, and shame on us for black-on-black violence."

Less than three weeks after the City College tragedy, Milton Mollen — then New York's deputy mayor for public safety — released his official review of the situation. His conclusion: "Almost all of the individuals involved in the event demonstrated a lack of responsibility."[19]

The report particularly skewered the police department for its delayed intervention in the situation, and for not summoning more officers earlier in the evening as it became clear that more than five thousand people had shown up to a gym that could hold only about half that total. Mollen also called attention to a damning radio transmission in which an officer on the scene said of the crowd, "They're not people: they're animals."

Diddy got slammed for letting inexperienced subordinates handle key aspects of a challenging event and not hiring enough outside security. But neither he nor Rosenblum ever faced criminal charges for the tragedy. In the end, Mollen's report laid much of the blame at the feet of the spectators themselves, excoriating the "crowd psychology" that led everyone to push into the gym "with a total disregard for their fellow attendees."[20]

As the events unfolded, Harrell stood by his protégé, and Diddy returned the favor at Uptown. Mary J. Blige and Jodeci's debut albums were both on their way to selling more than three million units apiece, and major labels had lined up to lure away the young A&R. Rather than depart, Diddy decided to launch his own imprint, Bad Boy Records, within Uptown. "The deal was significantly smaller than what it would have been had we gone with one of these other suitors," says Meiselas. "He was very loyal to Andre."[21]

But the workplace tranquility didn't last. Diddy brought in an army of two dozen unpaid interns to help him run Bad Boy, and soon he was cranking out as much music as the rest of Uptown.

According to Meiselas and others, Harrell began to feel threatened by his protégé, who appeared to be taking over his company. Diddy's attitude didn't win him fans among Uptown's other executives either. "I'm walking around the office with no shirt on, cursing white people out," explained Diddy at his 2016 Bad Boy Reunion show in Brooklyn. "I'm not understanding the rules of the game."[22]

And so, one evening during the summer of 1993, Meiselas came home to find an agitated message from Diddy on his answering machine. Harrell had fired him. Meiselas called right back.

"Congratulations," said Meiselas.[23]

"What are you talking about?" his client replied. "I got *fired*."

"This is the best day of your life. You were very loyal to Andre, but he's right. There are in essence two kings in the castle, and there are always major companies that are trying to do bigger and better deals with you . . . Time to move on."

One of Diddy's first stops was the posh Mark Hotel on Manhattan's Upper East Side, where he met with executives from EMI. Rob Stone, then a twenty-four-year-old who'd recently transitioned from selling jewelry on the beach to serving as EMI's head of crossover marketing (and would go on to cofound creative agency Cornerstone and music magazine *The Fader*), sat in on the meeting and still remembers how the unemployed impresario two years his junior walked in with the swagger of a middle-aged billionaire.

"When I talk on my records, that's so people know it's me, and they don't even have to hear the artist," Diddy explained, delineating his vision for creating and curating the Bad Boy sound. "They're going to know it's hot. They're going to know the record. They're going to like the record before my artist even starts spitting."[24]

Whoa: this guy is full of himself, thought Stone.

In addition to running his own label, Diddy wanted to be the vice president of urban music at EMI — where the label's top act was Vanilla Ice. When the execs asked him what he'd do with the "Ice Ice Baby" rapper, Diddy didn't hesitate.

"I couldn't fuck with that dude," he said, turning to Stone. "*Rob* knows I can't fuck with him. Know what they'd do to me in the streets?"

I've never met anyone like this, Stone recalls thinking.

Even in his early twenties, Diddy understood that Vanilla Ice had a certain value but would never be cool in the eyes of Bad Boy's intended audience. Remarkably, as the meeting continued, Diddy became even more outrageously self-confident—and started to dictate his own terms.

"When you guys get in a room with all them suits and you're going to decide what you're going to pay Puff, just when you get to a number that you think is going to make Puff happy, get crazy on top of that," he declared. "And then when you're there, I want whipped cream and a cherry on top."

That is the greatest thing I've ever experienced in my life, Stone thought. By this point, his bosses were laughing. But Diddy was dead serious.

"I don't even want to think about the money; that shouldn't even be an issue," he said, leaning forward. "Don't be coming at me with no n**ger money. Goodbye."

While Diddy and Jay-Z generally rented the mansions and auto-mobiles on display in their visuals in the mid-1990s, Dr. Dre and his West Coast brethren released videos featuring their own lavish residences and automobiles. They had done more than catch up to the prosperity of the East Coast. "It seemed like they were win-ning," says Branson.[25]

Dre produced every song on N.W.A.'s second album, *Niggaz 4 Life* (officially titled *Efil4zaggin*—its intended title spelled back-ward to appease censors), which, despite Ice Cube's absence from it, sold nearly one million copies in the week after its May 1991 debut. That same month, *Billboard* changed the methodology for its charts: instead of calling a select few record stores and ask-ing for anecdotal reports of record sales, as it had in the past, the publication turned to research outfit SoundScan, which tabulated the numbers with a system tied directly to the scanning of bar codes at checkout counters across the country. The Parents Music Resource Center — Tipper Gore's much-maligned obscenity watchdog — slapped *Efil4zaggin* with a Parental Advisory notice, but the move seemed to only make the album more popular: it debuted at number two on *Billboard*'s revamped charts and soared to number one in its second week, a clear indication that hip-hop was selling more than even record store owners realized.[26]

At this time, Dre wasn't quite the savvy businessman many now consider him to be. Jerry Heller remembered visiting the producer to help him with some financial housekeeping and finding an uncashed royalty check for $12,000, along with several others for similar amounts.[27] Still, after Ice Cube's departure, Dre became convinced he could create a better situation for himself than he had with Ruthless and N.W.A. "He had grown confident in his decision-making," his mother wrote. "Most important, he knew his worth."[28] And Dre concluded that working for someone else was a great way to be underpaid.

At around the same time, Dre had grown close to Marion "Suge" Knight — who, as a scab during the 1987 NFL strike, was a lineman for the Los Angeles Rams before catching on as a Hollywood bodyguard and then as manager of Dre's pal Tracy "D.O.C." Curry. Knight's nickname was a variant of "Sugar Bear" — ironic in light of his rap sheet: by the time he'd entered Dre's circle, he had already been arrested for shooting a man while stealing a car in Las Vegas, assaulting someone at Los Angeles International Airport, and using a pistol to break a man's jaw during an argument outside his house. Somehow, he had managed to get away with probation each time.[29]

With N.W.A.'s second album in the rearview mirror, Dre called Eazy to set up a meeting and discuss the group's future. But according to Heller and many others close to the situation, the undersize rapper arrived at Solar Studios as promised to discover no sign of

Dre. In his place, he found Knight, two bodyguards with baseball bats, and a set of papers clearing D.O.C., Dr. Dre, and his then girlfriend, Michel'le, a singer, to leave Ruthless Records. "You got to sign these," Knight allegedly said — before threatening to harm Eazy, his mother, and Heller. "You better off signing."[30]

Knight's attorneys did not respond to a request for comment for this book,[31] while Dre declined through a publicist.[32] In regard to the Solar Studios incident, though, the Dre-approved biopic *Straight Outta Compton* seems to lend credence to Heller's recollection; the superproducer's own words suggest that he approved of Knight's by-any-means-necessary attitude. "When he came in a room, he had a presence," Dre said in 1999. "I looked at it like this: he got the releases."[33]

Having Knight around to do some of his dirty work left Dre the space to focus on creating music, but he had a violent streak of his own. In 1990, he beat up journalist Dee Barnes after taking issue with a TV segment she'd done; Dre blamed her for including a verbal shot from Ice Cube directed at N.W.A. (Dre and Barnes settled out of court.) At around the same time, Michel'le accused Dre of domestic abuse, though the matter never went to court. (Since then, Dre has issued several blanket public apologies for his violence toward women. Barnes accepted; Michel'le didn't.)[34]

None of these incidents prevented Dre and Knight from inking Interscope Records as Death Row's distribution partner and financial backer in 1992. Jimmy Iovine, who had worked as a sound engineer for John Lennon and Bruce Springsteen, cofounded Interscope in 1990 and took an interest in Dre at the behest of John McClain, one of the label's other founders. Sensing a kindred audiophile, Iovine authorized Interscope to pay Dre a $750,000 advance for his first solo record and add options for up to four additional albums, which could make the deal worth $7.5 million more. Knight's scare tactics weren't enough to completely free Dre of his contractual obligations to Ruthless, which received a fee of $750,000 for his services and took a cut of royalties, too.[35]

Dre's hometown simmered just as his career came to a boil. The Rodney King riots of 1992 left vast swaths of Los Angeles in flames, and Dre's work with N.W.A. provided the soundtrack, with protesters chanting "Fuck the police!" outside the LAPD's downtown headquarters. Dre himself hunkered down in his mansion in Calabasas, on the outskirts of the city, and wrote "The Day the Niggaz Took Over." The aggressive exhortation toward black unity appeared on his solo debut, but Dre axed an N.W.A.-style song called "Mr. Officer," later saying, "Making money is more important to me than talking about killing police."[36]

The Chronic hit store shelves in December 1992, several months after the riots. Dre didn't feel the need to hog the spotlight, even on his own record. D.O.C. cowrote six songs on *The Chronic,* while youngster Calvin "Snoop Doggy Dogg" Broadus made the album's biggest assist. Dre had discovered him on a mixtape at a bachelor party, eventually bringing him in as a guest and/or cowriter on all but three tracks on *The Chronic.* Snoop's unmistakable flow—lackadaisical yet intense, the hip-hop equivalent of a karate master practicing drunken fist martial arts—combined with Dre's own laid-back lyricism to create a new hip-hop classic. Iovine later likened the partnership to that of the Rolling Stones' Keith Richards and Mick Jagger. (D.O.C. might've been Charlie Watts, but a 1989 car accident mangled his larynx, relegating him mostly to the role of ghostwriter.)[37]

Production-wise, Dre employed a Minimoog synthesizer on *The Chronic* to create the album's sonic trademark: a spooky whine that he mixed with George Clinton and James Brown samples and farty bass lines. This spawned the hip-hop subgenre known as G-funk. That letter stood for "gangsta," a word frequently employed but rarely defined in Dre's songs. He wasn't a member of the Bloods or the Crips and yet managed to create swaggering anthems that appealed to hard-core gangbangers and suburban white teenagers alike.

One such track, "Nuthin' but a G Thang," was perhaps the biggest hit on *The Chronic*. The song reminded Iovine of the Stones' "Satisfaction," but Interscope's radio team couldn't get DJs to play it, with one member saying, "They think it's a bunch of black guys cursing who want to kill everybody." So Iovine created a one-minute commercial cut and bought drive-time spots to air the track on fifty radio stations, leading to a deluge of listener requests. According to Iovine, "That's how that got on the radio."[38] Soon the *Los Angeles Times* was comparing Dre's artistry with that of Rock and Roll Hall of Famers Phil Spector and Brian Wilson.[39] "Dre was the first producer in hip-hop to put melody in records," Diddy later told VH1's *Behind the Music*. "He made 'em *songs*."

The Chronic sold three million copies its first year, but rather than sit back, Dre doubled down and went to work on Snoop's solo debut, *Doggystyle,* set for release on Death Row in late 1993. Dre invited Fab to come to Los Angeles and direct a music video for the young rapper's first single, "Who Am I?" (The answer, in a classic chorus set to the tune of "Atomic Dog" by George Clinton: "Snoop Daw-gy Dah-ou-awg.") Back then, Snoop was far from the goofy character known for starring in his own reality TV show and palling around with Martha Stewart, as Fab learned when he arrived at the video shoot in Snoop's hometown. "Long Beach was really a wild kind of gangsta haven," he recalls.[40]

Various gang members started to jockey for position in certain shots in the video's opening setup on the roof of VIP Records; soon fights were breaking out, and the police arrived on the scene. By the time Fab and his crew got to the next location, law enforcement helicopters were swarming overhead. The situation had gotten so far out of control that the artists were forced to put the video on hold. Dre, perhaps feeling guilty for wasting Fab's time — or possibly sensing an opportunity to surround himself with new creative inspiration — invited him to stay at his home until things cooled down.

Days stretched into weeks, and before Fab knew it, he'd been living with Dre for two months. He fell into the same routine as the superproducer and his entourage: wake up late, go to the studio, work on Snoop's album. "I was mainly interested in how he responded to directions," Dre said of Snoop. "That's always an important test with me. Talent gets you in the door, but there are other things I consider, like, 'Do I want to work with this guy?' "[41]

Once he'd had his fill of recording, Dre would often hit the gym—his house was packed with weight machines, stationary bikes, and StairMasters—and then summon a bunch of people to his backyard for a cookout. (The grill master was an ex-gangbanger from Texas who loved to explain how Lone Star State cooks don't use sauce but, instead, smoke their barbecue.) They'd blast *The Chronic* on Dre's sound system. According to Fab, there were always "a lot of hot chicks jumping in the pool nude."[42]

The two hip-hop legends also connected on a deeper level. Dre seemed genuinely interested not just in Fab's *Yo! MTV Raps* war stories but in his experience with New York's downtown art scene, and how he got connected with Warhol, Basquiat, and Blondie. For his part, Fab tuned in to Dre's creative process, learning that the producer initially hadn't liked several tracks on *The Chronic;* many of the album's songs only made the final cut after friends like D.O.C. urged him to keep them.

Eventually they got back to work on the Snoop video. Rather than focus on the rapper's gang-affiliated résumé, Fab decided to concentrate on his sense of humor and the images conjured by his name. He wanted to take the corny cartoon-dogs-playing-cards trope and apply it to Snoop's life. So Fab brought in trainers and their canine charges, setting up shots in which it looked as though the dogs were playing dice games. ("It was a nightmare working with these damn dogs," Fab told me.)

To add a technological flourish, Fab used his connections with digital postproduction houses to create an animation in which

Snoop would transform into an actual dog on-screen. With the bulk of the video in the can, he just needed to film Snoop one last time for the big setup: a girl petting the head of a Doberman, which would then morph into Snoop. But the rapper didn't show up—once, twice, three times.

"Dre, man, what's up with Snoop?" Fab finally asked. "You keep telling me he's going to show up."

Dre remained silent.

"What was it, man, a one eighty-seven?" asked Fab, jokingly employing the Los Angeles slang for murder.

Dre nodded his head, and Fab pulled him into a quiet corner.

"A couple of nights ago, Snoop and them was riding around," Dre explained. "He got into it and this guy got shot and killed."

Fab was stunned.

"Look, man, Snoop ain't going to be coming," Dre continued. "What they're going to do is, he's laying low. The VMAs is coming up...After that, he's turning himself in."

And that's exactly what happened. Fab cobbled together a video very close to his original vision, and Snoop eventually beat his charges. *Doggystyle* dropped in November 1993, and in addition to establishing the Long Beach rapper as a solo superstar, it marked the latest evolution of Dre as a producer. In just a few years he'd gone from hammering out the rugged, sparse beats behind *Straight Outta Compton* to crafting the mellow, menacing funk of *The Chronic* to spinning syrupy sing-alongs like "Gin and Juice" and "Who Am I" into legitimate crossover hits on *Doggystyle*. All that, coupled with the frisson of danger provided by Snoop's legal troubles, helped push the record to opening week sales of eight hundred thousand.[43]

To Fab, the whole episode seemed to be another example of Dre using controversy to attract attention to his and his artists' work. "Most of it was all theatrical," Fab says. "Most of the people in rap didn't do ninety percent of what they rap about, because they're just great storytellers and great actors...Dre was the architect who understood how to take this and theatricalize it."[44]

In the wake of his 1993 dismissal from Uptown, Diddy eventually earned offers from record companies including EMI, Elektra, and Sony. Ultimately, Clive Davis—who had discovered artists such as Janis Joplin, Whitney Houston, and Alicia Keys—lured Diddy to his Arista label with a pact that included a seven-figure advance for himself and even more for Bad Boy, including marketing funds, recording budgets, and total creative control over everything under the label's umbrella.[45]

That came in particularly handy when bringing on Notorious B.I.G.—whom Diddy had originally signed to Uptown after reading about him in *The Source*'s Unsigned Hype column. Biggie combined an unmistakably brawny flow with darkly comical rhymes about street life ("I got nines in the bedroom, Glocks in the kitchen / A shotty[46] by the shower if you wanna shoot me while I'm shittin'") and a knack for unexpected simile ("Your reign on the top was short like leprechauns"). He had a record ready to go when Diddy moved over to Arista but was still technically signed to Uptown.

"We've got to buy Biggie back," Diddy told Meiselas shortly after landing his new gig.[47]

"All right," the lawyer replied. "I'll negotiate."

"No," said Diddy. "I need it tomorrow because this thing has to come out yesterday. I don't want you to negotiate. I don't want you to haggle. I need this act...He's the greatest rapper since Ice Cube."

So Meiselas had a conversation with his counterparts at Uptown's parent company, MCA Records, and found that they were actually eager to rid themselves of the unproven rapper. In the end, Diddy got Biggie back for about half a million dollars, a deal that would prove to be one of the better bargains in hip-hop history.

Next, Diddy arranged a meeting so that he could play new music for the entire Arista staff. Before, his attire had typically mirrored that of his artists: athletic jerseys, Timberlands, and base-ball caps. But this time, he arrived buttoned up in a suit, ready with a plan to make Bad Boy a self-perpetuating hit machine. "Year one, it's going to be Biggie and Craig Mack," he said. "I'm going to come with my hip-hop to the streets... Then I'm going to introduce Faith and Total. My hip-hop artists are going to help introduce them."[48]

Diddy got to work promoting the first wave, at one point put-ting out a cassette with Biggie's single on one side and Mack's on the other, with packaging reminiscent of a Big Mac, and having copies passed out at hip-hop events.[49] Propelled by that sort of marketing — and the earworm "Flava in Ya Ear" — Mack's debut went gold. Biggie's first album, *Ready to Die,* went on to sell more than four million copies thanks to singles like "Juicy" and "Big Poppa." His gritty Brooklyn wit synergized with Diddy's flashy Harlem bluster to create an aspirational brand for listeners and art-ists alike. As rapper Jadakiss put it, "Getting on Bad Boy was like being the top pick in the draft, going to play with the Bulls when [Michael Jordan] was there."[50]

Diddy became the manager of a musical assembly line that aspired to be the Motown Records of hip-hop. Just as Berry Gordy had a team of songwriters and producers, Diddy helmed the Hit-men, crafting beats as a collective; the old days of the DJ at the cen-ter of the hip-hop ecosystem were over. As Tom Silverman recalls, "It was like an industrial revolution: 'Let's separate the beat-making and the music-making from the rappers, and let's market the rap-pers instead of the DJs.'"[51] Afrika Bambaataa saw the phenomenon as something darker — a "whispering devil that puts things in their ear and tells them, 'Go on and make this money without your DJ, your backbone that helped start you out.'"[52]

Meanwhile, Diddy was also reaching new levels as a convener of people. Chenise Wilson saw this firsthand when she walked into one of Diddy's gatherings — and noticed Frank Sinatra walking out. Coincidence? "I don't know, but he was in the building," she says.

"There wasn't nothing else happening there but the party. That's what Puff does. He brings people together to have a good time."[53]

Diddy had Sinatra-esque ambitions of his own. Shortly after Biggie recorded his debut single, "Party and Bullshit," Diddy was heading to an event with Wilson, chauffeured by his new driver.

"You know, I'm going to record my own album," he told her.

Wilson burst out laughing.

"No," he said. "I'm serious."[54]

Three years after the 1992 release of *The Chronic,* Jay-Z still hadn't launched a solo debut. A young photographer named Jonathan Mannion was among the first to learn that the rapper had plans of his own: Jay-Z and his business partners, Kareem "Biggs" Burke and Damon Dash, invited Mannion to propose cover art for *Heir to the Throne* — the working title of the record that turned into 1996's *Reasonable Doubt.*

After shopping the record to the major labels and getting turned down, the trio had decided to press on and release it through their own Roc-A-Fella Records. A classic Jay-Z triple entendre, the name references the glitzy lifestyle embodied by the world's first billionaire, John D. Rockefeller; the draconian drug laws bearing his family's name, which Jay-Z flouted to form the basis of his own fortune; and what might happen to a fellow who got in his way. Just as Ruthless had with N.W.A., Jay-Z and his partners wrangled a distribution deal from Priority Records, this time in partnership with another indie label, called Freeze.

Mannion brought an unusual style of negotiating to his first meeting at Roc-A-Fella's dingy downtown Manhattan office.

"I'm going to do [the album art] for three hundred dollars less than your lowest bid," the photographer declared.[55]

"What does that even mean?" asked Dash.

"It means if Cousin Jimmy's going to do it for a thousand dollars, I'm going to do it for seven hundred dollars. If someone's shooting for five hundred dollars, I'll do it for two hundred dollars. Someone offers you to do it for free, I guess I owe you three hundred dollars."

"I don't even get it."

"I just want my expenses covered—I have a very clear vision for what this should feel like," replied Mannion. "The Versace linen, speedboat, drug money, Miami, *Scarface*-y kind of thing? No, no, no, no. That's not where you need to be. You need to be... surveillance, John Gotti, well-dressed, sharp, tailored, Brooklyn, roots, smoking, steamy, black-and-white."

"That's it." Jay-Z had decided. "Let's go."

His look may have come together at the last minute, but the album itself overflowed with rugged beats by Christopher "DJ Premier" Martin and Clark Kent, along with guest appearances by Blige and Notorious B.I.G. The latter became friends with Jay-Z after Kent accidentally played Biggie the track for "Brooklyn's Finest," which he'd already promised to Jay-Z. The chunky wordsmith insisted on appearing on the track and, unannounced, accompanied Kent to his next recording session with Jay-Z. Biggie was so impressed by his new acquaintance's verses that he went home to work on his half of the duet before recording it two months later. (Jay-Z also inspired him to memorize his rhymes rather than write them down.)[56]

Two days after Jay-Z's initial meeting with Mannion, the rapper and Dash showed up with a new album title—*Reasonable Doubt*—and an understated black-and-white suits-and-fedoras wardrobe to match. The cover photo of an album known for its grim tales of the crime-ridden underworld was taken on the roof of a grand prewar building on Manhattan's sleepy Upper West Side. For interior shots, Mannion took Jay-Z to the derelict docks along the nearby Hudson River, where a cluster of Trump towers would soon sprout.

"He definitely lets people [talk], and he reads people in that way," says Mannion of Jay-Z. "He listens more than he speaks, and I think that when he does speak, it makes what he says... more calculated, or more carefully delivered."

The artistic and business calculations paid off handsomely. Jay-Z's dexterous rhymes and skillful rendering of a hustler's life went on to sell 420,000 units its first year (perhaps double that if bootleg street sales are taken into account).[57] The record "established Jay as one of his generation's premier rappers," wrote *Rolling Stone* in a review that placed *Reasonable Doubt* in the top fifteen debut albums of all time, ahead of work by legends like Bruce Springsteen and Jimi Hendrix.

As *Reasonable Doubt* took off, the Roc-A-Fella trio pressed Freeze and Priority for unpaid royalties. When the labels came up short, Jay-Z was able to arrange his release, along with the rights to his master recordings—a low-pressure task for someone accustomed to much higher-stakes negotiations in the street. The savvy move left him free to shop an already-hot album to major labels for a second run; Def Jam then brought him on board by purchasing one-third of Roc-A-Fella for $1.5 million. Jay-Z and his partners would retain two-thirds of their company, and therefore two-thirds of profits, while Simmons's label would pay for recording, videos, and promotion.[58]

Even after his initial success, though, Jay-Z told anyone who would listen that he had planned to release *Reasonable Doubt*—now widely considered to be one of hip-hop's best albums—and then fade back into the underworld,[59] a sort of hip-hop Keyser Söze maneuver, while perhaps leaving the task of running Roc-A-Fella entirely to Dash.

"Jay was very quiet for a long time," says Rosenblum, who planned the launch party for *Reasonable Doubt,* of the rapper's business chops. "Nobody knew that he was anything other than an artist."[60]

Branson and I have long since finished our glasses of Malbec, and he's now waxing philosophical about the difference between young Puffy, the eager party promoter he once knew, and grown Diddy, the calculating centimillionaire selling the Bad Boy dream on a global level. I ask Branson what set Diddy apart.

"I praise him," he says. "I call him Jimmy Clean Hands. You know what that reference is? You see *Once Upon a Time in America?*"[61]

He grins.

"There was a part where they had a labor leader that was dealing with elements of the mob," Branson continues. "The labor leader didn't want an affiliation with the mob...[Diddy] wants to be a part of certain things, and certain things he wants to not be a part of, like he doesn't have an affiliation with that. He had the affiliation when it chose to benefit him."

Branson speaks delicately about what exactly Diddy did or didn't want to be a part of, but his point is clear: the Bad Boy founder has long played a balancing game with his geographical identity. As Diddy's career evolved, he frequently invoked the *American Gangster* version of Harlem — his father's Harlem — in building his swaggering persona. But he lived a life that was becoming more and more like the Malbec and fancy cheese edition.

Suge Knight probed this paradox as he ascended the hip-hop hierarchy, testing Diddy and just about everyone else in his path. Like most bullies, he generally threw his weight around until someone had the nerve to stand up to him. That was Branson's read, anyway, after finding himself in Knight's orbit while dabbling in artist management during the 1990s. On one occasion, he hosted Knight for drinks at his Harlem speakeasy.

"Suge is not a scary guy," he says. "If I had the option to be in that same room, and a particular artist was a friend of mine, Suge wouldn't be putting that kind of pressure on him because I wouldn't allow it. Not no tough-guy stuff...Sometimes you can defuse a situation with a simple conversation."

Branson pauses.

"Some of these guys are not tough guys, they're not street guys, they're fucking musicians," he continues. "They might be in a situation where somebody might say something or act a certain way, and they could be a little scared."

"So the artists who got into these situations with Suge: it was less because of Suge, but more because they were artists?" I ask. "And he was a little bit..."

"A little more aggressive," says Branson. "They might not know how to handle that."

Studio Gangsters

If you take the Cross Bronx Expressway across the George Washington Bridge and drive west for two hours — as the skyscrapers of New York give way to the fragrant bogs of New Jersey, and then to the rolling hills of Pennsylvania — you might just have the pleasure of meeting someone even less likely than Robert Moses to spawn anything having to do with hip-hop. Her name is Voletta Wallace.

The Jehovah's Witness mother of Notorious B.I.G. makes her home on a hilltop in the Poconos. On the late summer day I drive out to meet her, she ushers me through her bright orange kitchen into a living room filled with plants — some real, some fake — and a plush, emerald-colored carpet. The green walls are covered with framed mementos of her son, mostly striking mafioso poses: a profile painting in which he's pulling a brown fedora down over his brow, a head-on shot of him wearing opaque sunglasses and puffing a cigar, a portrait of him sporting a pin-striped suit and a cane. The latter was left over from a VH1 Hip Hop Honors event — not that Voletta necessarily knows what that is.

"I had no concept of rap," she says, curling the words in her thick Jamaican accent. "I thought it was just kids making noise ... [My son was] in his room with his friends and I heard things and I would yell and scream, 'Will you stop that noise?' I guess they were laughing at me."[1]

Trim and sprightly in a white dress and fuzzy slippers, Voletta looks to be in her midfifties but is at least a decade older than that. She speaks slowly and crisply, rolling every syllable around in her mouth as though savoring a morsel of filet mignon. When she makes a particularly strong point, she lets her words linger in the air with the certainty of a true believer.

Voletta doesn't seem to care much for hip-hop music, but it's clear where her son got his love of the spoken word — something she first realized when he was eighteen and told her he'd gotten a record deal. "I'm hearing this name 'Puffy,'" she explains. "I'm hearing names that I never heard of before. I'm resenting those people…They're encouraging him to make music, and he can't sing." But Biggie was determined to convince her that he'd found his calling.

"Do you see this music, what I'm pursuing here, Mom?" he said.

"You don't know music," she told her son. "You can't even sing."

"Mom, I don't sing. I rap."

"Forget it. I don't want to hear about it."

"Ma, I'm going into the music business…You want me to be an upstanding citizen, to do good in life?"

"Yes. What mother wouldn't?"

"You want me to excel in something that's going to make you proud. That's what I'm doing."

Voletta smiles.

"He was so serious about it," she recalls. "I said, you know what? I'm not going to fight him anymore. He's over eighteen. I'm not going to fight him. 'Do what you want to do — you're happy doing it.'"

One morning shortly thereafter, Voletta turned on her radio and heard her son's voice.

"I thought, *My God, that's Christopher's voice,*" she says. "*And it sounds good.*"

She pauses.

"That was my best friend," she continues. "That best friend was also my son... He was the nicest, kindest, gentlest young man you would ever want to meet. That rugged thug persona you see out there? When he was around his mother and his mother's friends, he was a gentleman. The sweetest human being you would ever want to meet."

The popular understanding of the East Coast–West Coast feud that rocked hip-hop during its adolescence is, like most popular understandings of war, gravely lacking. And like most conflicts, this one was avoidable. Many East Coast acts had great respect for their West Coast counterparts, and vice versa. Eazy-E once found himself in an elevator with the members of Run-D.M.C.; in a sign of respect, the Queens legends started rapping "Boyz-n-the-Hood."[2] Even Biggie and Tupac were good friends before a series of unfortunate events turned them into mortal enemies.

The man often at the center of the violence was Suge Knight, unsurprising in the context of his Saddam Hussein–level early-1990s aggression, but a bit of a shock given the reputation he had prior to turning the rap world into his personal *Lord of the Flies* island. "He wasn't a problem guy at all," said Wayne Nunnely, who coached Knight during his stint as a defensive end at the University of Las Vegas. "You didn't really see that street roughness about him."[3]

Even some of those who dealt with Knight at the peak of his brutality have a similar perspective. "I've dealt with gangsters in City Island, where they threatened I was going to end up in the trunk of a car," entertainment attorney Donald David told me. "My sense is [Suge] is a studio gangster... not a professional criminal."[4]

Emboldened by his success in strong-arming Eazy to get Dre and his pals out of their Ruthless contracts, Knight began to realize that most of hip-hop's power players weren't actually gangsters either. East Coast moguls like Russell Simmons and Diddy grew up in middle-class, suburban settings; Biggie was a mama's boy who exaggerated his family's financial struggles. After he rapped on "Juicy" about being "the opposite of a winner" and asked, "Remember when I used to eat sardines for dinner?," a friend of Voletta's voiced mild shock at her culinary choices.

"Excuse me?" Voletta said.

"He said he had sardines for dinner, how poor he was," the friend replied.

Recalling the episode today, Voletta shakes her head: "The way he talk about this stuff? Oh, *please*."[5]

The same held true for his California counterparts. A relative of Dr. Dre once expressed surprise that he'd become a successful hip-hop artist, given that "he always seemed kind of square."[6] Even N.W.A.'s middle-aged Jewish manager could tell that the group's members weren't as dangerous as their lyrics suggested. "None of them had shot anyone in their lives," Jerry Heller wrote. "They were auto-documentarians, playing gangstas, playing bad guys."[7]

In some cases, they began to act the part. For Dre, that included instances of domestic violence and—in a span of just a few booze-fueled weeks in mid-1992—assaulting a record producer in Los Angeles and brawling at a New Orleans watering hole. This resulted in a sentence of sixty days' house arrest for Dre. "I was wild, the people around me were wild," he later said. "There was no one around to say, 'Yo, we don't need to do that. That's not cool.'"[8]

But Knight took all this to another level. At some point in the early 1990s, it seems to have dawned on him that he could threaten, intimidate, and bully his way to the top of the business—and not have to worry about anyone trying to stop him. The music business has always had its share of nefarious characters, but most executives still weren't accustomed to physical displays of force by three-hundred-pound former football players. For years, nobody really stood up to Knight, including Dre and Iovine.

Ominous rumors about Knight began to circulate as he started to throw his weight around with abandon. In one tale, the former bodyguard was sitting on an otherwise-dreary panel at an industry conference when someone lobbed him a vague question about his thoughts on the music business. "It's like the street business," he said, calmly placing a gun on the table. "And that's how I handle it."[9]

Another story had Knight showing up at Vanilla Ice's hotel room and holding the rapper over the edge of a fifteenth-floor balcony until he agreed to transfer $3 to $4 million worth of "Ice Ice Baby" publishing rights to one of Knight's cronies. "Signed 'em [over]," Ice later told ABC News. "And walked away alive."[10] Knight denied the story, but it bolstered his increasingly fierce reputation anyway. "I don't know if that became a wives' tale or if that was true," says *The Fader*'s Rob Stone of the hotel balcony story. "I remember believing it was true."[11]

Even as late as 1995, though, Diddy seemed to be on decent terms with Knight. "Me and Suge, we close…No problems or anything like that," he told *Vibe* that year for a story on Blige.[12] But tension bubbled in private. By the mid-1990s, insiders whispered that Knight was trying to encroach on Diddy's working relationship with Blige by becoming her manager; more quietly, some speculated that Knight was also dating the mother of Diddy's child.

Chenise Wilson remembers throwing a party with Diddy at a downtown New York club called the Grand at around this time, with Clark Kent serving as DJ. Suge and Dr. Dre rolled in before Diddy arrived, and Wilson alerted him. "Puff might have taken a long time to come host the party once he knew they was coming," she says. "Puff mostly tried to keep it easy, but Suge is a different kind of dude."[13]

Yet Knight and Dre stayed until the wee hours, and it seemed Diddy's brand of all-inclusive partying had won the day, at least until the *Source* Awards in August 1995. In the middle of the ceremony staged by one of hip-hop's leading publications, Knight sauntered up to the stage to accept the Motion Picture Soundtrack of the Year award for Death Row's *Above the Rim,* which featured acts including Dre and Snoop, as well as the recently incarcerated Tupac Shakur, whom Knight hoped to sign to Death Row.

"I'd like to tell Tupac keep his guard up, we ride with him," said Knight, clad in a bright red shirt, looking like a gang-affiliated Kool-Aid Man. "And one other thing I'd like to say: any artist...who don't wanna have to worry about the day the producer tryin' to be all in the videos, all on the records, dancing, come to Death Row."[14]

Stone was sitting toward the front of the crowd in the theater at Madison Square Garden and could hardly believe his ears. "That's where the first real altercation was between Puff and Suge," he recalls, before adding a point that many observers forget. "Puff just tried to defuse it. He's like, 'It's all love. There's enough [money] for everybody.' He was really smart about it. Then it just spun out of control."[15]

Wars of words and manufactured feuds involving celebrities have been around as long as show business itself. Old-time entertainers like Bing Crosby and Bob Hope exchanged barbs, calling each other an assortment of names, including "shovel head" and "mattress hip."[16] Similarly, early hip-hop had its share of verbal altercations: Kool Moe Dee versus Busy Bee, Rakim versus Big Daddy Kane. But none of them escalated in the way that the Death Row–Bad Boy feud did.

Knight's next step was to follow through on his plan to sign Shakur, already seething over a still-unsolved attack at New York's Quad Studios in November 1994. He was robbed and shot five times by a group of men in the lobby; Diddy, Biggie, and Andre Harrell were in a studio upstairs. Upon learning this—and hearing the Biggie track "Who Shot Ya," released two months after the incident—Shakur became convinced that he'd been set up, as he explained to *Vibe* magazine in 1995. Biggie's reported attempt to visit Shakur in the hospital didn't sway him, nor did the fact that the song in question had been written before the shooting and had been slated for a Blige album.

In Shakur's defense, the timing of the song's release was an incendiary move by Biggie and Diddy, given their proximity to such a high-profile shooting. And both were beginning to play the roles of the characters they'd created for themselves in an increasingly aggressive script. "[Diddy] just was looking to have fun and make people happy and dance and make money—and then, unfortunately, he had to deal with the other things," says Meiselas. "It just wasn't in his personality to back down."[17]

For Biggie, the gun-toting outlaw image went beyond "Who Shot Ya." In "I Got a Story to Tell," released in 1997, he brags about sleeping with an NBA player's girlfriend—and robbing the basketball star at gunpoint when he comes home. Astonishingly, Diddy confirmed the tale in 2016. (The victim: late New York Knicks forward Anthony Mason, who stood six foot seven and two hundred and fifty pounds in his prime.)[18]

Shakur similarly seemed to be transforming into the violent, misogynistic protagonist present in many of his songs. On Valentine's Day of 1995, he landed in an upstate New York jail after being sentenced to one-and-a-half to four years for sexually abusing a groupie in a hotel room. The rapper maintained his innocence and was given the option to leave prison pending appeal, but he didn't have the $1.4 million needed to post bail. He spent several months locked up—until Knight, with Iovine's backing, cut a check and sent a white stretch limo to drive him to a private jet bound for California, where a spot on the Death Row roster awaited him. Though Shakur had previously been signed to Interscope and was simply shifting to its partner label, the September 1995 agreement placed him in a new, sinister milieu. "I know I'm selling my soul to the devil," he allegedly told a confidant.[19]

Shakur touched down on the West Coast and immediately went to the studio to start recording for his new employer. Dre played him the track that would become "California Love" and asked Shakur what he thought of it. Shakur liked it so much that he went directly into the booth and laid down his vocals: "Out on bail, fresh out of jail, California dreaming / Soon as I step on the scene, I'm hearing hoochies screaming..." Shakur recorded a flawless verse the very first time around, and to add emphasis through what's known as overdubbing—making the track sound heavier—he went back and recorded it again. Remarkably, he matched his own cadence and inflection, word for word, without writing anything down. "That's some incredible shit," marveled Dre.[20]

Knight agreed, and when Shakur's double album *All Eyez on Me* debuted at the top of the *Billboard* charts months later, the bail-out move looked as brilliant as the diamond certification the record eventually earned. Shakur may have recognized that he'd sold his soul to a malevolent force, but by the time he got out of jail, he was feeling rather devilish himself. He reserved his most caustic words for Diddy and Biggie, whom he still blamed for the attack in New York. Shakur released "Hit 'em Up" in the spring of 1996. The vitriolic takedown opens with a suggestion that Shakur had sex with Biggie's wife: "I ain't got no motherfucking friends—that's why I fucked your bitch, you fat motherfucker." Shakur and a handful of associates proceed to skewer their East Coast rivals in verse before Shakur closes with a rant.

"Fuck Biggie, fuck Bad Boy as a staff, record label, and as a motherfucking crew, and if you want to be down with Bad Boy, then fuck you, too!" he screams. "Die slow, motherfucker, my [forty-four magnum] make sure all y'all kids don't grow!"

Like many of Death Row's personalities, the Tupac that emerged in the mid-1990s looked nothing like the version that had existed previously. "He wasn't a gangster," says Jeff Weiss, coauthor of the book *2pac vs. Biggie,* who blames the rapper's transformation on Knight. "It was honestly Suge versus the world. I think Tupac was sort of his weapon. He was the cavalry. Like a nuclear-armed cavalry."[21]

This particular cavalry-human had always been caught between several disparate worlds. Tupac's mother, Afeni Shakur, was an active member of the Black Panthers—and successfully defended herself after she was tried with a group of comrades in the early

1970s for conspiring to bomb public buildings.[22] Shortly after dodging a life sentence, Afeni gave birth to a boy: Lesane Parish Crooks (he didn't meet his biological father until he was in his twenties). She soon changed his surname to reflect her marriage to Mutulu Shakur, a radical who robbed banks with former members of militant groups like the Weather Underground and ended up on the FBI's most-wanted list. Afeni gave her child a new first and middle name, too, drawing inspiration from Túpac Amaru, the last ruler of the Incas, who resisted colonial rule in the sixteenth century, and Túpac Amaru II, who led a rebellion against the Spaniards some two hundred years later. (Both Amarus were eventually executed by colonial authorities.)[23]

Beginning his life in New York, Tupac was forced to adapt to constantly changing surroundings. His mother developed an addiction to crack cocaine and always found herself short on cash; she moved Tupac and his half-sister, Sekyiwa, between homeless shelters and rough parts of Harlem and the Bronx. A sensitive, thoughtful child who enjoyed writing poetry and reading, Tupac didn't fit in; neighborhood kids teased him for having long eyelashes and high cheekbones, and for his inability to fight. Salvation came in the form of a move to Maryland, where Shakur was admitted to the prestigious Baltimore School for the Arts, a free charter school. There he studied ballet in addition to traditional academics.[24]

At school, he befriended a young Jada Pinkett (long before she became a famous actress) and started rapping—ironically, in retrospect—as MC New York. But during his senior year, just after Shakur had finished his college applications, his mother got evicted and he was shipped across the country to a family friend's home in a public-housing complex in crime-ridden Marin City, California. Upon reaching the West Coast, Shakur experienced something worse than teasing when neighborhood gangs repeatedly jumped him. His mother relapsed and he dropped out of the local high school; to make ends meet, he started working for a local drug dealer. But as Shakur recalled in the 2003 documentary

Tupac: Resurrection, after two weeks, "the dude was like, 'Give me my drugs back,' because I didn't know how" to sell them.

Shakur kept writing poetry in private and began to hone his skills as a rapper. By 1991 he'd caught on with the group Digital Underground, initially as a dancer and hype man, and soon found himself on the tour on which Jay-Z was performing a similar role for Big Daddy Kane. "The guy I met who was in Digital Underground, he was so well-spoken and so sweet," says Rosenblum. "[With Death Row], it's like he was playing a role and a character, because that's not the guy I met."[25] Adds Fab: "With an arty bunch of dancers, or pro-black, Afrocentric folks, or some real street corner cats, he could ingratiate himself and just blend in and become a leader within those groups."[26]

Like Shakur, Biggie was a good kid who grew up in a tough neighborhood, Brooklyn's Bedford-Stuyvesant, long before it became a haven for yuppies priced out of Park Slope. After his father left, Voletta worked as many as three jobs at a time to spoil her only child, taking him on summer trips to her native Jamaica and buying him the latest video game systems. (He'd charge his friends, who already knew the portly grade schooler as "Big," a dollar apiece to rent the games.) Biggie attended Queen of All Saints Middle School and earned excellent grades, moving on to high school at Bishop Loughlin Memorial, which counts former New York mayor Rudolph Giuliani and onetime NBA star Mark Jackson as alums.[27]

Because the Wallaces weren't Catholic, they didn't receive the school's faith-based discount, and the financial strain eventually caused Voletta to enroll Biggie at Jay-Z's public alma mater, George Westinghouse. Biggie started to lose some of his mama's boy tendencies at the school, a training ground for rappers who honed their craft in the cafeteria — and for drug dealers and stickup kids who moved in the shadows. "There was a lot of fear," recalls Salvador Contes, who went to Westinghouse at around the same time as Biggie and Jay-Z. "Lights were always busted... You never went to that first-floor [staircase] because everything was pitch-black. You knew someone was waiting there."[28]

Drawn by the prospect of fast money, Biggie soon became one of those nefarious characters. His mother never figured it out, despite finding a curious dish in his room one day. "Wow, did I serve Irish potato?" she asked herself before taking the plate downstairs and washing off the white powder. Years later, she read her son's account of the event in a magazine: evidently, she'd thrown out his cocaine supply; he had to dig through the garbage to recover it.[29]

Biggie dropped out of high school in 1989, aged seventeen. More like Jay-Z than like the ill-fated dealer Shakur, he followed the laws of supply and demand — all the way to North Carolina — to find the best market for selling crack cocaine. Two years later, the law caught up with him and he was arrested, but his mother bailed him out. He returned to New York, and to his other main extracurricular activity: rapping. Biggie met Shakur for the first time after playing a show in Maryland in 1993, and they became friends; Voletta remembers Shakur calling the house and referring to her as "Ma." Later that year, Big Daddy Kane invited the young rappers to join him onstage at Madison Square Garden, and they traded freestyle verses. Biggie even introduced Shakur to Easy Mo Bee, who'd go on to work with Shakur on his next record.[30]

"Tupac and Biggie were friends," recalls Rosenblum. "I knew all the promoters and all the clubs, so we ran around [New York] and I would go up to the doors or whatever, and we would dip in... They would bum-rush the stage and do these performances."[31]

So how did the two rappers' relationship sour so quickly? It all came down to Shakur's belief that Biggie and Diddy had set him up at Quad Studios — a theory whose roots appear to lie at least partially in the childhood trauma of constantly getting picked on — and Suge Knight certainly didn't try to disabuse him of the notion. In Knight, Shakur had found a modern take on the *Arabian Nights*–style genie: a three-hundred-pound gun-toting golem who could grant wishes of freedom, physical protection, and boundless wealth.

"He was a studio gangster...He happened to be a big guy physically. He figured out how to manipulate," says Rosenblum of Knight. "Suge sold [Shakur] the dream and he manipulated him...He's like a poison dart. He fucked up a whole era of hip-hop."

Knight may have started out as a studio gangster, but he gradually turned the myth he'd created for himself into reality more than any one of his peers, broadcasting his exploits to earn an increasingly fearsome reputation. He strengthened his ties to the notorious Bloods gang, opening an appointment-only nightspot in Vegas called Club 662 (on a telephone keypad, the numbers can spell m-o-b, shorthand for "member of the Bloods"). Back in Los Angeles, Knight would throw massive parties for the Death Row crew at rented mansions in the Hollywood Hills; he'd hire a shady operator known as Party Man to set up illegal gambling on one floor and arrange for scantily clad women to perform sexual favors on another.[32]

On one occasion, the cops showed up at around midnight to break up Dre's birthday party. Knight had just arrived — only to discover that there were no women in the building — and had his goons throw Party Man into a limo. Dre's onetime right-hand man, Bruce Williams, driving in the car ahead of them, remembers seeing the limo rocking back and forth with the force of the beating unleashed upon Party Man. When they arrived at their next destination, Dre, who'd been increasingly skipping out on Death Row–related activities, disappeared into a hotel room with his latest conquest. Knight demanded a full refund from Party Man, who came up short. "They took Party Man to the bathroom," wrote Williams, "and fucked him up so bad he didn't even press charges."

This was the milieu into which Shakur landed upon his arrival in Los Angeles, and he played the part, covering himself in tattoos; one was of a machine gun, another the phrase "THUG LIFE."[33]

In 1996, the increasingly bellicose Shakur shelled out for a quarter-million-dollar military vehicle: a black Hummer H1 outfitted with off-road wheels, three sirens, and a diamond-plated bumper.[34] His first encounter with Biggie since the Quad attack came while he was sitting in the truck after the *Source* Awards in Los Angeles; he rolled down his window and saw Biggie standing with some Crips that Bad Boy had reportedly enlisted for protection. "West Side! Fuck y'all!" shrieked Shakur. Guns were drawn, but no shots were fired, and members of the Nation of Islam stepped in to defuse the situation. "I looked into his eyes," Biggie later recalled. "And I was like, 'Yo, this nigga is really buggin' the fuck out.' "[35]

Knight catered to Shakur — and likely stirred up his paranoia — by fortifying the Death Row offices. There were security wands, pat-downs, and a giant bank vault–style door. Recalls concert promoter Kevin Morrow: "You'd have to have a police battering ram to get through there."[36] The fortifications were also for effect, and Knight made sure to broadcast his label's fearsome image with signals powerful enough to cross oceans. Fab 5 Freddy remembers attending a fashion show in Italy during the mid-1990s and discovering a European publication's cover story on Death Row. The article opened with the terrified writer in Knight's office, being told not to step on his rug (Bloods red, of course), and cowering in front of a pair of snarling dogs. "That was a part of this mythmaking thing that he kind of poured gasoline on," says Fab.[37]

As with any good Hollywood villain, Knight occasionally exhibited another side of his personality. He gave away turkeys at Thanksgiving and presents at Christmas to the less fortunate, donated school supplies and even his old shoes, and held elaborate Mother's Day bashes. At one, the hundreds of guests in attendance were treated to performances by Shakur and the Isley Brothers; one year, all attendees received gold chains featuring a miniature Death Row logo.[38]

Despite the occasional Robin Hood gesture, Knight seemed to prefer darker imagery — he even had an old-fashioned electric chair installed at Death Row's headquarters — and his vision eventually made it to the silver screen via the N.W.A. biopic *Straight Outta Compton*. Director F. Gary Gray noted that Dre suggested the details of scenes in the film that depict the depravity of Death Row, including one in which the producer finds Knight puffing on a cigar while a dog attacks a man who's been forced to strip down to his underwear. "He said, 'This is what's going on in Death Row at that time. It was a circus — pit bulls, violence.'...Facts are so much more interesting than fiction sometimes."[39] Says Fab: "It's always, to me, been like he's living in a bad gangsta movie."[40]

All of this finally pushed Dr. Dre to his breaking point. Two other life events had also placed things in sharper perspective: he'd gotten engaged to girlfriend Nicole Threatt, and he'd just done five months in a Pasadena jail after a drunk-driving charge violated his parole for a previous offense.[41] Real danger lurked around the corner of every platinum-plaque-encrusted wall at Death Row, and Dre didn't want any more run-ins with the law. "It turned into a fucking Don Corleone thing," Dre said. "It made me say...'Is this the life I wanna lead, or do I wanna be a businessman, be able to take care of my family, chill out, have fun, and make money while I'm sleeping?'"[42] So in the middle of 1996, Dre walked away from the company he'd cofounded, leaving his master recordings and Death Row equity in Knight's hands.

Through it all, Knight seemed to show no compunction about his actions, real or implied. If anything, his story got worse the more he told it. When Eazy-E contracted AIDS in the mid-1990s, the diminutive rapper's N.W.A. bandmates, including Dre, put aside their differences and came to visit him in the hospital during his last days. Knight, on the other hand, danced a figurative jig on the rapper's grave — and possibly implicated himself — during an appearance on Jimmy Kimmel's late-night show years later.

"They get blood from somebody with AIDS, and they shoot you with [a syringe], so that's a slow death," said Knight with a chuckle, chomping on a cigar, shoes up on Kimmel's desk. "The

Eazy-E thing." Some of Eazy's children have gone on record saying that they believe this is what happened to their father. When asked about this theory, Ice Cube said, "I can't say they're crazy, because I don't know for sure."[43]

Like most bullies, though, Knight had a way of backing off when someone had the pluck to stand up to him. Months before Dre left Death Row, Williams remembers arriving on time for a meeting with Knight and leaving after an hour when he hadn't shown up. Knight called him in a huff five hours later, threatening him over his departure. "I don't care about all that," Williams told him, and hung up. A friend at Death Row later called to tell Williams that he'd been on speakerphone and overheard by the label's staff. Shortly thereafter, Williams asked Dre if he should be worried about Knight. "Suge likes you," Dre said. "He says you're the only one who's got nuts."[44]

Leland Robinson, son of Sugar Hill Records founders Sylvia and Joe, shared a similar anecdote. Death Row sampled a song whose rights were owned by the Robinsons, and Joe didn't look kindly on it. "He told [Knight] what the deal was; the check was there in twenty-four hours," says the younger Robinson. "They was two kinds of people. One was a studio gangster, and one was the real gangster."[45]

The money kept pouring in for gangsters, studio and otherwise, and big labels like Interscope responded by expanding recording budgets. Tommy Boy chief Tom Silverman remembers his company doing $21 million in profits on $50 million in billing in 1992—and Interscope making just $500,000 on $100 million in Death Row–fueled billing. But as budgets soared from $50,000 per album in the late 1980s to $50,000 per song just a few years later, companies like Silverman's got edged out.[46]

"The major labels reached into hip-hop and made it impossible to compete," he says. "They're in the market share business, not in the profit business. Indie labels can't really spend two million dollars to make one million dollars, but the majors do it all the time."

An indie label like Silverman's might invest $5,000 on an advance for an up-and-coming act and make $50,000, or perhaps turn $25,000 into $1 million, with a bit of luck. Major labels, on the other hand, could afford to spend six or even seven figures to launch an act; if they failed, there was still plenty of money pouring in from massive back catalog sales as consumers gobbled up CDs, often duplicates of vinyl albums they already owned. Another difference: for a small label, one or two big-budget flops could ruin the company. But hip-hop had taken off, creating gaudy revenues for major labels, as well as for the rappers whose voices propelled hit songs and the producers who collected as much as $50,000 per track.

Even record store owners were finding new ways to make money. SoundScan, the arbiter of weekly record sales, generated its numbers by gathering figures from a portion of retailers and extrapolating the totals. But since the data outfit published the names of the retailers who served as recorders, Machiavellian music business operators often bribed store owners and employees with cash or free inventory to scan certain records multiple times. Silverman recalls his company doing that for one particular artist who ended up being scanned for more albums than Tommy Boy had actually manufactured.[47]

Time Warner wanted a piece of the hip-hop action, too, and paid $100 million for a 50 percent stake in Interscope, doling out the first $20 million in 1992 and the remaining $80 million in early 1995. By then, though, the explicit lyrics of Interscope's Death Row acts had prompted protests from varied voices, including Republican presidential candidate Bob Dole and C. DeLores Tucker, the chairwoman of the National Political Congress of Black Women, who made a career of campaigning against rap music. Battered by boycotts, Time Warner began to explore a sale of its Interscope stake, which would rid the media giant of its association with Death Row.[48]

In February 1996, just days after Shakur released his raunchy *All Eyez on Me* — on one track he described his favorite sexual positions before pronouncing Dole "lame" and calling Tucker a "motherfucker" — Time Warner sold its Interscope stake to record company MCA for a whopping $200 million. MCA was a record label, not a mainstream consumer-facing company like Time Warner, and as a result, it seemed less of an interesting target to decency crusaders and politicians. And despite the controversy, Time Warner had been able to flip the parent of Death Row for twice its purchase price.

Publicly, Shakur continued to up the ante with his lyrical attacks, most notably with "Hit 'em Up" in the spring of 1996. Jay-Z got involved in the conflict, calling out undisclosed parties for "too much West Coast dick-licking," while Shakur lobbed a grenade at Jay-Z in a track released after his death, rapping, "I'm a Bad Boy killer; Jay-Z die, too."

But even Shakur privately seemed to be growing concerned about the level of violence following him at Death Row. He'd been dating Kidada Jones, the daughter of superproducer Quincy Jones, who started talking to the rapper about getting a fresh start at another label, where he could focus on music and his burgeoning career as an actor; with roles in *Juice* and *Above the Rim* already under his belt, he had a handful of others in the pipeline. Some sources close to Shakur say that he admitted to being unhappy with his record deal in the final months of his life; at around the same time, he fired his lawyer, who was also Death Row's official attorney. Many observers took this as a sign that Shakur wanted to jump ship. He also had about 150 unreleased tracks in the Death Row vault, and some believe Knight feared that his top artist would leave and take those recordings with him.[49]

On September 7, 1996, Shakur was fatally shot in Las Vegas while sitting in the passenger seat of a black BMW 7 series. The driver? Knight, who left the scene with barely a scratch. In the wake of Shakur's killing, Snoop Dogg left Death Row, publicly blaming Knight for his friend's demise. Others shared his opinion. In addition to scores of online conspiracy theorists, people who were actually in the Death Row crew have made their views clear. "I just don't see how all these hard-core niggas who had been around Suge and Pac all that time—always packin' heat—could let a car dump on them, in a lot of traffic, and *no one* got one shot at the assailants," wrote Williams. Still others pointed to Orlando Anderson, a Crip with whom Shakur and Knight had brawled earlier that night, as the assailant. Says author Jeff Weiss: "Kind of in general, it's not a good idea to beat up Crip members."[50]

It wasn't long before Biggie suffered the same fate as Tupac. Leaving the Soul Train Awards in Los Angeles on March 8, 1997, Biggie and Diddy hopped into a pair of SUVs. Biggie sat in the passenger seat in the front vehicle—and moments after leaving the ceremony, a gunman pulled up alongside him and fired seven shots into his chest. He died at Cedars-Sinai Medical Center shortly thereafter.

Investigations into the murders have pointed toward corrupt current and former employees of the LAPD, members of the Crips and Bloods, and, perhaps most prominently, Knight himself. Retired LAPD detective Russell Poole became the first to accuse officers in the force's Rampart Division—home to dozens of officers revealed to have had ties to the Bloods and to Knight, who paid off-duty cops to serve as Death Row security—of conspiring to murder Biggie, but he died of natural causes before he could make much progress with the case. (Poole was also convinced that Shakur's killer had come from within Death Row.)[51] The documentary *Biggie and Tupac* suggests that Knight believed Shakur had been preparing to sue Death Row over unpaid royalties and had commissioned his murder, later ordering a hit on Biggie to make Shakur's death seem like part of the East Coast–West Coast feud.

In 2008, journalist Chuck Philips sourced FBI files in a *Los Angeles Times* exposé connecting an associate of Diddy's to the 1994 attack on Shakur at Quad Studios, but the documents were later discovered to be fake. Implicating Diddy in Shakur's killing, as some have tried to do, seems far-fetched. If one ascribes a real-gangster murderous streak to the erstwhile reality TV star, a key question remains: why would he go through the effort of ordering a hit on Shakur and not kill the more menacing Knight? Speculation that Diddy played a role in Biggie's death is even more illogical. Unlike the prolific Shakur, the rotund rapper left behind only enough material to fill two studio albums. Diddy profited from them, to be sure, but if he were cold-bloodedly calculating the spoils of assassinating his best friend, surely he would have concluded that the returns on a full career of records and joint touring would have been far greater. And Diddy's eventual solo success, boosted by Biggie's verses on his debut album, was far from guaranteed. "I don't think anyone really saw that coming," says Weiss. "I mean, you know, he was a backup dancer."[52]

With Death Row's artists fleeing the label—and the world of the living—Knight began a steady decline, propped up by only Shakur's posthumous albums. (Seven were released through Death Row and/or Interscope, and six went platinum.) In 2005, a California judge directed the label to pay $107 million to Lydia Harris, the (now ex-) wife of incarcerated drug kingpin Michael "Harry-O" Harris, who claimed to have helped fund Death Row in the early 1990s. Knight forked over just $1 million before filing for bankruptcy in 2009.[53] The accoutrements of his empire were soon auctioned off, from his copy of the Bible ($325) to the Death Row electric chair ($2,500). Perhaps appropriately, the latter was sold to the owner of a company called Hostility Clothing.[54]

All the while, violence continued to surround Knight. He earned a sentence of nine years in prison in 1997 for having racked up eight arrests and six probations since 1987, but he got out after five years. He ended up back in jail in 2002, after the authorities stopped by the Death Row headquarters and found him associating with gang members, thereby violating his parole. Released again in 2003, he almost immediately landed a ten-month bid for attacking a parking lot attendant in Hollywood. He largely avoided incarceration for the next decade, but still managed to get into plenty of trouble: he reportedly paid an associate to punch Dr. Dre at the Vibe Awards in 2004, got shot in the leg at a Miami party in 2005, ended up in the hospital after a fight in Arizona in 2009, and got shot six times at a nightclub in 2014. (Reportedly, he strolled to the sidewalk under his own power to wait for the ambulance.)[55]

Fittingly, the altercation that resulted in Knight's latest lockup occurred on the set of the N.W.A. biopic *Straight Outta Compton*. He drove up in his truck and got into an argument—and proceeded to run over two men, injuring Fab's friend Cle "Bone" Sloan and slaying businessman Terry Carter, and then fleeing the scene. "It was simple. He was trying to kill my man," says Fab. "He killed somebody else by mistake."[56]

A surveillance camera captured the incident; gruesome clips of the event are widely available on the Internet. Knight claimed that he had acted in self-defense, and pleaded not guilty to charges including hit-and-run, attempted murder, and murder. As this book went to press, he was in jail, awaiting trial. Biggie and Tupac's cases remain unsolved.

"Nobody went to jail for either murder," laments rapper Too Short. "We killed our heroes. Those are our number one guys. What the fuck?"[57]

Voletta Wallace had never listened to one of her son's albums all the way through until one particularly tough day in the late 1990s, a couple of years after his death.

"I was here by myself one day...and I was hearing such negative things about him," she sighs. "'He's a drug dealer millionaire who don't know what to do with money.' 'You live by the sword, you die by the sword.' It was awful. I was hurting. I said, 'You know what?' I'm going to put this album on."[58]

She sat down and played *Life After Death* — "the one with 'Hypnotize,'" as she calls the album — and found herself getting to know a new side of her son. Initially afraid of what she might uncover, she instead ended up relishing the chance to hear his voice telling stories she hadn't yet heard, even if she didn't appreciate the subject matter. As she listened to the record from beginning to end, it almost seemed that he was there, talking and joking with her, once again.

"I cried like a baby...I said, 'My God, that's a very talented young man,'" she remembers. "That album gives me more respect for the rappers, because I was judging them, too. I was judging them. Here are these kids with their ugly clothes, their ugly hats. They dress terrible...I told my son once, 'You look terrible.' I said, 'If you're going on national TV, please don't embarrass me.'"

In the end, she's become fiercely proud of her son and his musical legacy, despite the fact that much of it contradicts the beliefs to which she clings. She still doesn't buy much of what others have said about Biggie, especially the darker theories of his role in the Death Row feud. Perhaps it's just a case of a loving mother refusing to believe anything negative about her son, but Voletta views the entire conflict as a mirage created by record labels and the media.

She remembers one particular conversation with her son about Tupac. "Christopher, why are you hanging around with him and he's saying such terrible things about you?" she asked. "He goes, 'Ma, I approached Tupac and all Tupac said [was], "Hey, I'm just selling music."'...I don't think my son resented Tupac...I don't think Tupac resented my son either."

Though that's possible, it does seem that real enmity flared between the two artists in the final years of their lives, even if they had no desire to inflict violence upon each other. After Biggie died, Voletta did her best to move forward, even reaching out to Afeni Shakur to try and build a more peaceful legacy for their sons; the two became good friends before Afeni passed away in 2016.

Voletta has gotten over her initial distaste for Diddy, too — she's having lunch with him tomorrow, she says — partly because of the grace with which he handled her son's death; he was always check-ing in on her and asking if she needed anything. "He was there for me," she explains. "He really grows on you. He's a sweet kid. Some-times I want to slap the daylights out of him, but he's a sweet kid."

Ask her about Knight, though, and it's as if a thundercloud immediately passes overhead. The mere mention of the man seems to test the faith that tells her to leave judgment to a higher power, and with considerable effort, she does.

"What I read about him is very dark," she says. "I believe if you do wrong, if you murder, whatever you do, there is an Almighty above. I call him Jehovah." Her voice rises now, crackling with righteous conviction, and suddenly she's addressing Knight directly. "You will get your day, because judgment is His," she continues, gazing skyward. "He sees your wrongs and he sees your good, too. Whatever you do, you will get it."

At this moment, she's speaking with such electric confidence that if she told me Jehovah was going to unleash a monsoon right there in the living room, I'd grab an umbrella. Instead, she looks back at me.

"Right now, if he's a good man...I hope he is," she says. "If he's a bad man, let him deal with God."

CHAPTER 5

Aftermath

I interviewed Diddy several times before this book came about, and perhaps the last word I'd use to describe him is "nervous." In person or over the phone, alone or in a group, he exudes swagger the way a lightning bug emits neon glow. Take, for instance, his 2013 proclamation when he decided that my estimates of his wealth for *Forbes* had reached an appropriate level: "You started learning how to count right, I see," he told me. "Thank God!"[1]

You'll imagine my surprise, then, when I meet up with him in Austin, Texas, shortly before our main stage keynote discussion at the 2014 edition of the music-tech-film conference South by Southwest—and I find him worrying. Sweating slightly through his dark brown shirt, perhaps selected to disguise precisely such an eventuality, he almost pleads with me to tell him that he's going to be fine onstage; it hasn't occurred to me that he'd be anything but. Perhaps to hide his concern, he dons a wholly unnecessary pair of sunglasses as we stroll onto the dais.

"I just want to tell y'all that I'm nervous up here," he informs the crowd of a few hundred people crammed into a stuffy conference hall. "The louder that y'all are clapping makes me not nervous, so you know."[2]

To be fair, the setup of the stage is a bit anxiety-inducing. Our awkwardly angled leather chairs—which face the audience but cause us to twist our necks to the side every time we look at each other—are more restrictive than the open stages across which Diddy is accustomed to stomping at shows. We've further complicated the eye contact situation by agreeing to accept questions from the audience via Twitter in real time, which requires me to spend much of the interview looking at my phone instead of my conversation partner.

Once we make it past the pleasantries, we delve right into Diddy's latest venture: the multiplatform cable network known as Revolt. It emerged in 2012 when Comcast handed four moguls—including Diddy and former NBA star Magic Johnson—the keys to their own realms as part of a promise to bolster minority ownership after the company bought a chunk of NBCUniversal. Revolt started with its own channel, available in Comcast's ten-million-plus cable boxes, and roughly tripled that number upon striking a carriage deal with Time Warner. According to Diddy, that made his network's launch the biggest since Oprah Winfrey's OWN.

I ask him about his inspiration for deciding to add a cable channel to an empire that by this point encompassed music, fashion, spirits, marketing, and startups. For Diddy, the answer goes back to his late friend Biggie, who he says dreamed of something similar as far back as the mid-1990s.

"We just always discussed not having to count on radio or any of the video music channels to be successful," Diddy explains. "And we didn't know that this day right here would come. But we always had a discussion about how we can take the power into our own hands."

Then he starts waxing philosophical about what Biggie's career arc could have been, both musically and commercially.

"He probably would've been an R & B singer . . . He loved Luther Vandross," says Diddy. "We probably would have put in a bid for Hennessy or something. He would have had Hennessy, I would have Cîroc."

Aftermath

It's a bit difficult to imagine Biggie transitioning from a career as a rapper known for glorifying brutal mafia dons (and occasionally finding himself in the middle of real-life violence) to that of an R & B crooner with interests in cable television and high-end spirits. The same could have been said of Diddy — and yet that's exactly how his narrative evolved, starting shortly after the loss of his friend.

The violent deaths of Biggie and Tupac put a serious damper on hip-hop's spirits, but as often happens when musicians pass away unexpectedly, sales exploded. By the end of the 1990s, the genre outpaced even country music in America and was climbing charts in untapped markets from Scandinavia to New Zealand.

Diddy had emerged as hip-hop's most visible face, and the one best positioned to monetize the genre's popularity. In 1996, with his star rising, he had negotiated a new Bad Boy deal that guaranteed him double-digit millions in the form of bigger budgets and a fifty-fifty split of profits. He was also given a chance to release his own album, *No Way Out,* a notion that had initially caused Arista's executives to balk.[3]

But in 1997, when Diddy launched the lead single "I'll Be Missing You," an ode to Biggie set to Sting's "Every Breath You Take," it became the first rap song to premiere atop the *Billboard* Hot 100. With Diddy rapping the verses and Biggie's widow, Faith Evans, singing the chorus with fellow Bad Boy act 112, the song helped Diddy's album move 561,000 copies its first week, eventually racking up sales of over seven million.[4] (A source close to the rapper confirmed that Sting only cleared the sample after securing 100 percent of the publishing for "I'll Be Missing You.") New pal Jay-Z appeared on two of the album's tracks, Biggie graced four posthumously, and Bad Boy freshman Mase showed up on "Been Around the World" and "Can't Nobody Hold Me Down." (The latter gave a nod to hip-hop's early days with its prominent sample of Grandmaster Flash and the Furious Five's "The Message," though the materialistic thrust of the Bad Boy song offered a very different sort of takeaway.)

The reception for the album, though, was by no means universally positive. The *New York Times* gave Diddy a backhanded compliment at best by noting that "people, even tone-deaf people, love to sing along with" his music.[5] *Entertainment Weekly* gave "I'll Be Missing You" a grade of D, excoriating the song as a "maudlin 'tribute'" that "gives lie to those who claim hip-hoppers are above self-serving sentimentality."[6] Perhaps to blunt such criticism, Diddy gave his $3 million in profits from the single to Biggie's family.[7]

Knowing he'd get flak for his materialistic boasts and his reliance on other songwriters and producers throughout the LP, Diddy preemptively devoted a chunk of album time to skits by the Mad Rapper, a fast-talking fictional firebrand who first appeared on Notorious B.I.G.'s *Ready to Die.* The character complained that, despite having four albums under his belt, he still lived with his mother while rappers like Diddy drove around in fancy cars and filmed $500,000 videos. On *No Way Out,* the Mad Rapper was joined by his brother: a new character called the Mad Producer, who criticized Diddy's abilities behind the board ("He ain't no real producer!") and his songwriting talents ("A thousand niggas write for him!"). This self-deprecating counterpoint to Diddy's grandiosity proved to be a clever move. Says Rob Stone: "You couldn't really get mad at him, because then you were the angry rapper."[8]

Diddy knew that hip-hop was an aspirational genre; he simply took the aspirations higher, and found a huge market for his message. A series of songs that Diddy rapped on, produced, and/or released through Bad Boy held the top spot on the charts for forty-two weeks of 1997.[9] His Puff Daddy and the Family tour grossed $15 million that year, perhaps not as much as it would have with Biggie on board, but still the most in rap history to that point. Diddy personally pocketed $53.5 million in 1998, thanks mostly to an outsize advance from Arista.[10] Diddy plowed a chunk of his gains—about $2.5 million, according to reports—into a modernist East Hampton mansion designed by Charles Gwathmey. The brightly painted house stood on an isolated plot overlooking Gardiner's Bay, seven miles from the more desirable (and pricier) real estate on the Atlantic coast closer to town.[11]

Next, Diddy decided to flip the notion of whiteness on its head. He'd taken his Harlem swagger and Timberland boots to suburban America; now he was going to put the violence of the mid-1990s behind him by exerting his cultural clout on one of the country's wealthiest Caucasian enclaves. He had his new home slathered in white paint and appointed its interior with fine Italian furniture. It would serve as the backdrop for an annual bash with a dress code more rigid than that of the snootiest country club: the White Party.

"The whole concept of the White Party and it being super strict — like you couldn't come in cream or whatever — was all him," recalls Rosenblum, who helped Diddy plan what quickly became the hottest invitation in the Hamptons. "It had an energy and it was beautiful."[12]

Diddy threw his inaugural soiree in 1998. Thousands of white Christmas lights hung in the trees around the house; mermaid-costumed women swam in the pool and bartenders were trucked in from New York to pour Cipriani's famed Bellinis. Hot-air balloons rose from the beach at sunset and sunrise. Guests ranged from hip-hop nobility (Russell Simmons, Jay-Z, and Andre Harrell — Diddy had recently hired the man who'd been his boss at Uptown) to mainstream stars (Martha Stewart, Howard Stern, Donna Karan, and Donald Trump). "If you couldn't get into the White Party, your summer was ruined," says Stone. "You'd see grown men leave the party and come back . . . If their shorts had blue trim, they'd go find white shorts and come back."[13]

Rosenblum remembers staying up until four or five in the morning the day before each iteration of the party, working with Diddy to perfect the setting, all the way down to moving pieces of furniture a few inches one way or another. His vision amazed her. "A lot of people—and particularly men—would not be so confident," she says. "And particularly rappers in the nineties would not be so confident, in their thought of *This furniture must be arranged this way* or *I don't like the way this looks* or *This isn't pretty enough.*"[14]

Nor would they insist on all-white flowers, or an all-white dress code. But then they wouldn't be Diddy, who was redefining the art of celebration for a new generation. He was also upending sociocultural customs as a young black man throwing a white-clothing-only party in one of America's most economically segregated vacation haunts, leaving revelers of all races begging to get in. As Simmons points out, Diddy never believed the color of his skin should dictate where he spent his time.

"He don't mind where he hangs out," the Def Jam cofounder explains. "He might like cultural stuff that is based in urban culture, but there's nothing about him that's going to stop him from going into any door or hanging out anywhere."[15]

That attitude is part of the reason many in Diddy's orbit during the late 1990s still trace the through line of fake-it-till-you-make-it American ambition from F. Scott Fitzgerald's most celebrated character to hip-hop's most ostentatious impresario. "There certainly was a Bad Boy dream," says Rosenblum. "[The White Party] was this thing, it was mansions and chicks and jet-setting and the life. In a funny way, it's *The Great Gatsby* for the nineties."

Meanwhile, in California, Dr. Dre took a literal approach to the end of the Death Row–Bad Boy conflict, founding a new label called Aftermath. With Interscope backing him once again and Suge Knight out of the picture, Dre set out to emphasize quality over quantity: his label launched just five albums in its first five years; all of them went platinum.

The first of those was *Dr. Dre Presents…the Aftermath,* which featured seven Dre-produced tracks and three songs on which he rapped; there were also guest appearances by New Yorkers including Nas and KRS-One. The latter offered an incisive summary of the 1990s rap wars on the track "East Coast/West Coast Killas": "Cacophony of small-talent rappers, claimin' a coast over instrumentals / Ain't got no real street credentials."

The presence of such lines, along with the names of Dre's album and label, revealed his immediate goal: to move past boundaries of coast and label — as well as the accompanying violence — and get back to making money. Just as Jay-Z had done earlier that year with the founding of his own record label, Dre tried to model himself after America's first billionaire, anointing himself a "young black Rockefeller" in "Been There, Done That." Perhaps in an effort to further distance himself from Death Row's misogyny, and from his own admitted history of violence toward women, Dre praised his new bride's entrepreneurial pluck later in the song: "My woman's independent, makin' dough by the caseloads."

He also set about rehabilitating his East Coast connections, accompanying Iovine to New York during the fall of 1996, shortly after Shakur's death. Dre was riding high from his appearance on the chart-topping R & B classic "No Diggity." (Iovine had convinced producer Teddy Riley to record the song with Blackstreet and Dre instead of giving it to Michael Jackson, as Riley had initially planned.[16]) The mellow crossover hit about giving listeners "eargasms" was an excellent way to further remove himself from the Death Row era and rebrand himself for audiences on both sides of the country.

Rob Stone, working as a consultant for Interscope at the time, took Dre to do an appearance at one of New York's underground hip-hop radio stations, where he got a warm reception, and then to Rockefeller Center for his *Saturday Night Live* performance. In the greenroom, they sat with Iovine and watched a few innings of a World Series game; the New York native Iovine revealed his own standards of perfection when one of the Yankees made an error.

"If I was Joe Torre, I'd fire him," Stone remembers Iovine saying. "I'd run right out on the field and fire him in front of everyone. You can't make that kind of play in the World Series."[17]

Iovine didn't have to take any such measures when Dre went on and performed "Been There, Done That." In the midst of the stirring rendition, a familiar figure sidled up to Stone: Diddy. Much like his erstwhile rival, Diddy wanted desperately to smooth things over — and that wasn't necessarily a given with Iovine, who'd been heavily involved with Death Row's rise and the signing of Shakur. "Yo, introduce me to Jimmy," Diddy said to Stone. "Tell him I'm a good guy. Tell him I'm cool."

"Puff wanted to just make sure Jimmy knew that he was a businessman and not all this other craziness, which was very smart and probably part of the reason he was there," Stone recalls. "Later on, they would end up doing a lot of business together. They're best of friends now."

There didn't seem to be any awkwardness that night between Diddy and Iovine, or between Diddy and Dre. "He was out," says Stone of the latter. "He was away from Suge."

At peace with himself and those around him, Dre could focus on what he did best: produce music and discover new talent. The biggest splash for his Aftermath empire was signing a bleached-blond, blue-eyed, twenty-four-year-old rapper from Detroit. When the urgent vocalizations of Eminem first wormed their way into the ears of Dr. Dre — courtesy of Iovine, who got his demo from an Interscope intern who'd heard the neophyte on a Los Angeles radio show — the producer tracked him down within twenty-four hours. Soon they were in the studio working on his debut, *The Slim Shady LP,* named for the rapper's sharp-tongued, sometimes violent, politically incorrect horrorcore alter ego — more Quentin Tarantino than Suge Knight. But in the booth, Eminem played the role of eager student. "Dre showed me how to do things with my voice that I didn't know I could do," Eminem told the *Los Angeles Times* in 2007. "I'd do something I thought was pretty good, and he'd say, 'I think you can do it better.'"[18]

Though Dre once spent seventy-nine consecutive hours in the studio, the duo completed the smash single "My Name Is" in about sixty minutes. Just as he'd done with "Who Am I?" on Snoop Dogg's debut, Dre made sure to pound the identity of his new protégé into the heads of audiences—the name of Eminem's alter ego, Slim Shady, is stated seventeen times.[19] Dre produced three tracks on Eminem's album, which would go on to sell 480,000 copies its opening week. Dre appeared on the album, as in life, in the role of the avuncular foil to Eminem's erratic adolescent, showing up on one song as his "motherfucking conscience," trying to talk the youngster out of making the sort of mistakes Dre once had. (Fascinatingly, the maturing Dre wouldn't let his young children listen to Eminem's music.)[20]

In Eminem, Dre found someone who actually had quite a bit in common with Shakur: he had grown up essentially fatherless in a rough neighborhood, had been raised by a drug-addicted single mother, had been scrawny and gotten picked on by neighborhood bullies. As an adult, Eminem inhabited multiple personalities: that of the clever lyricist challenging the norms of society, and that of the violent (and often misogynistic) nihilist. But unlike Shakur, Eminem had to overcome early doubters who didn't think a white guy could rap. In post–Death Row Dr. Dre he had a perfect ally, one who had grown tired of conflict and wanted to bridge divides to create provocative, meaningful art.

"I got a couple of questions from people around me…You know, 'He's got blue eyes, he's a white kid,'" Dre told *Rolling Stone* in 1999. "But I don't give a fuck if you're purple: if you can kick it, I'm working with you."

At the turn of the millennium, Diddy seemed to be "kicking it" in just about every sense of the phrase. *Forbes* writer Rob LaFranco (whose media and entertainment role I inherited years after he left the publication) learned this firsthand when he traveled to Atlanta in early 1999 to land an interview. The goal was to put Diddy on the cover of the first-ever Celebrity 100 issue, a chronicle of the top-earning names in show business. The only problem: LaFranco couldn't get a firm answer from Diddy's camp as to whether or not the interview would actually happen.

LaFranco arrived in Atlanta and spent his first night unsuccessfully trying to corner Diddy at the opening of his restaurant, Justin's (named for one of his sons). A few hours before his flight back to New York, LaFranco received detailed instructions via telephone from one of Diddy's handlers regarding what he needed to do if he actually wanted to talk to the twenty-nine-year-old superstar: "You need to go to the Omni Hotel... Walk into the front door. You go to the left, there's a set of curtains. Velvet curtains. You walk into those velvet curtains. There will be a guy standing at a desk. When you get to that guy at the desk, you say that you're there to see the King."[21]

This is total bullshit, LaFranco thought. But he had to try, so he pushed back his flight. On his seventh cup of coffee and already exhausted after staying up all night, he arrived at the Omni at 11:30 a.m. on Friday morning, walked past the velvet curtains—and, sure enough, found a man standing behind a desk.

"I'm here to see the King."

"Is the King expecting you?"

"I think that he is. Yeah."

The man vanished for a moment, and then returned and ushered LaFranco into an elevator. At the penthouse, the doors opened to reveal a raucous party. The rapper Juvenile danced with a group of revelers in front of a baby grand piano; Diddy's mother was there, too, clad in fur. On the sofa lay a pair of matching fur coats—a big one for Diddy and a miniature one for five-year-old Justin—but Diddy himself was nowhere to be seen. LaFranco ended up sitting by the fireplace for half an hour, talking to a screenwriter working on a Sean Combs biopic that never materialized. Suddenly, LaFranco felt a tap on his shoulder and turned around. It was Diddy.

"They tell me you want to talk to me."

"Puffy, we're going to put you on the cover of the entertainment issue. You're the top entertainer of the year."

"Yeah, yeah, yeah, just stick around for a little while," Diddy replied. "I can't do it now, but we'll see."

Then he disappeared into a bedroom with Kim Porter, his off-and-on girlfriend of many years. LaFranco had been sucked into the Diddy vortex and wouldn't emerge until the end of a weekend during which he and the mogul had crisscrossed Atlanta in a fleet of Lincoln SUVs and Bentley sedans, going from hotels to clubs and beyond. They stopped at a gym to meet Diddy's trainer, a former pro boxer; they tracked down famed lawyer Johnnie Cochran, with whom Diddy was thinking of starting a sports agency; they discussed his vision for Justin's, in terms of both menu (Diddy felt strongly about hush puppies and corn fritters) and vibe (he wanted it to be the sort of place where people would stand "outside with their fur coats, smoking cigarettes in the dead of winter"). There was even discussion of a Puff Daddy packaged food line.

But at that point in time, Diddy had homed in on music. It was a pivotal moment in his career as a recording artist, and particularly for his label. Bad Boy's biggest artist was dead, and Mase — its most promising up-and-comer — had just left the hip-hop world to become a minister. Diddy felt enormous pressure to make his second solo album, *Forever,* live up to its lofty name. So he had indefinitely rented a studio owned by Thom Kidd, an engineer whose résumé included working with artists from Gladys Knight to Elton John, for the sole purpose of recording this new opus.

LaFranco wandered around the studio, finding an entire room full of vinyl classics by everyone from Steely Dan to REO Speedwagon — and a seemingly unlimited quantity of 1970s R & B that looked particularly rifled-through. The building teemed with producers and songwriters in the vocal booth and outside it, loung-ing upstairs near the pool tables and big-screen TVs. In every cor-ner, there was a ghostwriter scribbling lyrics or a producer trying to convince Diddy to use one of his beats on the album, a realization of the Mad Rapper's and Mad Producer's prophecies.

"He would listen to it, he would give it a little bit of feedback — 'I kind of like that, but it's lacking a little bit,'" LaFranco remem-bers Diddy saying. "These guys would just kind of cycle through... You could almost believe that you were sort of in a Berry Gordy type of situation."

At the same time, a coterie of attractive young women spun through Diddy's orbit. One of them had a cold, so the rapper sent an intern out to get her some vitamin C. There was another—a University of Georgia student of Irish and Puerto Rican descent—who caught LaFranco's eye before he went into the studio. He went to try and find her after growing tired of waiting for Diddy to sit down for his interview. As he reached the second floor, he heard someone in Diddy's camp urging him back down: "No, Robbie, Robbie. No, no, no, no!"

At that moment, LaFranco looked across the upstairs room and saw the woman for whom he was searching—along with another familiar face.

"I see Puffy's head pop up over the couch in front of a big-screen TV," recalls LaFranco. "He was very clearly going to town."

LaFranco headed back downstairs, dejected and annoyed.

"Puffy's the only one in this room who's getting any action, and he's getting all the action," LaFranco remembers. "I'm kind of bored now. My editor's expecting me to interview this guy. The day comes to a close, uneventful...I don't even see Puffy."

The next morning, Diddy's entourage picked up LaFranco at his hotel and took him to the studio again. At the end of the day, Diddy finally deigned to sit down and talk. "Sorry," he said. "I had to take care of some shit."

For the rest of the interview, Diddy blustered brilliantly. "I'm gonna be bigger than [billionaire] David Geffen," he told LaFranco. "The torch has to be passed to somebody. That's the only reason I'm in the game."[22]

LaFranco couldn't help but be amazed at the young entrepreneur's ambition. Perhaps even more impressive was his frenetic pace, not to mention his ability to constantly function without sleep — a trait LaFranco also noticed while interviewing billionaires like Rupert Murdoch.

"[Diddy] was constantly on the phone, he was recording, he was singing, he was fucking, he was drinking, he was getting high, he was marketing," says LaFranco of his time with Diddy. "And he never slept. He was in the studio till two, three in the morning, then they'd go out to the club. The latest they ever got in was eleven in the morning. When was he sleeping?"

After completing the interview in Atlanta, Diddy returned to New York to do a cover shoot alongside Jerry Seinfeld, the subject of a profile in the same issue. Diddy demanded organic juices and smoothies, fruits, and a full soul food meal catered for twenty on-site, along with five racks of fur coats and Hugo Boss suits to choose from; naturally, he showed up in a Rolls-Royce. Seinfeld, by contrast, asked only for granola and strawberry yogurt and arrived in a cab with one suit thrown over his shoulder.

Despite their radically different approaches to the shoot, Diddy and Seinfeld hit it off and began to discuss the idea of collaborating on an album — Seinfeld would do comedy routines, while Diddy would produce music to fill in the background (the idea never came to fruition). In the end, for the photo that ended up on the cover of *Forbes,* Diddy wore dark pants and a white shirt bearing a Sean John Denim logo, turning the cover shot into a free advertisement for his new clothing line. The entire episode served to amplify Diddy's desired image: bigger, badder, and bolder than anyone in show business.

"Why he needed all the other clothing to set that up, I don't know," says LaFranco. "It's all about the show, right? That's the brilliance of Puffy."[23]

While Diddy swaggered his way to the top of the entertainment universe, Jay-Z faced a conundrum. The massive critical success — and relatively modest commercial performance — of *Reasonable Doubt* made it clear that he could have a tolerably remunerative career as a rapper and leave the streets behind. But to reach the top-most layers of monetary success, he needed to capture the attention of the mainstream.

"I can't be too deep. I have to spoon-feed 'em," he said one day while driving through Brooklyn, according to his cousin Briant "B-High" Biggs. "Once I spoon-feed 'em lightly, feed 'em sugar… then give them something more, some knowledge on top of that, then they'll take that and start growing."[24]

To provide some of that sugar, Jay-Z turned to Diddy. The Bad Boy chief and his stable of producers provided the bulk of the sonic work behind *In My Lifetime, Vol. 1,* and the gritty beats of Jay-Z's debut album gave way to glossier production. The record, which debuted in November 1997, is regarded as one of Jay-Z's worst, a clumsy attempt to court pop audiences. Though it sold 138,000 units its opening week, triple the opening week of *Reasonable Doubt,* top albums routinely debuted with sales north of 500,000 in the late 1990s heyday of the music business.

As much as he chased Diddy's sound at the time, Jay-Z also tracked his lifestyle. Jonathan Mannion, who continued to shoot Jay-Z's album covers, remembers the rapper picking him up one day in a Bentley convertible — the same model Diddy had.

"You own this, man?" asked Mannion.[25]

"Nah, I'm thinking about buying it. Puff has one, so I figure…" Jay-Z replied, trailing off. To Mannion, the move was a quiet sign of respect.

"It wasn't like, 'Fuck that guy, I'm going to have more than him.'

It was like... 'He's moving at the highest level, and if he has one, I should at least consider that one.' It was never from a position of, 'I'm beneath, he's above.'... Diddy and Jay, they're cool with each other, but they're definitely competitive."

For Jay-Z's next album, *Vol. 2... Hard Knock Life,* the cover features him standing in front of the car, a possessive hand on its hood and a scowl on his face. The record was lighter on Bad Boy guest appearances and instead prominently featured producers now known as Jay-Z's go-to beatmakers: Timbaland, DJ Premier, and Swizz Beatz, all of whom helped craft a critically acclaimed record that still had the pop prize very much in its sights, particularly with the title track. With its infectious sample from "It's the Hard Knock Life," from the musical *Annie,* the title song captured the mainstream imagination and, per SoundScan, helped Jay-Z once again triple the opening week sales of his prior album.

His friends at Def Jam had millions of reasons to urge him to crank out *Vol. 2,* the best-selling album of his career, less than a year after its predecessor. In 1998, Russell Simmons was in negotiations to sell the rest of his label to PolyGram; the year before, the Dutch company had offered $50 million, and then reduced the number to $34 million. Def Jam's executives realized that the size of the offer centered on a multiple of the label's revenues, not its earnings; in other words, to up the price, all they needed was to sell more records.[26]

So Simmons and Lyor Cohen leaned on their two biggest artists: Jay-Z and volatile Yonkers rapper Earl "DMX" Simmons. ("I thought DMX was greater than Jay-Z," recalls the Def Jam cofounder. "That's the difference between honing your talent and destroying it.") The latter's album went quintuple platinum. The former launched his quadruple-platinum debut in May 1998 — and followed it in December 1998 with a triple-platinum record, an unheard-of turnaround time in the record business, even back then. Releases generally followed a structure: put out an album's lead single, then the album itself, then the next single, and then the next, waiting for months in between each step as each song racked up radio spins, and then died down. At least that was the custom for much of the 1990s.[27]

"Jay-Z and DMX were amongst the first, I think, to ignore that goal; everybody followed suit," says Simmons. "You can't get out the seat for a year now . . . In hip-hop, if you get off your seat, somebody's sitting there."

That year, Def Jam did a record $175 million in billing — and in 1999, PolyGram bought the remainder of Simmons's company for $135 million. Cohen signed a five-year deal to stay on board as CEO, while Simmons kept the title of chairman. The pair added double-digit millions to their net worth, thanks in no small part to the efforts of Jay-Z and DMX.[28]

Says Simmons: "We sold it definitely because of those guys."[29]

Not to be outdone by his Def Jam rivals, Diddy departed from the music industry norm of shutting down his company over the holidays. Instead, he made his team truly earn their year-end bonuses. At one particular meeting two days before Christmas in the late 1990s, Diddy emerged from an elevator with his bodyguards wearing a mink coat, gaudy jewelry, and sunglasses. Then he went to get some apple juice, forcing his colleagues to wait for five minutes before his return.

"Y'all are mad as fuck, ain't you?" said Diddy, according to employee Jayson Jackson. "You see me sitting here with my fur and all of that and you['re] like, 'Fuck Puff.' But you know what? I dare one of y'all to come get it. I dare one of you to work harder than me . . . I come in here and work harder than you in the day, then go to the club and work. You think I'm in the club getting drunk? I'm looking at who's dancing to what, figuring out which song is working in what way, which DJ is making it hot. Tell me who's doing that more than me."

Holy shit, Jackson thought. *He sleeps no more than four hours a night. And every waking hour, he's figuring out how to make more money.*[30]

But the new year took Diddy's career trajectory in the wrong direction for the first time in quite a while. In March, he was charged with assault after allegedly bashing record executive Steve Stoute over the head with a champagne bottle. Diddy is said to have enacted this heavy-handed metaphor for rap's late-1990s excesses after Stoute refused to pull the plug on a video in which Diddy and Nas were shown being crucified. (Both rappers had willingly participated in the shoot, but the former apparently had second thoughts.) After Diddy publicly apologized, Stoute asked the Manhattan district attorney not to press charges; the Bad Boy chief's only punishment was a day at anger management class.[31]

In a bigger blow, at least to Diddy's ego, his album *Forever* climbed to number two on the charts but earned only a single-platinum certification, a far cry from *No Way Out*'s seven.[32] *Complex* named *Forever* number six on its list of the fifty all-time worst rap album fails, and Chris Rock cracked a joke about the record during his monologue at the 1999 MTV Video Music Awards: "Puffy got a new album called *Forever*. *Forever*? What you trying to say, Puff? *Forever*? You know if the album don't sell, the next one gonna be called, *How About Three More Months?!*"[33]

Later that year, Diddy found himself in an even worse situation. When gunfire erupted during a dispute at a nightclub he was attending with then girlfriend Jennifer Lopez, the two fled the scene with Diddy's bodyguard and driver. Police pulled over their vehicle after it ran a red light and discovered a pistol.[34] Diddy got charged with bribery and possession of an illegal weapon. In the year of legal wrangling and trial that followed, he denied carrying a weapon and offering his driver a $50,000 bribe to take the gun rap for him. He was eventually cleared of all charges, as were his bodyguard and driver. But his latest protégé, Jamal "Shyne" Barrow, also on the scene at the time, caught an assault conviction and spent nine years in jail.[35] (Barrow and his team did not respond to a request for comment.)

Lopez soon parted ways with Diddy, a move that left him humiliated. He reportedly tried to date model Naomi Campbell, and after she rejected him—she was engaged at the time—he begged her to appear in public with him so that the tabloids would think they were together. "Sean told Naomi that he desperately needed 'prestige' on his arm to recover his ladies' man reputation," a source told *Vogue*.[36] "In his mind, he's a pimp, lover, Casanova," says Chenise Wilson. "He's one of those who gets his feelings hurt really quickly, so he becomes the pimp persona in order to guard his feelings."[37]

Both his personal life and his financial empire seemed to be spinning out of control; though he avoided jail time, Diddy had to field civil lawsuits worth a combined $1.4 billion. His lawyers would eventually deflect most of them, but even after recovering from the violent associations of the mid-1990s, Diddy's reputation had taken another hit, jeopardizing his appeal to mainstream companies he was courting for new mass-market ventures (the line of packaged food he'd been contemplating, for instance).[38]

In order to reach the David Geffen–esque heights he was shooting for, Diddy would have to reinvent himself yet again. "If you're a dreamer, you're a visionary," he later explained to me. "People may know about five or six of the things you're pursuing, but you may have a thousand dreams in your head."[39]

Over the past hour or so in front of the packed room in Austin, Diddy has hooked the crowd with his usual unfiltered banter. But his words have taken on an increasingly instructive tone—this grown version of Diddy draws on the lessons and the swagger of his youth, mixing in the trappings of a life coach and a motivational speaker—and the crowd is eating up his advice, even when his outlook is less than optimistic.

"If you were one of those kids who are just graduating from

high school or college," I ask, "how would you do it if you were starting from scratch?"

An audience member rushes the stage and hands Diddy a CD, presumably a recording of her music, which he accepts before replying to my question.

"I want to give you an honest answer—I don't want to give you the schoolteacher answer. I would be scared to death," he says. "I would probably be doing the same thing that y'all are doing right now...Never letting go of your dream is the only thing I can say, but I can't sugarcoat it and say it's gonna be easy."[40]

We begin taking questions directly from the audience.

"If I go up to Revolt TV," asks one young man, "am I gonna get somebody to look at my videos and listen to my music? 'Cause I ain't gonna spend that train fare if I ain't gotta."

"What I'm gonna do is I'm gonna save you your train fare," says Diddy. "I'mma have somebody watch it and listen to it in the next fifteen minutes...[If] you put something up that's dope—it's just dope, man—it's gonna spread like the bird flu."

Next, a towering man who looks to be in his late thirties raises his hand and explains that he's an aspiring DJ with two ex-wives, four kids, and another on the way. His question: "What do I do now?"

"I'mma be Dr. Phil for you. Want to come up closer so you can get it?" asks Diddy. His "patient," who is nearly seven feet tall, walks up and sits on the mogul's lap. "Keep taking care of your kids, keep paying that child support so you ain't in trouble...You gotta be able to raise the kids and also put your all into it and know that you have a harder road than somebody that's seventeen, eighteen, nineteen trying to get into the game. And that's just real talk."

The DJ ambles off the stage, and a young woman asks the next question. "Back in the day I used to go by She-Diddy because I modeled my career after you," she says. "I want to be the next Diddy. Do you have any advice for kind of getting over that hump?"

"This is a great time in the world of business and in the world of media, and I think this is just a great time for women," he says.

"There has been a turn in the hiring process where women...Y'all will run the world."

As we wind down our talk, I decide to find out whose advice Diddy might want: "If you could have lunch with anyone in the world you've never met, who would it be?"

"Number one would probably be Steve Jobs, but we know he's not here," he says. "But I'm pretty sure he's figured out a way for me to have lunch with him one day. And I'm the worst with names, but I asked my staff this before I came: the brilliant woman who runs Facebook —"

"Sheryl Sandberg?"

"I would love to have lunch with her, because I feel like what she's trying to do to empower women and shake things up is the same thing I'm trying to do with youth culture," he says. "I think that that's somebody that I could learn from and that I can get inspired from. So if any of y'all know her, let her know Diddy wants to take her out to lunch."

CHAPTER 6

Fashion Fortunes

Russell Simmons stands out from his peers in the world of hip-hop—and the broader entertainment industry—in numerous ways, from his business savvy to his more recent embrace of yoga and veganism. (He's also set apart by the allegations of sexual assault leveled at him as this book was going to press; he has denied the accusations.) But the first thing you notice in person is that, unlike most big names in showbiz, the Queens-born tycoon shows up to appointments on time, or even early.

I roll into the lobby café at the Mercer Hotel in SoHo at 10 a.m. on the dot, only to find him already slurping up a bowl of sweet pea soup and a beverage that later shows up on my receipt simply as "Green Juice." Simmons is decked out in his trademark navy-blue New York Yankees cap, tilted jauntily to the side, and a pair of the still-chic Adidas shell-toed sneakers that Run-D.M.C. rapped about so many years ago. The centerpiece of his outfit is a patterned dress shirt by Argyleculture, his new fashion line. All in all, it's a representative sampling of his eclectic style, which for decades has combined his favorite aspects of street wear and yacht club attire.

The Mercer is an appropriate meeting spot. In March 1993, Simmons opened the flagship store for his first clothing line just a few blocks away. "When I started Phat Farm," he says, "there was no such thing as a black designer even doing fashion."[1]

Under Simmons's watch, Phat Farm made what he calls "classic, simple stuff that kids could wear the way they wanted." And unlike most other clothing chiefs at the time, he knew not only what kids wanted to wear but how to create new trends—argyle sweater-vests outside the golf course, for instance—and capitalize on them. At its late-1990s peak, Phat Farm raked in nearly $1 billion per year in retail sales.

Soon some of hip-hop's savviest operators went into the apparel business. Diddy launched his Sean John clothing line in 1998, and Jay-Z followed with Rocawear a year later. Both released sneaker lines as well. Dr. Dre nearly did, too, but found focusing on head-phones to be much more lucrative. It was Simmons who laid the groundwork for the rise in hip-hop's fashion fortunes.

When Simmons first started selling clothing, Dr. Dre had barely released one album, Diddy had just graduated from his Uptown internship, and Jay-Z hadn't left the drug business. The day Sim-mons's boutique in SoHo opened, Phat Farm was a drop in the proverbial bucket for a man whose businesses were grossing $40 million annually by the early 1990s.

"It's fun and I can afford to do it," Simmons told the *New York Times* at the time, after casually explaining that he started a cloth-ing line because he often dated models. "So if I lose a lot of money on it, I had fun. If I make money, I'll have even more fun."[2]

At the outset, Phat Farm's fifty-item catalog seemed to borrow heavily from established brands like Tommy Hilfiger, Ralph Lau-ren, and the Gap. The pieces, which ranged from $50 khakis to $650 leather jackets and were designed by a pair of untrained twenty-two-year-old graffiti artists, "could be worn by a sixty-year-old Jewish guy," Simmons liked to say.

But the SoHo shop (burnished by $175,000 in renovations) and the rural-meets-urban theme (complete with a bull mascot called Money Moo) combined with the European sensibilities of Simmons's partner — a Frenchman named Marc Bagutta — to create a brand that resonated with a new generation of upwardly mobile hip-hop enthusiasts. Attending fashion shows before founding Phat Farm sparked Simmons's thinking.

"Everybody would wear Tommy Hilfiger and Ralph, but they'd wear it a certain way," Simmons explains (and, by the way, have I heard he's been with many models?). "You'd look at Ralph's collection and you'd find one thing you liked."[3]

Simmons got tired of watching hip-hop tastes transform companies like Hilfiger into billion-dollar brands, he says. So he launched Phat Farm and packed its catalog with the sort of items that were selling. Not only did he increase the number of street wear items available on the overall market, but he jacked up prices. The Adidas sneakers that Run-D.M.C. rapped about were selling for thirty-eight dollars at the time; Simmons sold similar pairs for eighty dollars. Even Phat Farm T-shirts cost forty bucks.

"You sit there and you see all the areas that you affect," he says. "People come to you with their ideas about what you're affecting, about your cultural influence. You may learn to monetize that yourself."

Phat Farm's formula wasn't limited to its tony SoHo flagship. The brand showed up on shelves of independent outlets like Jimmy Jazz, V.I.M., and Dr. Jay's. These weren't actually black-owned businesses. (Jimmy Jazz was created by James Khezrie, the son of Syrian immigrants; V.I.M. was launched by the Israeli family behind Jordache jeans; and the head of Dr. Jay's is named Hymie Betesh — as likely to be a goy as Lyor Cohen. It's worth noting that none of these companies replied to my requests for comment.) The stores were located in places like Brooklyn and Harlem; in the latter neighborhood, Simmons remembers there being three Jimmy Jazz stores on a single block. That meant a lot, especially during a time when few big names in the fashion world dared venture into low-income neighborhoods.

"We try to give the customer what he can't get anywhere else in this area: brand names," explained Brooklyn-born Khezrie—who launched his company in 1988 and within six years had reached $30 million in annual revenue on sixteen stores, fifteen of them in poor precincts—in a 1995 interview with *Crain's*.[4]

This was especially important as Robert Moses–era urban planning moved shopping centers to the suburbs, exacerbating the decline of cities around the country. When inner-city customers went to local establishments to buy Phat Farm and other hip-hop-influenced clothing, that meant more cash flowing through communities with large black populations. Though the chains' owners hailed from other backgrounds, they generally hired locally and helped keep stretches of urban storefronts occupied.

"That was a meaningful moment in fashion," says Simmons. "We were sucking a lot of the wind out of the fashion industry."[5]

"When I was moving off the streets and tried to envision what winning looked like, it was Russell Simmons," Jay-Z wrote in his autobiography. "Russell was a star, the one who created the model for the hip-hop mogul that so many people—Andre Harrell, Puffy, even Suge Knight—went on to follow."[6]

And so, as Jay-Z began to consider his next steps after aligning Roc-A-Fella with Simmons's label, he looked to the Def Jam founder for inspiration. During the late 1990s, Jay-Z wore a lot of clothing by the European designer Iceberg; he often donned the brand at concerts, and soon he found his fans doing the same. So Damon Dash arranged a meeting with the company's brass, hoping to land an endorsement deal. He and Jay-Z demanded millions of dollars and the use of a private jet; the Iceberg executives offered free clothes.

Needless to say, there was no deal, and Jay-Z and Dash decided they would try the do-it-yourself approach. They hauled sewing machines into the Roc-A-Fella offices and hired people to stitch together early Rocawear prototypes. They weren't anywhere close to building something scalable: shirts took three weeks each to make. Finally they asked Simmons for advice, and he set them up with his partners at Phat Farm, letting them out of exclusive contracts so that they could work for Rocawear, too. "I wasn't their manager, but they were part of my company," the Def Jam founder says of Jay-Z and Dash. "A family."[7]

Soon Rocawear replaced Iceberg in Jay-Z's lyrics and on his person, and the fledgling brand became a real business. Jay-Z had discovered what would become one of the central tenets of his business: whenever possible, own the products you rap about; otherwise, you're just giving someone else free business. With that in mind, he went back to the studio, aiming to keep his album-per-year streak alive, this time no doubt feeling some pressure to match the career-best performance of his latest effort. But instead of continuing to chase a pop-oriented sound, Jay-Z embarked on another pattern that would serve him well down the line. Just when it seemed he'd gone totally mainstream, he tacked back to the gritty beats and subject matter that first catapulted him to stardom (with a couple of Rocawear references thrown in, of course).

On *Vol. 3...Life and Times of S. Carter,* he fully abandoned Diddy and his glossy production crew, setting the tone by positioning the DJ Premier–produced "So Ghetto" as the first full-length track on the album. In the song, he tells a tale of cruising in his car with a "bougie broad" who asks him to remove his do-rag — so he hangs a U-turn and dumps her back at the club. "I'm so gangsta prissy chicks don't wanna fuck with me / I'm so gutter, ghetto girls fall in love with me," he spits in the chorus.[8] He even recruited Dr. Dre for a guest appearance on "Watch Me," further down in the track listing.

Jay-Z wanted his new album to underscore his street credibility in every way possible, and when it leaked weeks before its December 1999 launch date, he took that notion a step too far. During a party at New York's now-defunct Kit Kat Club, he confronted Lance "Un" Rivera, the producer on *Vol. 3,* who Jay-Z believed was responsible for bootlegging the album. Jay-Z reportedly rammed a knife into Rivera's stomach after offering, as the story goes, a line that revealed lingering mafioso fantasies: "You broke my heart." Jay-Z turned himself in to the police; after a high-profile perp walk, he was charged with felony assault, eventually pleading guilty to a lesser charge and getting away with three years of probation.[9]

But little doubt remains over what happened that night. "I stabbed Lance Rivera," Jay-Z told the judge, according to numerous reports. Jay-Z, barely three years removed from street life, hadn't yet fully shed his former persona. "I was blacking out with anger," he said of the incident. Still, the episode came with something of a silver lining for Jay-Z—and a valuable lesson about the nature of publicity.[10]

"The hilarious thing, if any of this can be considered funny," Jay-Z wrote, "is that the Rocawear bubble coat I was wearing when they paraded me in front of the cameras started flying off the shelves the last three weeks before Christmas."

By the middle of the following year, the company was closing in on $50 million in annual revenue.[11]

By the time Jay-Z's brush with the law boosted his new clothing line in 1999, Diddy's Sean John brand had already been established for a year.

With the help of his lawyer Kenny Meiselas, Diddy modeled the Sean John deal after his Bad Boy pact, first finding equity partners: the Sinni brothers, who owned a vast real estate and apparel empire. They contributed financing and handled sales and manufacturing. Diddy oversaw the vision and design, once again making sure he had total control over the product as well as over the use of his name and likeness.[12]

"He never got caught up in, 'Okay, I have a clothing line, I'll put my mother in to run it, I'll put my sister in to be the designer,'" says Meiselas. "He's always done it in a real professional way with people who are experts and experienced in those businesses."

Diddy debuted his line at a Las Vegas trade show in 1998; much like Simmons, he was influenced by designers like Tommy Hilfiger and aspired to create clothing for the members of the hip-hop generation. "We wanted to give them fashion that represents them. We wanted to give them extremely multicultural and diverse fashion," he told the *Washington Post*. "We brought them fashion-tainment."[13]

Diddy's first hires were Neiman Marcus veteran Jeff Tweedy and Calvin Klein publicist Paul Wilmot; they often joined him at fashion shows, where he'd sit in the front row and observe what generated the most excitement. He announced Sean John's New York debut at a cocktail party at Bloomingdale's in 1999, arriving on the scene in a flurry of security guards and television cameras. Sean John revolved around Diddy, from its moniker (his real first and middle names) to its advertising (the Times Square billboards featured Diddy himself).

Far more than Jay-Z or Dr. Dre — or Simmons — Diddy used personal charisma to prop up his business interests. In 1999, for example, *Vogue* editor Anna Wintour hired photographer Annie Leibovitz to shoot him with Kate Moss on a bridge in Paris. One classic image featured Diddy, clad in a dark overcoat and a white suit, hand on his chin, seemingly evaluating the supermodel — as though she might not be good enough for him. Another captured Moss and Diddy, both robed in fur, stepping out of a pearly Mercedes into a horde of paparazzi.

This sort of publicity not only helped to up Diddy's glamour quotient; it also helped make him, and Sean John, a more mainstream brand. ("'Urban'...I would get insulted when they put us into [that] classification," he said. "They didn't do that with other designers.")[14] Soon Sean John was taking up shelf space in stores like Macy's alongside Calvin Klein and Tommy Hilfiger.

For Diddy, it was all quite the juggling act. Meiselas remembers him bouncing between songwriting sessions and recording studios for his Bad Boy artists while his Sean John employees presented the latest clothing designs for his approval. "I was always amazed by just how much he would do at one time," the lawyer says. "He was just so driven."[15]

In 2003, with Sean John grossing some $175 million annually and available in more than two thousand stores, Diddy bought out the Sinni brothers and teamed up with a new partner: billionaire Ron Burkle, who invested $100 million in the company.[16] Diddy kept a controlling stake and stayed on as Sean John's chief; in 2004, he captured the Council of Fashion Designers of America's Top Menswear Designer of the Year Award, the first time a black person had won.[17]

Both Diddy and Jay-Z had taken Simmons's blueprint and expanded it in a way that he couldn't as a behind-the-scenes mogul. But their debt to the Def Jam founder was clear. Says rapper Too Short: "Without Russell doing Phat Farm, and then giving [Jay-Z] the game for Rocawear, and then giving [Diddy] the game for Sean John, you're missing two moguls."[18]

While Dr. Dre's most notable contribution to the world of fashion would ultimately be a headphone line that became as much an accessory as a listening device, he did make one ill-fated foray into the clothing business. His mother convinced him to pony up startup funds for a his-and-hers loungewear line called Dre V Denee. (The *V* stood for her name, Verna; Denee is the middle name of Dre's sister.) Its target demographic: middle-aged couples who wanted something other than sweatpants to wear around the house. Verna hatched the idea with the best of intentions: she wanted to repay Dre for buying her expensive homes and cars by creating a business that would make her self-sufficient.[19]

Verna was a talented seamstress, a skill passed down from her Texas sharecropper parents; she'd had some success crafting African-print outfits and selling them to her husband's coworkers during Black History Month one year. But the Dre V Denee project was doomed from the beginning, from its clunky name to its outdated concept to its cringeworthy slogan: "Sexy appealing but not so revealing." The clothing line never got farther than a friends-and-family launch party at Verna's home, which was probably for the best. Dre's fashion moment would have to wait.

While Jay-Z and Diddy were getting into the clothing world—and out of all sorts of legal trouble—in 1999, Dre forged ahead with more musical masterpieces. He released his somewhat confusingly titled second studio album, *2001,* in November. The name didn't stop the record from achieving a sextuple-platinum certification in its first year. The album offered a rare glimpse into the world of Dr. Dre, who was becoming something of a recluse in his middle age. In an era when top acts like Jay-Z put out a new album every year, Dre had waited seven years for his follow-up.

As always, keenly aware of his own strengths and weaknesses, he focused on producing—and turned to Eminem, Snoop Dogg, and Jay-Z to cowrite songs like the self-affirming ballad "Still D.R.E." All three rappers tried to pen verses for that track, but Jay-Z conveyed the essence of being the superproducer better than Dre himself with concise summaries ("Still taking my time to perfect the beat / And I still got love for the streets") and obscure throwbacks ("It's not a fluke, it's been tried, I'm the truth / Since 'Turn Out the Lights' from the World Class Wreckin' Cru").

"He understood what he was writing for. He took and embodied the whole situation as far as writing for Dr. Dre," Snoop said in 2012. "We all took a shot at it, but we all couldn't come up with nothing as dope as Jay-Z."[20]

In the broader business, though, nobody could top Eminem at the dawn of the new millennium, at least when it came to music sales. The rapper's second major label effort, the Dre-produced *Marshall Mathers LP,* dropped in 2000 and earned a rare diamond certification for sales of more than ten million units in the United States, easily better than Jay-Z and Dre's career bests. Eminem went on to sell thirty-two million albums during the ensuing decade, more than any other artist, dead or alive—two million more than the Beatles during that period, and nearly 60 percent more than number ten Jay-Z.[21]

During the summer of 2000, Dre and Snoop headlined the Up in Smoke tour, along with Eminem, Ice Cube, and several others. Kevin Morrow, who ran the House of Blues in Los Angeles and organized Eminem's first show, served as promoter; though many in the industry had been deterred by the violence that had shaken hip-hop a few years earlier, Morrow realized that the genre had crossed back into the mainstream.

"You started to see record sales that were so huge you really knew, 'Wow, this isn't a black thing anymore; this is multicultural,'" he recalls. Just as he'd done in the era of N.W.A., Morrow took a professional approach to concert planning, going into "real buildings with real security and real marketing budgets and real sound and lights...We made it safe."[22]

Fans responded, and the forty-four-date excursion went on to gross more than $20 million. But what impressed Morrow most of all was the genre's reach, which extended to cities far beyond the tour's route. "Every little kid in friggin' China or anywhere in Asia, or Europe, wanting to wear his baggy pants and the oversize T-shirts and wearing the Air Jordans? I don't know anyone doing that in country, in blues, in jazz," he says. "There's no musical genre anywhere that's changed the world like hip-hop."

Dre had emerged as a go-to producer for all manner of artists, including Gwen Stefani, Mary J. Blige, and even sometime rapper Shaquille O'Neal. The NBA Hall of Famer spent time in the studio with Dre, whom he describes — tongue perhaps in cheek — as "the Michael Jordan of hip-hop." He also affirms the producer's reputation as a perfectionist. "You go in there and he never messes around," Shaq says. "And everything has to be nice and crisp."[23]

Shaq remembers Dre repeatedly going back over each part of the song they were working on and meticulously tightening up its individual components. Like many of Dre's creations, though, the song never came out; according to Shaq, the labels involved couldn't agree on a release date. He remains hopeful, however, that the track will one day make its debut. "I still have it in my archives," says Shaq. "That shit was banging."

By 2001, Dre's new label was worth over $100 million, at least on paper, after Interscope paid him $35 million for a 30 percent stake. Perhaps the best part of the deal: it bound him and Iovine even closer together, strengthening what would become the most lucrative relationship in each of their respective careers.[24]

Just as Dre and Diddy bolstered their own brands — and bottom lines — by bringing other artists into their respective stables, Jay-Z signed a raft of rappers to Roc-A-Fella in the new millennium. Among them: Memphis Bleek and Beanie Sigel, each of whom would go on to release three gold-certified albums for the label. Jay-Z also must have noticed that there were plenty of rappers, including the belligerent Sigel — born in Philadelphia, he called himself the Broad Street Bully — still making careers off aggressive lyrical imagery. Eminem emerged as the most outrageous of the bunch; many of his songs depicted elaborate fantasies of killing himself or others.

The brutal epoch that had taken the lives of Biggie and Tupac was over, but violence lived on as a viable — and profitable — theme. Though Jay-Z's altercation with Lance Rivera may have helped sell records and Rocawear items, it had nearly cost him his freedom. And so, for his next move, he launched a lyrical offensive that never placed himself or anyone else in real danger, but brought unprecedented attention to his music by challenging Nas to a fight for hip-hop's crown.

The Queens-bred emcee had been floundering since *Illmatic,* and he and Jay-Z had been sending low-level snipes at each other for quite some time. So at New York's 2001 Summer Jam concert, Jay-Z took it to another level with "Takeover," a song that called out the Nas-affiliated crew Mobb Deep, ending with a shot at his soon-to-be-chief rival: "Ask Nas, he don't want it with Hov!" (Jay-Z had recently given himself this godly nickname, a shortening of "Jay-Hova.") Nas responded with a radio freestyle in which he questioned Jay-Z's drug-dealing résumé.

Jay-Z hit back with the release of his album *The Blueprint,* which included "Takeover"—and a new verse in which he pilloried Nas, aiming one of his most pointed barbs at the rapper's fashion exploits. Nas had appeared in ads for designer Karl Kani, prompting Jay-Z to call him a "fag model" (a curious choice for Jay-Z, himself a budding clothing mogul who occasionally appeared in Rocawear ads). In addition to hurling homophobic slurs, Jay-Z also declared Nas's rap career over, questioned his business acumen, and even alluded to an affair with the mother of Nas's daughter.

"It was literally Ali-Frazier," says MC Serch. "It was two guys in their prime going toe to toe. Nas was the underdog because he had put out two subpar albums and didn't have a real sense of direction. Jay was a beast, but no one would ever doubt Nas's prowess as an emcee."[25]

Nas responded with "Ether," considered by many to be the most devastating diss track in hip-hop history. He simultaneously excoriated Jay-Z for his physical appearance and his lyrical treatment of Notorious B.I.G. "First Biggie's your man, then you got the nerve to say that you better than Big," Nas rapped. "Dick-sucking lips, why don't you let the late great veteran live?" He saved his best for last: "Queens niggas run you niggas, ask Russell Simmons!"

Jay-Z countered with "Supa Ugly," a graphic retort filled with vivid descriptions of his exploits with Nas's ex, whom he called out by name. "Since you infatuated with saying that gay shit," Jay-Z rapped, "yes, you was kissing my dick when you was kissing that bitch." He also bragged about having had sex with the woman in question in the back of Nas's Bentley and leaving condoms in the baby seat. The lyrics were so over-the-top that Jay-Z's mom made him apologize to Nas.

Fans are divided on who won the battle, but both artists won the commercial war. Jay-Z's *The Blueprint,* whose sound was driven by a young producer by the name of Kanye West, went double platinum despite having been launched on September 11, 2001; Nas's *Stillmatic* also topped the two million unit mark. Most importantly, the verbal spat never escalated into physical violence. Though hiphop's kings still had some growing up to do, they were certainly moving in the right direction.

"Hip-hop was a cultural shift," says Kevin Liles, who served as president of Def Jam during the height of the Nas–Jay-Z tiff. "It wasn't just a sound...It's one thing to just put out records that sound good that sell a lot. It's another thing where, because I said this in a record, a company grew twenty percent."[26]

That's exactly the sort of thing Rocawear and Sean John experienced as Jay-Z and Diddy continued to flaunt their own brands in songs and videos, at posh parties, and on Times Square billboards. At their peak, both clothing lines were doing several hundred million dollars a year in retail sales, as was Phat Farm. But the field had gotten crowded. On top of the street wear lines Fubu, Mecca, and Eckō Unltd, a host of rappers launched their own clothing lines, from Eminem's Shady Ltd. to Nelly's Apple Bottoms. The Wu-Tang Clan, which had started its own Wu-Wear line in the mid-1990s—and opened several brick-and-mortar stores—even launched a special-edition sneaker with Nike in 1999.[27]

But the influx of mainstream interest had a downside. As department store shelves swelled with new arrivals, the big sellers started steeply discounting popular street wear. That put pressure on stores like Jimmy Jazz, V.I.M., and Dr. Jay's, many of which declined during the 2000s. "We let Macy's put them out of business," says Simmons. "We didn't know any better."[28]

Simmons and Jay-Z both knew enough to get out—and get paid—at the peak of the hip-hop fashion boom. In 2004, Simmons sold Phat Farm to half-century-old Sears supplier Kellwood for

$140 million, retaining his role as chief executive and grabbing an array of lucrative performance incentives. His then wife, Kimora Lee Simmons (yes, another model), who'd become the face of women's line Baby Phat, stayed on as well; Kellwood's chief noted that this brand had better potential for growth than the original Phat Farm.[29]

Meanwhile, sensing an opportunity, Jay-Z and the two partners to whom Simmons had introduced him paid a reported $22 million for Damon Dash's Rocawear stake in 2005. Two years later, publicly traded clothing giant Iconix bought the rights to the brand for $204 million, with Jay-Z staying on as chief of product development and marketing; the deal also called for him to get up to $35 million in Iconix stock if Rocawear met certain sales goals.[30] Diddy's reaction: "I need a billion for mine."[31]

Jay-Z's nine-figure haul came on top of a $5 million annual guarantee for his continued marketing efforts, according to industry sources—not bad, especially considering that the entire world economy collapsed about a year after the sale, and buyouts of this sort essentially ceased to exist for several years during the downturn. Simmons still marvels at the two sales.

"I don't know why they bought it," he admits of the Phat Farm deal, offering a similar explanation for Iconix's purchase. "When they bought Rocawear, it was a brick. They bought it at the end of its life. Both of us got out at the right time."[32]

Diddy dialed back his involvement in Sean John, too. In 2010, he reached an agreement to make Sean John sportswear available exclusively at Macy's, where it has done well over $1 billion in sales to date. Terms of the deal were not released. "I got my start at Macy's when I was sixteen, selling shirts and ties," Diddy told the *New York Post* in 2010. "To come full circle like this is a dream come true."[33]

In November 2016, with Sean John doing annual retail sales of $450 million, Diddy finally joined Simmons and Jay-Z in pulling most of his money out of the clothing line he'd founded. He sold his controlling stake in Sean John to apparel giant CAA-GBG Global Brand Management Group for an undisclosed sum, keeping a reported 20 percent stake. (I estimate that he received about $70 million pretax for the one-third or so of Sean John that he sold; his team would not confirm the terms.) Said Diddy: "Our new partnership with CAA-GBG provides us the opportunity to reach the millennial customer on a global level."[34]

The agreement called for Diddy to remain involved with the marketing of the brand and for Sean John to continue its exclusive sportswear pact with Macy's. Simmons takes a darker view of hip-hop's relationship with the apparel business. "Sean John is the only brand [left]," he says. "We really had built up a nice industry that a lot of kids aspired to be in. Now it's completely destroyed."[35]

Simmons may be right, at least when it comes to mass-market street wear. But the next generation of hip-hop acts is already building on the foundation laid by the likes of Phat Farm and Rocawear. Fashion-focused stars from Kanye West to A$AP Rocky have pushed out their own collections, with an eye more toward the runway than the racks at Macy's. This approach may not be as remunerative as Diddy's or Jay-Z's was, but what it lacks in profitability, it makes up for in prestige—a currency that's becoming perhaps more valuable than the dollar in the upper echelons of hip-hop.

Simmons has finished his sweet pea soup, and only a smidge of his Green Juice remains. If his Yankees cap and shell-toed sneakers are a reminder of his past, his meal is a harbinger of the health-oriented future he's trying to create.

As hip-hop has grown up, Simmons has done things like shelling out $30 million to build a yoga studio in front of the trendy Soho House in Los Angeles, where he moved in 2015. (He even convinced Diddy to give yoga a try, though it doesn't seem to have stuck.)[36]

Hollywood is Simmons's focus these days, along with his new

portfolio of lifestyle brands, including Argyleculture and an energy drink called Celsius. He holds a "significant" stake in the publicly traded company — whose share price has more than doubled since he bought in — along with billionaire Li Ka-shing (a perennial contender for the title of Wealthiest Man in Asia; also, a lock for Best Name for a Rich Person).

"So fucking strong," says Simmons of the beverage. "I go to hot yoga class after a Celsius. It's unbelievably powerful."[37]

I tell Simmons I appreciate that he's taken the time to sit down with me.

"Thank you," he says. "What's the book? The name of it?"

"We're leaning towards *3 Kings*."

"Oh, that's good," he says, pausing to ponder Diddy, Dre, and Jay-Z. "They just said, 'Why don't I do it myself?' It's funny that in the other industries, people didn't do it. All the rock stars, they never did it."

To be fair, there are a few rockers, including Sammy Hagar and Gene Simmons (no relation to Russell: the Kiss star was born Chaim Weitz in Israel), who have never been afraid to shill. But for the most part, the Def Jam founder is right: musicians tend to downplay anything having to do with money.

"They're afraid," I offer. "They don't want to be seen as sellouts."

"Oh, yeah," says Simmons, as if suddenly remembering the aspirational energy at the core of the movement he helped invent. "That's how they do it. That's hip-hop."

CHAPTER 7

A Fourth King?

The first time I interviewed 50 Cent, I was in my twenties and living with three friends in a four-bedroom, one-bathroom Manhattan rental. By contrast, thirty-four-year-old 50 had reportedly paid Mike Tyson $4 million for a Connecticut mansion with nineteen bedrooms and thirty-five bathrooms — just another perk of the 2003 album *Get Rich or Die Tryin'*, which made him hip-hop's newest superstar.[1] According to Tyson, parties went on for days because he simply couldn't find his guests to inform them that the festivities had concluded.[2]

I ended up sitting down with 50 after kicking off *Forbes*'s fulltime hip-hop coverage in 2007; one of my earliest assignments was to write a story on the topic of the rapper and his entourage. My editor envisioned a photo shoot featuring all the characters he believed 50 employed, like a guy whose sole job was to carry an umbrella. (Diddy had someone like this on his payroll many years earlier.) It took a while to convince this editor that 50 generally showed up at meetings with a less sexy group that included a lawyer, a brand manager, a publicist, and a business manager. At the photo shoot, all four walked into a boardroom and started to debate who should stand where. Clad in snakeskin boots, designer jeans, and a Yankees cap, 50 ultimately hopped up and stood on the conference table, arms folded, no smile. His employees took their places in office chairs behind him, hands clasped—no nonsense, all business.

Following the shoot, 50 told me about his plan to become hip-hop's first billionaire. He explained that, in addition to pouring his entertainment-related gains into accounts monitored by brokers at Morgan Stanley and Goldman Sachs and throwing money into "golf courses in China," he'd been working on a deal with South African metals mogul Patrice Motsepe. He said he'd visited the billionaire at one of his mines, and the two had traveled a mile below the earth's surface. There, 50 gazed longingly at the glistening walls—packed with platinum, palladium, and iridium—and started maneuvering to land an equity stake in the mine in exchange for committing to a joint venture with Motsepe that would eventually bring 50 Cent–branded precious metals to market around the world.

"Things that people wouldn't actually expect me to be involved in," he said with a grin. "I've got a diverse portfolio."[3]

Indeed, 50 Cent was one of the challengers that Diddy, Jay-Z, and Dr. Dre faced to win hip-hop's cash crown in the second half of the aughts, perhaps the most formidable of their entire run. And though he couldn't match their staying power, his example would serve as a valuable blueprint, thanks in large part to his striking one of the biggest deals in hip-hop history to that point.

As was also true with this book's titular kings, 50's wealth as a young adult came in sharp contrast to his socioeconomic status as a child. Born Curtis Jackson III in Jamaica, Queens, and raised during the crack epidemic of the 1980s, he was just eight when his drug-dealing mother was murdered, and he began selling cocaine only a few years later. He'd been arrested three times by age nineteen, surviving several potentially deadly encounters along the way, one of them after he purchased an $80,000 Mercedes-Benz 400 SEL V12 sedan. One evening, a pair of gunmen who'd followed the car ambushed him in front of his grandmother's home; after escaping the attack, he started looking for an alternate career path.[4]

"I decided to write music, 'cause my son's mom was pregnant at the time and I had to make some changes," 50 told me. "So I ended up selling the car, and the money I got back from the actual vehicle we lived off of."

His first musical break came in 1999, when he landed a record deal with Columbia and gained a measure of regional fame for his first single, "How to Rob," a song in which he half-jokingly delineates how he'd relieve all sorts of entertainers of their cash. Suggestions include robbing his own producers, kidnapping Diddy's girlfriend and holding her for ransom, and putting four bullets through the door of Jay-Z's Bentley. The latter responded with a potent line: "Go against [me], your ass is dense / I'm about a dollar, what the fuck is 50 Cents?"[5]

Far from ending 50's career, the attention only elevated him (and likely contributed to Jay-Z's more recent philosophy of not responding to provocation, so as not to give challengers free publicity). Days before the planned 2000 launch of his first album, *Power of the Dollar,* 50 was again waylaid—and ended up taking nine bullets. He survived the strike, but his record deal didn't: executives at Columbia, wary of the violence surrounding the rapper, dropped him from the label.

"When you get hurt as bad as I got hurt when I was shot, either your fear consumes you or you become insensitive on some level," 50 explained. "And people interpret my aggression in that period as gangster...when it was more like a response to being in the most vulnerable spot I've been in."[6]

As 50 nursed his wounds—including a shot to the mouth that gave his speech an almost Don Corleone–esque slur—he plotted his comeback, pumping out furious new mixtapes. In 2002, Eminem heard his driver playing one of the songs and alerted Dr. Dre to the Queens rapper's talent; the duo flew 50 to Los Angeles for a meeting and signed him to a five-album deal, shared between Aftermath, Interscope, and Eminem's Shady Records. The rapper says he spent the first $300,000 of his $1 million pact on trademarking "50 Cent" and "G-Unit," which would become the name of his own record label, clothing line, and sneaker brand.[7]

Dr. Dre and Eminem served as executive producers on his next album; Eminem appeared on several tracks and Dre produced a handful, including 50's biggest hit, "In da Club." The song typified Dre's musical evolution from the 1990s to the 2000s, when the producer more frequently traded his Minimoog's funky whine for relentless beats and sinister strings. As always, his exacting standards underpinned every detail, even those as minute as the seemingly ad-libbed spoken intro for "In da Club" (in which 50 spits a syncopated "Go! Go! Go! Go! Go! Go!" before sliding into the chorus: "Go shorty, it's your birthday, we're gonna party like it's your birthday..."). In reality, Dre carefully constructed the section in the studio, barking out a vocal instruction here or flicking a knob there.

"Even though 50 would change up his vocals, there would still be repetitive parts—almost made the song boring—while we waited for the hook to kick in," noted Dre's erstwhile right-hand man, Bruce Williams. "So the producer adds a counter rhythm, a slight *nin-nih-nin-nih* pattern to speed things up. Now it's good."[8]

Thanks to Dre's attention to detail and 50's aggressive rhymes, Eminem was so excited about the album that, even as he released his own record-breaking work, the music of his protégé surged to the top of his mind. At a party for 2002's *The Eminem Show,* which sold 284,000 units its opening week and 1.3 million the week after in the United States alone, 50 talked to the elder rapper, who couldn't contain his enthusiasm. "He was like, 'Yo, man, [your music] is it,'" 50 recalled. "'This is the next big thing.'"[9]

Shortly thereafter, *Get Rich or Die Trying* debuted atop the *Billboard* charts with opening week sales of 872,000 en route to a total north of six million in the United States and easily double that sum worldwide; both Eminem and Dre shared in the spoils. It was the best-selling album of the year and remains the most popular effort of 50's career. He's well aware of the magnitude of the accomplishment.

"I mean, [look at] Tupac," he says. "They got to kill you for you to do these kind of numbers."[10]

Diddy wasn't selling records on a 50 Cent level — or at all, really — in the early 2000s. In 2001, he formally changed his name to P. Diddy (he dropped the *P* several years later)[11] and released *The Saga Continues...*, an album about as tedious as its ellipsis-laden title suggests. But that didn't really matter: making a living by selling records was so twentieth century.

Diddy scored his first true smash of the century with the reality television program *Making the Band,* in which he served as both executive producer and star. His goal in the show, launched in 2002, was to craft a hip-hop supergroup by handpicking the most promising, dedicated contestants as cameras rolled. That made for some entertaining television as Diddy assigned outlandish tasks, most memorably dispatching a handful of contestants from Manhattan to Brooklyn just to fetch him some cheesecake. ("I am an asshole sometimes," he once admitted to me.)[12]

That same year, 150 of Diddy's closest friends, family members, and acquaintances received a hand-delivered DVD inviting them to travel to Morocco to celebrate his thirty-third birthday as special guests of the country's royal family. Apparently, Diddy had told a friend that he wanted to hold the celebration in the Dominican Republic. The friend happened to know the king of Morocco, and the monarch convinced Diddy to change his plans.[13]

And so, in the fall of 2002, two Royal Air Maroc jetliners arrived in New York to carry Diddy and his revelers — including Fab 5 Freddy, Naomi Campbell, Tommy Lee, Jessica Rosenblum, Andre Harrell, and Ivana Trump — to North Africa (another plane transported guests from Paris to Morocco). Upon reaching cruising altitude, Diddy's voice rang out over the plane's public-address system: "Our forefathers came over on a slave ship and we're returning on a charter!"[14] Dancing began; champagne popped; joints were smoked.[15]

Fab believed that the king footed the bill as part of an elaborate public relations campaign. (The Moroccan embassy's culture and media team did not respond to a request for comment.) Indeed, the drums of war were beating: in the wake of the attacks of September 11, 2001, the United States had invaded Afghanistan and was preparing to move into Iraq as well—and the instability, though quite far from Morocco, threatened to taint even the countries on the periphery of the Middle East. Hosting a very public birthday bash for one of America's best-known celebrities seemed a means of reminding tourists that Morocco was still a safe vacation destination.[16] After Diddy's crew landed, the party continued for three days at the king's palaces; guests were ushered around the country via motorcade and entertained by jugglers, acrobats, and snake charmers.[17]

"They treated us like we were literally heads of state," Fab recalls. "They had this whole beautiful itinerary...this thing by this amazing river. They had these indigenous Moroccan people making bread with big tents with all the rugs and pillows scattered— like, traditional shit. Camel rides and ATV rides...Perhaps the best party I've ever taken part in."[18]

Diddy returned to the States reinvigorated. Spurred by the success of *Making the Band,* he turned his focus to film and television. He went on to executive produce reality shows like *Run's House* and *I Want to Work for Diddy,* as well as the Biggie biopic *Notorious,* which grossed $44 million on a $20 million budget. As an actor, he landed roles in films like *Get Him to the Greek* and *A Raisin in the Sun* (he starred in the latter on Broadway as well). *Making the Band* would continue through 2009, spawning acts like Da Band and Danity Kane, which Diddy then signed to Bad Boy. He thrived in these new roles. In most of them, he really only needed to play himself.

"I'm sorry 'bout the cheesecake thing," he told me in 2014. "I really would go to Brooklyn to get cheesecake if somebody told me to — that's just the truth."[19]

Both Diddy and 50 Cent owe much of their wealth to the beverage business — and to fully understand how and why that happened, it's important to know hip-hop's historical impact on this particular industry, starting with soft drinks. There's perhaps nobody better equipped to illuminate that connection than longtime Coca-Cola exec Darryl Cobbin.

During his early adulthood in the 1980s, Cobbin watched his heroes like Kurtis Blow and, later, Heavy D appear in Sprite commercials on BET. While attending business school at Clark Atlanta University, he became obsessed with the idea of landing a gig at Coca-Cola and using hip-hop to turn Sprite into an international powerhouse brand. Cobbin managed to get a job offer from the beverage giant in 1991. The only problem was that Coca-Cola had a system: new employees showed up, proved themselves, and were then sent to work on specific brands, not the other way around. Cobbin told his recruiter he wanted to change that — and that he had eight other job offers.[20]

"If I don't get on Sprite, I'm not coming," Cobbin said.

"Well, you know what?" came the reply. "If you do that, you will be viewed as a troublemaker before you even walk through the doors. You don't want to do that, Darryl."

"I do."

A few days later, the recruiter called back with some news: Cobbin could work on Sprite right away if he joined Coca-Cola.

"As far as I know, this is the only time anyone has said, 'I want that brand, and I'm out if I don't get that brand,' " he recalls. "This gives you some indication of how much I believed what was possible on Sprite with hip-hop."

Cobbin arrived to find a brand that had lost its way. Sprite's business had been in decline for nearly a decade, pinning its turnaround hopes on new commercials featuring Macaulay Culkin — fresh off a starring turn in *Home Alone 2* — and the tagline "I Like the Sprite in You." The spots were aimed at what Sprite thought were its key customers: young kids and their parents, who were willing to buy the clear lemon-lime soda for their offspring because it was caffeine-free and didn't stain clothes when spilled.

As Cobbin started leafing through Sprite's sales numbers, however, he discovered that there were pockets of adults throughout the country, mostly black and Latino, with whom Sprite performed well. "You have to dig into the data to get beyond the averages," he says. "If you put a man on a table, and you put his head in an oven and his feet in a freezer, he might have an average temperature. But he'd be uncomfortable as hell."

Cobbin concluded that Sprite had made a mistake by aiming its marketing almost exclusively at white suburban grade school kids and their parents. Instead, he asked a question: what if the brand repositioned itself, using its hip-hop heritage to grow its share of the black and Latino market *and* the white market at the same time? Cobbin began by doing some focus group research on the brand. He found that the customers who appreciated Sprite tended to like it for what he calls the five *c*'s: crisp, clean, clear, cool, and caffeine-free.

To him, those were all attributes that resonated especially well with members of the hip-hop generation. "Crisp" and "clean" could be tied to the notion of dressing sharply. "Clear" could reference a what-you-see-is-what-you-get sort of attitude. "Cool" could mean refreshing in a physical and stylistic sense. "Caffeine-free" could imply that someone has his or her own unique energy. Cobbin linked this notion with three words — "Trust Your Instincts" — which Sprite's ad agency then turned into the iconic slogan "Obey Your Thirst."

Cobbin appealed to Coca-Cola's executives to fund the cam-

The home of DJ Kool Herc—and the birthplace of hip-hop—in the South Bronx, present day. *(Photograph by Zack O'Malley Greenburg)*

Afrika Bambaataa at New York's Roseland Ballroom in 1982. *(Photograph by Cutman LG / Courtesy of the Universal Hip Hop Museum and From Now Until Music LLC)*

A 1980 flyer promoting hip-hop founding fathers Grandmaster Flash and the Furious Five, among others. *(Photograph by Peter Nash/ Courtesy of the Universal Hip Hop Museum)*

Hip-hop pioneer Fab 5 Freddy and Blondie lead singer Debbie Harry, whose 1981 single "Rapture" became the first number one song to feature rap vocals. *(Photograph by Bobby Grossman)*

1980s royalty, from left to right: Lynda West, Donnie Simpson, Michael Schultz, Buff Love aka the Human Beat Box, Kool Rock Ski, Sugar Ray Leonard, Prince Markie Dee, and Charles Stettler. *(Photograph by Steve Friedman)*

From left: Pete Nice, Eazy-E, Dr. Dre, and MF Doom partying in Los Angeles in 1990. *(Photograph by Michael Berrin)*

Jay-Z's childhood home—the Marcy Houses in Brooklyn—at present day. *(Photograph by Danielle La Rocco)*

From left: Lonzo Williams, Dr. Dre, DJ Yella, and Cli-N-Tel during the brief 1980s heyday of the World Class Wreckin' Cru. *(Courtesy of Lonzo Williams)*

Core Consumer: Male Youth Thought and Style Leaders Who Are and Who Others Recognize as "Cool"

Positioning: "Cool" –
- Leading Others Through a Confident. Charismatic, Honest and Edgy Attitude
- Trusting Your Instincts, Being Active. Being Yourself (Real)
- Participates in "Cool" Activities such as Sports, Music, Technology

Objectives: (1) Recruit 7.5 Million New Users, and
            (2) Increase Frequency of Consumption

National Tools: Contact: Andy Lewis - 404/676-7169
- 12 Month UTC with 3 Phases
    (1) 10/96 - 2/97   NBA
    (2) 3/97 - 9/97   Music/Fashion
    (3) 10/97 - 12/97 "Cool" Holiday

Local Activation Properties/Associations: Contact:
- NBA   Oscar Budejen - 404/676-7739
- Hip Hop   Darryl A. Cobbin - 404/676-4523
- Snow Boarding   Work in Progress

Brand Team
- Darryl A. Cobbin 404/676-4523   • Marcia Huff 404/676-4159
- Mike Glennon 404/676-7828

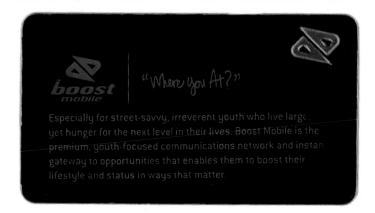

boost mobile | "Where you At?"

Especially for street-savvy, irreverent youth who live large, yet hunger for the next level in their lives. Boost Mobile is the premium, youth-focused communications network and instant gateway to opportunities that enables them to boost their lifestyle and status in ways that matter.

The two-sided card Darryl Cobbin presented to Coca-Cola brass in the early 1990s, spawning a marketing plan that forever linked Sprite and hip-hop; below, his follow-up years later at Boost Mobile. *(Courtesy of Darryl Cobbin)*

Diddy gracing the cover of *Forbes* in 1999 alongside Jerry Seinfeld. *(Courtesy of Forbes)*

Beats headphone collaborators Dr. Dre and Noel Lee, chief of Monster Cable, during happier times. *(Courtesy of Noel Lee)*

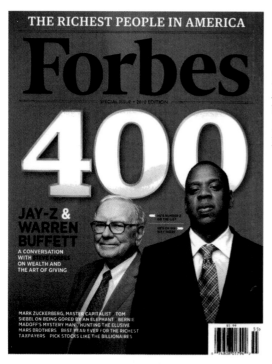

Jay-Z on the cover of *Forbes* in 2010 with billionaire Warren Buffett. *(Courtesy of Forbes)*

Diddy and Lee, who also forged a headphone connection. *(Courtesy of Noel Lee)*

The Oslo headquarters of Jay-Z's Tidal streaming service. *(Photograph by Zack O'Malley Greenburg)*

Grandmaster Flash (left) and Afrika Bambaataa, present day. *(Photograph by Emmanuel Adarkwah)*

paign. Typically, the beverage giant's flagship product got 80 to 90 percent of the company's advertising budget, leaving the employees representing the rest of its brands to fight for scraps by presenting seventy-five-page strategy outlines. Cobbin took a different tack, printing up business cards that simply explained what hip-hop was and how it would help Sprite on a quarter-by-quarter basis. His message: he would sell the brand by leveraging the burgeoning cultural movement—and make its executives a lot of cash. Says Cobbin: "I got big boy–big girl money in that meeting."

That meant spending on talent. For the first time, Sprite brought on black voice actors to do its commercials, along with venerable hip-hop group A Tribe Called Quest. Though the company briefly continued to run two sets of ads—one targeted at white consumers, one targeted at black consumers—the latter version quickly became its primary mode of marketing.

Just as Cobbin had suspected, the hip-hop-based approach resonated across demographic groups: "Obey Your Thirst" kicked off in March 1994, and by the end of the year, the brand had grown 8.9 percent. The following year, it grew 18 percent; in 1996, 23 percent. Throughout the mid-1990s, Sprite nearly tripled its volume, revenue, and profits over a five-year period. Much of that occurred in the midst of the Bad Boy–Death Row conflagration that made Interscope's corporate overlords sell the company. But the soft drink industry wasn't so closely tied to gangsta rap, and executives decided not to abandon hip-hop.

"Were the people nervous? Yes," says Cobbin. "When you're en route to tripling a business that wasn't growing, nervousness gets dismissed quickly...Sprite would not be what it became and what it is today without hip-hop."

Sprite continued to grow through the turn of the new millennium, at which point Cobbin moved to a global strategy role. He replicated his U.S. plan in places from South Africa—where the brand keyed on Kwaito, a local genre that included elements of hip-hop and house music—to Norway. That's where Sprite brought on

Tommy Tee, an Oslo native who'd grown up on graffiti art and Melle Mel en route to becoming the godfather of Scandinavian hip-hop, to lecture its European marketing teams about the genre's international presence. "I remember them being totally surprised [about] the traditions we already had established," says Tee. "That we already had generations of different performers in every part of the culture over here."[21]

Along the way, Cobbin inspired a young Coca-Cola executive named Rohan Oza, a marketer of Indian descent who was born and raised in Africa and then educated in the United Kingdom and the United States. Oza started working on the Sprite brand in the late 1990s, under Cobbin's wing. ("He was my Jedi master on Sprite," Oza says of Cobbin.) Like his mentor, Oza quickly recognized the marketing power of hip-hop, and he put together a series of popular anime-inspired commercials in 1998.[22]

In the spots, the evil King Zarkon declares war on the rap world: "This hip-hop culture of yours is making a big buzz around the universe," he says. "And I'm not feeling it. The break dancing, the graffiti art, the rhyming, the DJing—it all has to go!" The only way to save hip-hop is by getting its disparate forces—Common from the Midwest, Goodie Mob from the South, Fat Joe from the East, Mack 10 from the West—to unite as the super-robot Voltron. With the help of spiritual leader Afrika Bambaataa, this happens in the spot: Voltron defeats Zarkon's robot, and hip-hop wins. The message is clear: in the wake of the violence of the mid-1990s, different factions needed to put aside their differences (and drink some Sprite).

As time went on, Oza became a crucial conduit for one of those unifying goals: deal-making.

👑 👑 👑

As 50 Cent set about building an empire of his own, he got significant assistance from his manager, the late Chris Lighty. He grew up in the Bronx River Houses, like Bambaataa, and later went to work for Russell Simmons's management company. Lighty helped forge the connection between hip-hop and big brands: he put LL Cool J in a 1997 Gap commercial and linked A Tribe Called Quest with Sprite.[23] He also served as Diddy's music manager for a spell, though nobody has ever managed the mogul's career in its entirety. ("Managers have existed, but really only for Puff Daddy the artist and really not in the traditional sense of…a manager being somebody who kind of tells an artist what to do," says Meiselas. "More of kind of like a right hand, who would help him execute on the artist side.")[24]

Lighty recognized 50 as a kindred spirit—a chameleon who could ramp up the tough-guy act or the smooth-talking boardroom diplomacy as the situation demanded. "There's a deeper side to 50 Cent, a deeper business side that people don't normally see," Lighty told me in 2009. "It was done his way, and not the way that people [expected]."[25]

The rapper's rise may have been rooted in his experiences in the streets, but his interests and influences soon grew much wider. For example, he became a devoted watcher of the History Channel. He was particularly struck by a special on six-man guerrilla units; the image stuck with 50 and inspired his G-Unit empire. He used the same name for his clothing line, which soon ended up on store shelves next to Jay-Z's Rocawear and Diddy's Sean John, and for a sneaker that followed the former's S. Carter edition. Both shoe lines were created by Reebok in an apparent attempt to make up for losing the LeBron James sneaker sweepstakes to Nike when he went pro in 2003.[26]

Jay-Z's shoe came first. His understated white low-top, inspired by a vintage Gucci sneaker, made him the first nonathlete to strike such a deal with the brand. Rather than sign a traditional endorsement deal, he structured the agreement as a fifty-fifty joint venture with Reebok, with the rights to the logo and trademark eventually reverting to him. For the sneaker's debut, Reebok wrapped a private jet in S. Carter imagery and sent the rapper across the Atlantic to give press conferences on tarmacs across Europe in order to create buzz.[27]

The shoe became the fastest-selling model in Reebok's history, only to be eclipsed shortly thereafter by 50's sneaker; both were promoted in a minute-long commercial. ("I rock Reeboks, man / If it ain't the G-Unit, it's the S Dot, man," raps 50 before Jay-Z adds, "See how we cross-brand? We boss about it, man."[28]) The verses may have been corny, but the deals were huge wins for Reebok, which was purchased by Adidas-Salomon for more than $3 billion in 2005. Fittingly, the company behind the original hip-hop sneaker deal had now gobbled up the latest shoemaker to be boosted by the genre.

Meanwhile, Rohan Oza had moved on from Coca-Cola's Sprite to its Powerade brand, spending a lot of time in New York in order to visit NFL and NBA executives. On his trips, Oza kept seeing Vitaminwater in shops; intrigued, he started drinking it, and quickly got hooked. He loved that the different flavors were tasty but had only half the amount of sugar as other beverages he consumed. So when the founder of Glacéau, Vitaminwater's parent company, offered him a job as CMO—complete with equity in the company, then based in Queens—Oza accepted. "If I didn't, I'd probably get fired from Coke anyway," he says. "My makeup is much more suited to an entrepreneurial world than it is to corporate America. I intimidated too many people."[29]

Upon Oza's arrival at Glacéau in 2002, he decided that he wanted to bring on someone with a similar reputation: 50 Cent. A friend of Oza's introduced him to Lighty, who set up a meeting with 50 in 2004. Oza hoped to convince either the Queens-born rapper or Jay-Z to become a part of the brand, but his first meeting with the former went so well that he never asked the latter. A fitness enthusiast from the same borough as Glacéau, 50 immediately took to the product.

"I can't pay you that much," Oza warned.

"No problem," replied 50. "I'm going to bet on myself."

The rapper became the face of Vitaminwater, receiving $5 million and 5 percent of the company for his troubles.[30] Oza wouldn't confirm the numbers but said that the payment was "predominantly equity." "[If] I don't give the exact numbers out, 50 doesn't beat me up, which I think is a pretty fair deal," Oza says. He notes that the rapper invested additional cash in the company beyond the equity he received; Lighty, who negotiated the deal, also got a piece.[31]

Very quickly, 50 became the straw that stirred Glacéau's drink. He created his own flavor, Formula 50, and appeared in commercials. In one, a pair of tuxedoed commentators introduce 50 as the conductor of a televised performance of Beethoven's Ninth Symphony. "Since he began drinking Vitaminwater Formula 50, he feels he's up to the task," says one of the announcers. The rapper takes a sip of the concoction and leads the orchestra in a mash-up of Beethoven and "In da Club." Even in spots for other brands like Reebok, 50 insisted in holding bottles of Vitaminwater.

It's hard to quantify how much 50's involvement boosted Glacéau, but the company's numbers certainly exploded in the years after he came on board. In 2005, Vitaminwater sold just over thirty million 192-ounce cases; the following year, that number doubled. The company clocked revenues of $355 million in 2006 and projected a $700 million haul in 2007. That sort of performance convinced Coca-Cola to buy Glacéau for just over $4 billion that May.[32]

The rapper's reported 5 percent stake left him in excellent shape: sources close to the deal confirmed that 50 took home roughly $100 million after taxes. But 50 wasn't satisfied. "People were talking about how much money I made, but I was focused on the fact that $4.1 billion was made," he later told me. "I think I can do a bigger deal in the future."[33]

Jay-Z had his own guerrilla inspiration at around the same time. In the waning days of 2001, he released his first live album, *Jay-Z: Unplugged,* recorded with the Roots as part of MTV's series

Unplugged. On the cover, he sits on a drum in front of Questlove, whose 'fro pokes out above Jay-Z's left shoulder, just enough to be recognizable but not so much as to take away any of the spotlight. A more surprising face in the photo: Che Guevara, whose image appears on Jay-Z's shirt. The late Marxist likely wouldn't have been thrilled to be associated with the gaudy chain dangling from the neck of the arch capitalist, but no matter.

"The spirit of struggle and insurgency was woven into the lives of the people I grew up with in Bed-Stuy, even if in sometimes fucked up and corrupted ways," Jay-Z later wrote. "Che's failures were bloody and his contradictions frustrating. But to have contradictions — especially when you're fighting for your life — is human, and to wear the Che shirt and the platinum and diamonds together is honest."[34] As Jay-Z would put it on his song "Public Service Announcement" two years later: "I'm like Che Guevara with bling on: I'm complex."

Jay-Z increasingly embodied those contradictions, both in his personal life and his business life. In the former, his old friends were being replaced by glitterati; the likes of Foxy Brown and Jaz-O had given way to Gwyneth Paltrow and Bono. At around this time, Fab 5 Freddy ran into Jay-Z at a Robin Hood Foundation gala, where the rapper had just gotten a tour of a Basquiat retrospective; the guide had mentioned that Fab had been close with the painter.

"I saw Jay at this benefit, he came over and was like, 'Man, oh my God...Basquiat, I didn't know that was your man...You need to break this shit down for me!'" Fab remembers him saying. "That would lead to seeing him develop this passion and love for fine art."[35] Jay-Z has since been growing his collection, which includes works by Warhol and Basquiat; he dished out $4.5 million to buy a painting by the latter in 2013.[36]

When it came to business, there seemed to be a growing divide between Jay-Z and Damon Dash. The latter's confrontational approach had been an asset in the early days but became an impediment as Jay-Z soared higher up the A-list. In 2002, while Jay-Z was vacationing in the Mediterranean, Dash fired several Roc-A-Fella employees and gave rapper Cameron "Cam'ron" Giles the title of vice president without consulting Jay-Z; upon his return, Jay-Z reversed the move, escalating tension with Dash.

In 2003, Jay-Z made another move sure to upset Dash: he decided to retire from his career as a performer. It seemed that he'd gotten tired of rap after putting out an album every year since his 1996 debut, and perhaps grown a bit jaded. "I dumbed down for my audience to double my dollars," he rapped on "Moment of Clarity," from his supposed swan song, *The Black Album*. "They criticize me for it, yet they all yell 'Holler!'" Dash may have found some solace in the fact that Jay-Z put together a plan to milk his farewell for all he could, driving buzz for the album and padding Roc-A-Fella's coffers in the process.

There was more to the scheme than just music. Jay-Z planned the launch of his S. Carter sneaker to coincide with the album's release and opened his 40/40 Club in Manhattan's Flatiron district at around the same time. That summer, he gathered some of his newfound NBA friends—including Kenyon Martin, Tracy McGrady, Lamar Odom, John Wallace, and Jamal Crawford—to form a team to play in the Entertainers' Basketball Classic, a Harlem street ball tournament that stretched through the dog days. He also started negotiations with Doug Morris, then chief of Def Jam parent Universal, to become a full-fledged record executive at the end of the year.

To maximize marketing opportunities, Jay-Z decided to create a documentary about his ride into the sunset, focusing on the basketball tournament. Though Dash fancied himself a movie maven—producing Roc-A-Fella's bizarre, quasi-pornographic, straight-to-video flick *Streets Is Watching* in 1998—Jay-Z went in a different direction, bringing on Fab 5 Freddy to direct his film. The hip-hop pioneer would meet Jay-Z and his team at the 40/40 Club on game days, and they'd all hop on a bus emblazoned with the S. Carter sneaker logo and head up to Harlem as cameras rolled. Guests on the bus ranged from Diddy to *The Fader*'s Rob Stone to Jay-Z's new girlfriend, a young singer named Beyoncé Knowles.

After Team S. Carter lost the first game, it became clear that too many of these visitors were trying to backseat coach. "You got nine guys on the team and there's nine coaches," Stone remembers telling Jay-Z's colleague Mike Kyser. "Get one fucking coach." Later that night, back at the 40/40 Club, Jay-Z sidled up to Stone. "I got to get rid of eight coaches, huh?" he said. Stone was amazed. "The guy pays attention," he says.[37] Jay-Z consolidated coaching power in Juan Perez—who, along with his wife, Desiree, had partnered with him on the 40/40 Club—and would continue to be a key part of the rapper's inner circle.[38] Jay-Z also began to take a more proactive role himself, personally calling and emailing players to make sure they'd be there for games.[39]

Team S. Carter cruised through the Rucker Park season, setting up a championship matchup against rapper Fat Joe's Terror Squad team, which boasted NBA stars including Stephon Marbury and Ron Artest (who, despite his famously cantankerous attitude, later changed his legal name to Metta World Peace). On the day of the final game, Jay-Z met Fab in a downtown recording studio and prepared to head up to Harlem. Just as they were about to leave, though, the lights went out—and didn't come back on for another twenty-four hours or so. It was the blackout of 2003, which left some fifty-five million people without power across the northeastern United States and Canada, rendering a nighttime basketball game impossible.

Jay-Z immediately faced a dilemma. A private jet waited to take him and Beyoncé to Europe for their first major vacation as a couple; they had to be back in the States by the end of August for the MTV Video Music Awards, where many of their songs, including their new duet, "Crazy in Love," were up for awards. He could cut the trip short and come back for the rescheduled final game or relax with his new girlfriend. He did the latter.

It wasn't easy for Jay-Z to throw himself so fully into a relationship—by his own admission, he'd found it hard to trust people ever since his father abandoned him; in his business dealings and his romantic relationships, Jay-Z was "always suspicious." But in 2003, he found some personal closure when his mother helped arrange a meeting with his estranged dad, who was terminally ill (and passed away several months later). "That was very defining," Jay-Z told *Rolling Stone* two years later. "I got to let it go. I got to tell him everything I wanted to say."[40]

While Jay-Z worked on overcoming his hang-ups and winning the hand of pop's top superstar, his Rucker team wound up forfeiting the last game. ("My niggas didn't have to play to win the championship," Fat Joe bragged on "Lean Back" the following year.) Fab hoped to release the documentary anyway, but Jay-Z pulled the plug, not wanting to be seen as anything less than victorious. Losing the documentary pained Fab; for his subject, the episode was something best swept under the rug. And because Jay-Z didn't call attention to it, most observers to this day think of 2003 not as the year Jay-Z lost the Rucker Park tournament but as a positive turning point in his career. "It was the beginning of him becoming this more grown Jay-Z, if you will," says Fab. "The business ventures became more pronounced and diverse... He became more of his own thing."[41]

Jay-Z's plans included outflanking his Roc-A-Fella cofounders. After Def Jam bought out the trio's remaining equity for $10 million, a head-spinning game of musical chairs consumed the seminal hip-hop label. Kevin Liles, who'd worked all the way up from intern to president at Def Jam, followed his mentor, Lyor Cohen, then head of the label's parent, Island Def Jam, to Warner Music Group. Cohen then tried to lure Jay-Z to his new company as an executive. Says Atlantic Records chief Craig Kallman, who worked under Cohen at the time: "I know Lyor would have loved to have Jay-Z in Warner."[42]

But it wasn't meant to be. Universal, which owned Island Def

Jam and, by extension, Def Jam itself, brought in executive L.A. Reid to run the former — and Jay-Z to head the latter. In this role, he came to oversee all of Def Jam's labels, including Roc-A-Fella, which meant becoming the boss of his old partners Dash and Burke. "It's just business," Jay-Z reportedly told Dash, who subsequently left the label and evaporated into obscurity. (Burke was arrested for drug trafficking in 2012 and spent four years in prison.)

Under Jay-Z's leadership, Def Jam went on to launch acts including Kanye West, Rick Ross, and Rihanna. But perhaps his most brilliant move was signing an old foe. In November 2005, Jay-Z held the ominously titled "I Declare War" concert at the New Jersey Nets' home arena in East Rutherford (he had recently purchased a small stake in the NBA team). On a stage set to look like the Oval Office, complete with a large desk and mock Secret Service agents, Jay-Z tore through his set, pausing only to bring out special guests including West and Diddy. He closed with one final surprise: Nas, who joined him to perform Jay-Z's song "Dead Presidents," which samples a Nas track.

"All that beef shit is done, we had our fun," he said onstage. "Let's get this money."[43] Within months, he'd signed Nas to Def Jam; their duet, "Black Republicans," appeared on Nas's next album, which sold 355,000 copies in its first week.

Ever the trendsetter, Jay-Z had moved hip-hop away from the aggressive lyrics of 50 Cent and his ilk, finding that unity could be much more remunerative. Others followed his lead. In 2006, for example, West Coast rapper Xzibit released "California Vacation" — which featured Bloods and Crips rapping on the same track in the form of the Game and Snoop Dogg — with Xzibit delivering the core message: "From what I see, red and blue can make green."

At the same time, the overlapping Venn diagram of subgenres known as Backpack Rap and Conscious Rap, which include bookish acts like Common and Lupe Fiasco, began to take shape. Jay-Z noted on his triple-platinum *Black Album* that, in the wake of a recent $5 million payday, he hadn't been rhyming as thoughtfully as

Common. But it turned out that rapping about the perils of violence and capitalism could be lucrative, too. I once asked Common about the Jay-Z line. His response? "I've made more than $5 million."[44]

The last time I interviewed 50 Cent, we sat high above the icy Manhattan streets in a SiriusXM studio where he was about to do some promo work for his latest album, *Animal Ambition*. But more than the music, he remained focused on scheming a way to make his next Vitaminwater-esque score.

Though the precious metals deal he'd dreamed up in South Africa never came to fruition, 50 had taken equity stakes in a number of companies closer to home that he in turn promoted heavily. Among them: Street King (a performance-boosting shot meant to compete with 5-Hour Energy), Effen (a vodka brand aspiring to challenge Diddy's Cîroc), and Frigo (maker of the $100 climate-controlled boxer brief). But he spent the most time obsessing over headphone maker SMS, short for "studio mastered sound."

This proved surprisingly problematic for his mentor, Dr. Dre, already committed to a headphone line of his own. After 50 made a music video and saw the final cut, with his SMS hat blurred out, he decided that he'd had enough and left the company that launched him to superstardom in favor of an independent distribution deal in February 2014.

"Interscope is Beats Records," he told me. "There's no artist that has a marketing budget supporting what they're actually doing that doesn't have Beats headphones in the actual visual to support that brand, that company. So when I invested in SMS Audio, it kind of made people afraid."[45]

But unmoored from Dre — and from Lighty, who died of an apparently self-inflicted gunshot wound in 2012 — 50's punches, both musical and entrepreneurial, just weren't landing. *Animal Ambition* sold a mere 47,000 first-week copies during its summer 2014 debut; by that point, 50 hadn't played more than a dozen shows in a year since 2010 (after averaging more than thirty annually over the prior eight years, according to Pollstar). In 2015, he got hit with multimillion-dollar lawsuits from Sleek Audio ($18 million, for a headphone deal gone bad) and from a woman named Lastonia Leviston ($7 million, for posting a sex tape featuring her, in an apparent attempt to get back at rival Rick Ross, who had fathered a baby with Leviston).[46]

The rapper's equity stakes were worth millions on paper, but with his cash flow dwindling and a list of money pits like his Connecticut estate drinking up his Vitaminwater windfall, the lawsuits caught 50 in a liquidity crunch—and he declared bankruptcy in the spring of 2015. As part of the settlement, he agreed to pay a court-designated disbursing agent $7.4 million up front (presumably, the remaining total of his liquid assets) plus $6 million from the planned sale of his mansion and another $10 million gleaned from his annual earnings at a minimum of $2 million per year. Sleek Audio would receive $17.3 million, Leviston $6 million.[47]

In an interview, 50 told Larry King that it was a "strategic" move. The rapper did not respond to a request for comment on the matter. But 50's filing served a strategic purpose indeed: though it shaved only a couple of million dollars off the total he owed his creditors, bankruptcy meant that he could pay them off a bit at a time instead of being forced to sell stakes in early-stage companies all at once. Beginning shortly after his filing, he demonstrated his resolve to get out of debt by increasing his annual gig count by about 50 percent while averaging $360,000 per city, according to Pollstar. He also launched an even more expensive underwear collection with Frigo ($150 for the "Nano Stitch" boxer brief, which is covered with images of lions with crowns on their heads) and a re-upped for a fourth and fifth season of the Starz television show *Power,* which he both acts in and produces.

Perhaps most importantly, 50 received a windfall of $14.5 million after winning a malpractice suit against the lawyers who negotiated his deal with Sleek (he initially sought $75 million in damages). By 2017, it seemed that this unfortunate chapter in 50's financial history was on the verge of early resolution.[48]

Dr. Dre, meanwhile, seemed to have barely noticed the departure of his onetime protégé. He'd filled up his schedule putting the finishing touches on the masterpiece of his career as a businessman—and the end result would make 50's Vitaminwater deluge look like a mere droplet by comparison.

CHAPTER 8

The Beats Generation

Noel Lee is a man who knows how to make an entrance. Accompanied by an entourage of a half-dozen or so, he rolls into the sky lobby dining room of the Marriott Marquis in Times Square on a gold Segway accented with flames and then settles into a banquette beneath a towering waterfall in the center of the room.

Lee sports a navy blazer and a black T-shirt bearing the logo of his company, Monster Cable, which he founded in 1979 after working as both a professional drummer and a laser-fusion design engineer for a nuclear weapons research outfit. There, according to Lee, he was exposed to toxic doses of radiation that led to the development of a nerve disorder that prevents him from walking—hence the Segway, which he prefers to a wheelchair. The greatest breakthrough of his career came when, frustrated that most stereo systems were wired with the same cables used for household lamps, he designed a high-performance cable that enabled crisper, stronger sound.

Monster still peddles these trademark cables along with speakers and headphones. The company does not disclose its financial performance, but Lee says he expects annual revenue to top $1 billion within the next five years. Most recently, he's teamed up to create a range of products, including Monster DNA with Swizz Beatz, ROC headphones and speakers (no relation to Jay-Z's Roc Nation) with soccer star Cristiano Ronaldo, and, most famously, Beats by Dr. Dre. These experiences have taught Lee lessons he never could have learned in engineering school.

"What is popular in hip-hop is popular for every white kid in suburbia and every Korean kid doing a rap...and all corners of the world," he says. "It affects the vernacular of how you speak, so the word 'motherfucker' means 'good,' or it could be bad. That's what I learned."[1]

A waitress comes by to take our orders; I ask for a mac and cheese, making sure to request a separate check for myself, per journalistic custom.[2]

"I'll write that in our memoirs," says Lee. "'Couldn't even buy Zack a mac and cheese.'"[3]

"You're not allowed to buy him anything," one of his lackeys pipes in.

"Shut up, will you please?" says Lee.

I can't tell if he's actually annoyed, and neither can his employee.

"Sorry, boss," he says.

But Lee is just getting started. Swatting down members of his retinue is part of his personality, as is pontificating about hip-hop and, occasionally, referring to himself in the third person.

"Guys like Dre and Jay, they've extended beyond their time... Diddy, too, but not in the musical sense," he says. "Let's take Dre... How does somebody who doesn't put out music become the richest hip-hop artist? Well, guess what? Noel Lee put that in the driver's seat for him."

Dr. Dre and Jimmy Iovine see things a little differently from Lee, as I learned the afternoon when I first met them in 2011. A small group of reporters gathered at an airy loft in midtown Manhattan to cover the launch of Beats' latest offering, and Iovine gave some opening remarks. With Dre at his side, he explained the genesis of Beats: he and Dre were walking along the Pacific Ocean one day in

2006 when the latter said he wanted to start a shoe line; he even had an offer on the table from a major brand.

"Fuck sneakers," said Iovine. "Let's sell speakers!"[4]

It's a great Hollywood line from a great Hollywood story. But as is often the case with such tales, there's quite a bit more to it—namely, the extensive involvement of Lee. His son, Kevin, who initially turned him on to hip-hop (and later went on to found his own Sol Republic headphone line), was the one who suggested sitting down with his future Beats partners. "Dad, we've got to hook up with Jimmy and Dre," Kevin said. Lee's response: "Jimmy who? What does he do? And Dre—isn't he done?" But Kevin prevailed and helped set up a meeting. According to Lee, Iovine was indeed convinced at first that speakers were the way to go.[5]

"Jimmy," said Lee. "Nobody buys speakers anymore."

"What do you mean, 'Nobody buys speakers'?"

"Big speakers—you can't take it with you. Everything is portable," Lee replied. "Kids don't listen to speakers. You got to do headphones."

Iovine quickly came around and Dre became the face of the product. Lee agreed to have his company design, engineer, manufacture, and distribute the headphones; he'd pay a royalty to Iovine, Dre, and Interscope, who would collectively provide marketing and own the brand. Iovine and Dre held the lion's share of equity, with Interscope parent Universal possessing a large chunk as well. Lee eventually negotiated a 5 percent stake in Beats. Smaller pieces went to artist Will.i.am and NBA star LeBron James, both of whom would go on to play a key role in Beats' development.

Of course, the entertainer who contributed the most to the project was the one who gave it his name. Dre actually came up with the Beats by Dr. Dre moniker, according to Lee and others close to the company. He also defined the company's guiding principle, a pure product of his passion for "perfecting the beat," as he once rapped. "Apple was selling $400 iPods with $1 earbuds," Iovine later recalled. "Dre told me, 'Man, it's one thing that people steal my music. It's another thing to destroy the feeling of what I've worked on.'"[6]

Lee developed nearly one hundred prototypes before passing a dozen or so to Dre and Iovine for their input. Dre used 50 Cent's "In da Club" to test different iterations, eventually settling on a bass-heavy version that made Beats the first headphones truly designed for hip-hop. He and Iovine envisioned the "Beats curve," a thumpy sound profile that would extend across all the products they'd build together.[7]

"It was the first time anybody had heard that bass — Sennheiser didn't do it, Bose didn't do it, Sony didn't do it," says Lee. "They were still doing studio or orchestral stuff, but they weren't doing hip-hop... The kids, when they listen to music, they want to hear it like they hear it in the club."

Dre tested out other genres on the headphones, too, listening to everything from Sade to Kraftwerk to make sure that both soul and electronic music sounded right. Yet Lee worried that they'd turned up the bass too far (many audio purists would later agree with that assessment) and sought the counsel of Will.i.am. "Will, I'm not quite happy with the bass," Lee remembers saying. The artist's response: "Don't touch it. You've got magic."[8]

Getting retailers to sign on wasn't quite so easy. Beats debuted in the middle of the great recession — not exactly the best time to be selling $300 headphones. Dealers didn't believe that an aging rap star who hadn't released a solo album in a decade would be enough to move the needle. So Lee went to work convincing Brian Dunn, then the chief executive of Best Buy, that Beats would be not just the next big product but the next big category.

Dunn was an unlikely ally. He started out at Best Buy in 1985, selling televisions in Minnesota to make some money over the holidays, but when VCR technology hit, he found himself in the middle of a consumer electronics industry revolution and stayed on with the retailer. He worked his way up the ladder, running a store, then a district, and then a region; he eventually ascended to the rank of COO and took over as Best Buy's chief executive in 2009.[9]

By that point, Dunn had heard of both Lee and Iovine, and when the former reached out to discuss Beats, he listened eagerly. Dunn remembers going to Lee's Bay Area office, replete with curtains and couches reminiscent of a Moroccan casbah, and wrapping a Beats prototype around his ears. It took one session to hook Dunn. Shortly thereafter, Lee brought him into a meeting with Dre and Iovine. Dunn had been involved in his share of celebrity meet and greets by this point. But as Iovine articulated his vision for marketing the headphones while Dre obsessed over sound and fashion, Dunn realized that he'd stumbled upon something different.

"Dre talked about what it was going to mean, how the industry would get behind it," Dunn recalls. "Talked about, 'People pay a lot of money for Nikes; they're going to pay money for great headphones that have a great sound, that have some cachet to them.'"

Best Buy became the first big retailer to stock Beats, but before the headphones could really take off, sales associates had to learn just what they were selling. Lee and his team went in to explain that they needed to know their competition for consumer dollars—and, as Dre had advised Dunn, it wasn't Sennheiser or Bose.[10]

"Do I buy the Beats or the Air Jordans?" says Dunn. "That's the consideration set."[11]

Much like Dre, Jay-Z chased a period of musical dormancy—and, some would say, decline—with one of the most lucrative deals of his career. His three-year "retirement" from life as a rapper hadn't gone as planned, nor had his comeback: in 2006, Jay-Z returned with *Kingdom Come,* his lowest-selling album in nearly a decade. His follow-up, *American Gangster,* inspired by the Denzel Washington movie, fared even worse. Both records did claim number one spots on the *Billboard* charts, and Jay-Z shrugged off his critics, saying that his music had become too "sophisticated" for many to appreciate.[12]

He announced on Christmas Eve of 2007 that he was stepping

down from his role as president of Def Jam. His contract, worth some $10 million, had expired; he reportedly wanted more money to stay, and Universal, the corporate parent of his label, declined to give it to him. It seemed that he longed for more than a raise: his position had confined him to music, at least in his day job, at a time when he felt compelled to flex his entrepreneurial muscles even more broadly.

"At Def Jam I wanted to bring the entire culture into it," he later said. "I wanted a fund so I could do other things aside from signing artists, like buying a television station or a club where we can develop these artists, or putting out some headphones...I don't think at that time they could really get their mind around that."[13]

Within days of his Def Jam departure, the rumor mill had Jay-Z and Beyoncé teaming up to form a new superlabel at Apple. It was a fascinating possibility, but ultimately, one of his fellow kings would sign an industry-altering deal with Steve Jobs's company first. Jay-Z and Beyoncé had a different sort of union in the works: on April 4, 2008, the duo finally tied the knot at their Tribeca penthouse amidst friends, family, and fifty thousand orchid blooms imported from Thailand.[14] The marriage legally solidified a relationship that had already paid dividends for both, giving Beyoncé some of Jay-Z's street cred while bringing him to her broader pop audience.

That same month, Jay-Z took his next step professionally, agreeing to a ten-year, $150 million deal with concert giant Live Nation that would encompass music, touring, and his thirst for outside business ventures. The pact included $50 million up front plus $10 million for each of at least three albums, $20 million for certain licensing rights, $25 million meant to finance Jay-Z's investments, and $5 million per year for five years to cover the creation of Roc Nation, a multipurpose entertainment company whose profits would be shared with Live Nation.[15] As part of the deal, Jay-Z received 775,434 Live Nation shares (worth more than $30 million today), plus an option to purchase 500,000 more at $13.73 per share (a discount of more than 60 percent at recent prices).[16]

At the time, record labels wracked by the piracy-induced decline in music sales were beginning to claw back revenue by insisting that new "360" deals include a provision giving them a cut of artists' touring dollars. Jay-Z wasn't interested in that sort of arrangement, so he turned the template inside out and went directly to a concert promoter. "The record company is not in the touring business," Jay-Z later said. "So why would an artist sign with you when that's not your area of expertise? [Live Nation] is the biggest concert promoter there is, and there's just so many different aspects we're into to make ourselves successful: touring, producing, publishing, clothing, movies."[17]

Jay-Z and Live Nation would share ownership of Roc Nation evenly.[18] He'd found a partner who would let him do exactly what he couldn't at Def Jam — while paying him handsomely and letting him retain ownership. All the more remarkable was Live Nation's decision to give a rapper a deal on par with those of its two biggest legacy pop and rock acts: Madonna (ten years, $120 million) and U2 (terms weren't disclosed, but Live Nation's chief said that the Irish rockers' twelve-year pact resembled Madonna's).[19]

"[Hip-hop] just hadn't translated into the live arena very well," says Gary Bongiovanni, chief of touring data outfit Pollstar. "Part of it is that you have to do something of a dynamic stage show [to make it more than just] a guy talking into a microphone."[20]

Randy Phillips, then chief of Live Nation's main rival, AEG, had similar thoughts when the Jay-Z deal went down. When *Rolling Stone* writer Steve Knopper called him for a quote, he offered an honest appraisal. "I said I would never have made the Jay-Z deal," Phillips recalls. "Part of it was I was jealous that I was never asked to even bid on the deal, but I said Jay-Z is no U2, in terms of what I thought the potential was [for] the earnings and the touring...That's what got printed."[21]

Not long after the story came out, Phillips was taking in a concert from a luxury box when a tall figure in a hooded sweatshirt materialized between Phillips and the door. "So," a familiar voice said. "You don't think I'm as good as U2?"

"I looked up and I could barely see him, but I could tell in the voice it was Jay," recalls Phillips. "My exit was blocked, so I had to engage. And so I said, 'Look, it was taken out of context, as you know. Frankly, I would never have made that deal. Not that you ever asked me.'"

The two parted ways, and Jay-Z spent the next several years trying to prove critics like Phillips wrong, usually boosting himself by teaming with artists who had fan bases different from his. He got help from his 2009 album, *The Blueprint 3,* which included "Empire State of Mind," the New York anthem he recorded with Alicia Keys, which became one of his biggest hits. The song quickly reignited Jay-Z's touring career, and he hit the road for a sixty-two-date excursion, his average gross soaring past $1 million per night.[22]

In addition to launching solo tours following his own album releases, he teamed up with Kanye West for the Watch the Throne tour, which ran from October 2011 to June 2012, grossing roughly $75 million on fifty-eight shows, and then with Justin Timberlake for the Legends of the Summer tour the following year, pulling in $69 million across fourteen sold-out concerts. In 2014, Jay-Z and Beyoncé sold out all twenty-one dates on their On the Run tour from Pasadena to Paris, doing $110 million in ticket sales. The total was more than that of any hip-hop tour to that point; Live Nation shared in the spoils at every step.[23]

"That's one of the best deals they've ever done, because of the type of business and how Jay keeps reinventing himself," says Kevin Morrow, who promoted Dre and Snoop's Up in Smoke tour. "This guy's a genius. [He says] 'Oh boy, if my sales are diminishing, even by ten percent, I'm going to go grab Eminem or Kanye West or Beyoncé.'...He is so smart when it comes down to, 'How am I packaged? What is my brand? Where am I going to play?'"[24]

Years after the *Rolling Stone* story came out, Phillips ran into Jay-Z once again—this time at a Who show at the Barclays Center in Brooklyn. The AEG executive walked over to Jay-Z and shook his hand.

"I apologized for being wrong," Phillips recalls. "I was totally wrong. His deal turned out to be a home run for both him and for them."[25]

It makes sense that, of all three kings, Dre launched a headphone line that truly resonated with people. Diddy was the flashy impresario and Jay-Z the brainy lyricist. Dre, on the other hand, had carved a niche for himself as the quiet perfectionist so obsessed with sound quality that he'd released only two solo studio albums by that point in what was already a quarter-century career.

Dre's stamp of approval helped Beats headphones get off the ground despite continued lukewarm reviews from audiophiles unenthused by the product's sometimes-overwhelming bass and hefty price tag. But the audiophiles weren't his target. Beats aimed to attract young music fans who'd never bought fancy headphones before, serving up the product with a side of sex appeal. In 2008, Beats adorned the ears of LeBron James and his U.S. teammates at the Beijing Olympics and started popping up in every Interscope music video — hundreds of them — on or around the bodies of artists including Lady Gaga, Justin Bieber, Britney Spears, Will.i.am, Miley Cyrus, and Nicki Minaj. Some musicians got their own headphone lines (most notably Bieber's JustBeats and Gaga's Heart-Beats). According to Noel Lee, acts allowed the headphones to be placed in their videos without receiving additional compensation, let alone equity. "You did a video with Interscope, you got the headphones," he says. "[Artists] would say, 'What are these?'" The response: "Don't ask. Just put them in the video."[26]

The broader headphone business soon came to reflect the success of its newest entrant. From 2008 to 2009, industry-wide sales surged from 59 million units at $490 million to 68.7 million units at $648 million, marking a 32 percent jump in revenues. The average unit price also increased by 14 percent, from $8.30 to $9.43. That might not seem like a lot, but it was quite a feat year over year, especially given that it occurred during the depths of the great recession.[27] Boosted by all the free product placement, Beats suddenly accounted for nearly one-third of the market, racking up revenues of $180 million in 2009.[28]

Dre's success spurred other hip-hop acts to create headphone lines of their own: Soul by Ludacris, 50 Cent's SMS Audio (Timbaland was among its investors),[29] and Roc Nation Aviator, a collaboration between Jay-Z's new company and Skullcandy. In the meantime, Iovine plotted to maintain Beats' marketplace dominance, sometimes checking with dozens of people before making decisions. Dre obsessed over keeping Beats cool, weighing in on everything from commercials to font styles, generally relying on his gut and vetoing anything "corny" or "cheesy." His dismissals would come in short, simple bursts: "I'm not feeling that." But Iovine recognized the value of the company's "cultural barometer," as one colleague called Dre. "Once you try to describe cool, you run the risk of going perpetually to noncool hell," said Iovine. "The whole premise is not to talk about it."[30]

Just as Nikes were as much a fashion statement as an athletic necessity, Beats—with its flagship Studio line available in a rainbow of colors—soon became equal parts accessory and audio device. "We changed the way headphones are a part of lifestyle," says Lee. "It established headphones, where it's cool to wear headphones around the neck even though they may not be plugged in."[31] Adds Dunn: "It's not about the sound, solely; it's about the fashion."[32]

In August 2011, with Beats' annual revenues rocketing toward $500 million,[33] the company got an incredible infusion: handset maker HTC paid $300 million for a 51 percent stake. With new cash came new products—for example, the understated Beats Executive headphones and the Beats Pill, a modern take on the boom box—and brand extensions galore. There were HTC cell phones with Beats Audio, Beats-branded laptops from HP, and even a deal with Chrysler to put Beats speakers in a new edition of its sporty Charger sedan.

"What Dre did was smart," says MC Serch, who lives in Detroit and has done some work in the auto industry. "Dre is seen as an audio guy...Putting the Beats Audio into computers, expanding the Beats brand—that makes sense. I don't know if you've heard that Beats Audio in the Dodge Charger. That shit bumps."[34]

By the middle of 2012—a year in which Beats would clear $57 million in profit on $860 million in revenue[35]—Dre and his partners had grown rich enough to buy back half of HTC's stake. They also decided to cut out Monster as the product's manufacturer and distributor, taking the reins themselves. Lee was shocked. "They knew nothing about manufacturing," he says. "They knew nothing about engineering...Dre is not that kind of an engineer."[36]

Beats plowed forward aggressively, buying streaming service MOG for $14 million that year[37] and raising $60 million to transform it into what would become Beats Music in 2013.[38] The cash came from a list of investors including billionaire Len Blavatnik, the owner of Warner Music Group; by the time Beats Music launched, industry insiders believed that streaming had already overtaken MP3s as the dominant music medium.

With Blavatnik on board and Universal holding a sizable stake in Beats, the company's fledgling service had buy-in from two of the three major record labels. It placed Iovine and Dre tantalizingly close to completing a trifecta that would allow the service access to an all-you-can-eat music menu. New executives hired the same year—including Ian Rogers, the former chief of music software company Topspin, and Trent Reznor, the audiophile front man of industrial rock group Nine Inch Nails—were indicative of Dre's continuing focus on sound quality.

"Beats was always about helping people rediscover the magic in the experience of listening to music," said Iovine at around the time his company's streaming service launched. "Now that we are well along the way to addressing the quality of audio playback with Beats headphones and speakers, [Beats Music] allows us to reintroduce the same magic into the process of music discovery and consumption."[39]

Lee didn't believe that Beats would be able to achieve anything without Monster's expertise; a new streaming service wasn't enough to change his mind. At this point, his stake had been diluted down to 3 percent, and he decided to sell it back to his partners for about $20 million. His message to his former partners: "You guys got no exit strategy."[40]

At least that's how Lee frames it. Some insiders say that his son, Kevin, was the one responsible for giving up Monster's stake in Beats. Lee strenuously denies this: "He had nothing to do with me giving up my shares."[41] Regardless of whose choice it was, the move would end up costing Lee roughly $70 million in pretax profits.

While Diddy had discovered his twenty-first-century groove in the television world with *Making the Band* and, later, *I Want to Work for Diddy,* his music career was heading in the wrong direction.

In 2004, he took part in the Super Bowl halftime show that ended with Janet Jackson and Justin Timberlake's "Nipplegate" scandal, wherein Jackson's breast was bared for a split second on national television. The revelation spurred 540,000 people to file complaints with the FCC. (It also inspired a young PayPal programmer, frustrated because he couldn't find any clips of the slip online, to create a video-sharing service that eventually became YouTube.)[42]

After selling 50 percent of Bad Boy to Warner for $30 million in 2005,[43] Diddy released his third solo album, *Press Play,* the following year. The record failed to move one million units, despite decent reviews. In the four years that followed, he became disillusioned with the music industry and turned his focus almost entirely to his other business ventures and his reality TV career. "I went through, like, a year and a half of being uninspired, and I just hit a wall. I was just like, *Why am I getting up out of bed?*" he told me in 2014. "Music is such a part of my life…I just didn't feel like people had the passion that I had."[44]

Diddy's next release would be a concept album called *Last Train to Paris,* recorded under the name Diddy–Dirty Money with singer Kalenna and *Making the Band* winner Dawn Richard, from Danity Kane. The album, a moody mix of electropop and hip-hop, follows Diddy as his character travels from London to Paris, searching for a lost lover. Famous friends including Swizz Beatz, Timbaland, Lil Wayne, Drake, Justin Timberlake, and Wiz Khalifa contributed to tracks, and others, from Anna Wintour to Tommy Hilfiger, popped up on spoken-word interludes.

The album performed modestly from a commercial standpoint and received mixed reviews: the BBC dubbed it "a seriously impressive artistic statement,"[45] while *Rolling Stone* put it on a list of 2010's biggest musical disasters.[46] The record did include a single cowritten by a committee featuring Jay-Z; the song earned multiplatinum certification and kept Diddy's name in the music conversation.

Diddy also attempted to cross-promote his new record, teaming up with Dre's headphone company to release Diddybeats, a $179 pair of earbuds that came with a free track from *Last Train to Paris* and a travel case inspired by his Sean John fashion line. "Dre and I wanted to design an earbud that was a combination of great style and powerful sound," said Iovine. "Diddy was the perfect choice for this because he's a pioneer in marrying music with fashion."[47] For his efforts, Diddy received a small financial interest in Beats, according to sources close to the negotiations.

But Diddy's tiny leather-and-aluminum earbuds—available only in black, white, and pink—were barely visible when in use. Without the ability to make a bold fashion statement, they never took off like Dre's brightly colored, over-ear monsters. The biggest problem for Diddybeats, according to Lee, was that Diddy simply "didn't believe in it"; the Monster chief says that Iovine "kind of dragged him along."[48] By this point, Diddy had established strong friendships with Dre and Iovine. He also struck a deal with Interscope to distribute Bad Boy's music at around the same time.[49]

Yet, for whatever reason, Diddy just didn't go all-in on the earbuds. "You have to live it," Lee explains. "You have to wear it around your neck all the time. It has to be part of your lifestyle, and it wasn't for him."[50]

Diddy had his eye on a different sort of product: Cîroc vodka (more on this in chapter 9), which commanded his attention on a constant basis and would be nearly as rewarding for him as Beats was for Dre.

As Dre prepared for the launch of his Beats streaming service, his headphone line had gobbled up two-thirds of the hundred-dollars-and-up market, simultaneously dwarfing and lifting brands like Bose and Sennheiser.

"It didn't just cannibalize sales and elbow other guys out; it grew the whole category," says Dunn, who saw the effects of Beats first-hand at Best Buy. "All of a sudden, headphones were much more than just these little earbuds."[51]

The effects of such dominance showed up on Beats' balance sheet. By 2013, the company zoomed toward $1.2 billion in annual revenues. This helped to lure yet another massive investment, this time from the Carlyle Group, one of the world's largest private equity companies, which poured $500 million into Beats in September.[52] (A spokesperson for the firm declined to make an executive available for comment.)[53]

The size of the stake Carlyle had purchased wasn't publicly revealed, though most reports at the time said that the agreement gave the firm less than half of the company, valuing Beats at more than $1 billion. By Lee's math, though, the deal gave Carlyle about one-third of the company, implying a $1.5 billion valuation.[54] The infusion also allowed Beats to buy out HTC's remaining 25 percent stake and repay a $150 million note held by the handset maker, whose primary business had faltered in the face of challenges by competitors like Samsung.[55]

A report by the research firm PrivCo later suggested that Beats was also having a bumpy time—much more than anyone on the outside ever realized—despite its gaudy revenue numbers. Apparently, after taking manufacturing in-house, Beats experienced a cash crunch and teetered just days from bankruptcy before coming up with a nine-figure loan. "By 2013, Beats Electronics was a distressed business by any standard," said the late PrivCo chief Sam Hamadeh. "The company was in a corner until Carlyle stepped in."[56]

The Carlyle investment also gave Beats the funds it needed to keep expanding. That was especially important given the focus on its new streaming service. Beats Music celebrated its official launch in January 2014 with a concert at the Belasco Theater in Los Angeles, fronted by Dre, Diddy, Eminem, Nas, and Ice Cube. Inside, superstars from Drake to Pink mingled with label chiefs and talent agency executives at the oversubscribed show.[57]

There were no reports of Apple executives in the crowd, but the computer giant was clearly watching. On May 8, the *Financial Times* reported that Apple had agreed to purchase Beats for $3.2 billion; that night, the grainy YouTube video of Dr. Dre's impromptu celebration lit up the Internet. As the end of the month neared, though, the deal still hadn't been completed—and Beats' founders worried that Dre's public actions had spooked the secretive tech giant. "I thought the deal could blow," Iovine admitted in the HBO documentary *The Defiant Ones,* in which Dre called the episode one of the most embarrassing moments of his life. Says Lee: "I could see [Apple CEO] Tim Cook going, 'What's this guy doing?'"[58]

Three weeks later, though, the deal went through—for a final price of $3 billion. "No traditional valuation measure applied to Beats as a business justifies the price," wrote PrivCo's Hamadeh. "We must assume Apple and Tim Cook have grand plans that we're not privy to."[59]

A clue can be found in Apple's annual report from 2014. According to the document, the Beats buyout included $2.6 billion in cash and about $400 million in stock that "will vest over time based on continued employment with Apple."[60] In other words, the tech giant structured the deal to include a centimillion-dollar carrot to keep Beats' founders in its fold. And that's perhaps the most fascinating part of the purchase. Though many experts believe that the existing business of Beats headphones and the potential of its nascent streaming service were enough to justify the deal on Apple's end,[61] others think that the company mainly wanted to get Beats' founders onto its executive roster.

"Apple's Beats Deal Is Happening, and It's a Dre Acquihire," blared a headline on TechCrunch. "They want Jimmy and they want Dre," a source told the publication. "He's got fashion and culture completely locked up."[62] Some went as far as to suggest that Cook saw the duo as a partial replacement for Steve Jobs, who'd passed away in 2011. "He's saying, 'I'll try to replace [Jobs] with five people,'" U2 front man and venture capitalist Bono told the *New York Times*. "It explains the acquisition of Beats."[63]

Indeed, Iovine had befriended Jobs — who believed that people would always want to own their music rather than stream it[64] — a decade or so before the Apple founder's passing. Jobs helped persuade the Interscope chief to allow unbundled songs to be sold in the iTunes Store, a crucial step in Apple's insertion into music's ecosystem. In 2015, Iovine told *Wired* that when he and Dre founded Beats, he hoped to someday be acquired by Jobs. "Apple got the best people in pop culture," Iovine said. "Whether it succeeds or not, it's the beginning of what the future should look like."[65]

Other reactions filtered in from Beats' early team. Lee, who'd sold his stake in Beats for barely twenty cents on the dollar just months earlier, began the painful process of digesting the multibillion-dollar transaction. He believed that Apple did the deal so that the company could tie the headphones to iPhones and iPads, perhaps replacing the headphone jack on the products with its Lightning connector and producing Beats products exclusively for that type of hardware.[66] On the other end of the spectrum, Will.i.am got a multimillion-dollar payout — likely in the low to mid eight figures — and mused on the social impact of Dre's deal.

"It's not just good for the company; it's good for the culture," he said. "You have to look at it like...kids in inner cities not only dream about being athletes and musicians, but now entrepreneurs, and bringers of new, disruptive, cool lifestyle products. A whole new spirit just popped from this one announcement."[67]

The Apple buyout also underscored the value of Iovine's advice to Dre—to reject that sneaker deal—so many years earlier. Amazingly, the best way to do battle with Nike's Air Jordan for consumer dollars turned out not to be launching a shoe line, but creating a revolutionary brand of headphones.

As far as Lee is concerned, the Beats deal is one that should be held up as an example for young entrepreneurs—but not in the way Will.i.am suggested.

"I call it Beware of the Sharks, because when you're not successful, nobody will touch you," he says as we wrap up our interview. "When you're successful, everybody comes out of the water, and Monster was a very successful company before Beats."[68]

Lee arrived at this conclusion several months after the completion of the Apple deal, he says, reflecting on his role in creating Beats. As he saw it, he'd paid the company some $200 million in royalties over the years for headphones he'd manufactured; rather than partnering with Jimmy and Dre, he could have simply used that money to hire entertainers to shill for his own products.

Going back through the timeline, he fixated on what happened when he negotiated his 5 percent stake in Beats, before HTC bought 51 percent of the company. Lee claims the contract that gave him equity also had a change of control provision that would require Monster to forfeit its intellectual property rights to the headphones and all its dealer lists—an event that he insists the HTC investment triggered. Says Lee: "When I looked at all of the happenings, and the business that occurred, and the time they occurred, I said, 'I think we've been scammed.'"

And so, in January 2014, Lee filed a lawsuit in California alleging, among other things, fraud and deceit, breach of duty of trust and confidence, unfair competition, breach of fiduciary duty, and violations of the California corporations code. The suit demanded a jury trial and unspecified damages.[69]

Lee believes that the entire HTC deal was "a sham transaction" designed to cut Monster out of the picture, and that Beats had a deal in place with Apple long before 2014 — he insists that Carlyle knew about a planned Apple pact before investing in Beats in 2013. "We had put all our eggs into building that Beats basket," says Lee. "We got screwed on that deal... We had to lay off people, close factories, all that kind of stuff."[70]

The authorities weren't swayed. A few months after our meeting, Los Angeles Superior Court judge William Fahey dismissed the main claims in Lee's suit. Fahey ruled that Beats' actions were permissible under the contracts they'd signed with Monster as sophisticated investors.[71]

But even before losing the case, Lee was already plotting his next moves, telling me of a new business model — "Beats on steroids" — and speaking of plans to team up with other artists and athletes to create future products. Above all, though disappointed with the way the Beats scenario had turned out, he clearly hasn't lost his taste for doing business with centimillionaire rappers.

"I would love to help Jay-Z," he says. "I'm the business guy. I'm the retail guy. I'm the one who has the connections for mass markets."[72]

Jay-Z, though, already has such connections — not just in the headphone business, but in the spirits world, where he and Diddy turned their attentions while Dre bolstered Beats.

CHAPTER 9

Grape Expectations

Lower Manhattan is home to the center of the financial universe, the fifty-dollar truffle-topped personal pizza, and Lyle Fass, a man who knows more about the business of alcohol than anyone I've ever met.

Fass got his start working at liquor stores before becoming a personal wine buyer for megawealthy clients. Through his company, Fass Selections, he now makes his living selling reds and whites to thousands of loyal buyers who've signed up for his email list. Twice a year, he places orders with European producers and brokers; the bottles are shipped to a warehouse in California, and then directly to customers. It's a good setup for Fass, who never has to touch the product, and for his clients, who get biannual deliveries of top-tier wine for well below retail price.[1]

"It's like Christmas for adults," he explains after greeting me at the door of his financial district home-office in sweats and a T-shirt, sporting a salt-and-pepper beard and black glasses. Despite Fass's enological inclinations, his walls are lined not with bottles but with sneakers. Shoe boxes are stacked floor to ceiling in some places, and wire racks blossom with brightly hued pairs of kicks from Nike to New Balance, Diadora to Le Coq Sportif. Old-school hip-hop blares in the background.

But tonight we are here to talk spirits — not sneakers — specifically, Cîroc, the vodka for which Diddy has shilled to the tune of hundreds of millions of dollars over the past decade, and D'Ussé, the cognac peddled by Jay-Z more recently. I've brought Fass a medium-size bottle of the latter — in addition to talking, there will be some tasting. He opens it up, takes a sniff, and crinkles his nose. "Going to have to save that for later, or it will ruin our palates," he says. Also on the menu: a selection of eight different Cîroc flavors in fifty-milliliter containers.

"The terminology is called 'nips,'" says Fass. "I worked on the counter of many stores that sell such small bottles like this. You are getting a person that literally needs to open that right as they're walking out the door of your liquor store."

Fass is not one of these people. He's got experience peddling all sorts of spirits but tends to look down on any beverage with alcohol content over 14 percent. He is as opinionated as he is irreverent. "Wine is the only truth," he says. "Everyone's like, 'Oh, I'm a hard liquor connoisseur.' I'm just like, 'You're a fucking drunk.'" I tend to agree, which is partly why I decided to interview him for this chapter. (His grape expertise is especially relevant given the beverage portfolios of Jay-Z and Diddy; we'll get into that shortly.)[2]

In any case, Fass insists on lining up the flavors as he would at a wine tasting, starting with lighter options and moving toward heavier. He places Cîroc's flagship Snap Frost variant first, and then the fruit flavors, finishing with Cîroc Amaretto. He also warns that, as with marathon wine tastings, it's best to spit out the product once it's been sampled, lest the taster become too incapacitated to judge the next offering. He cracks open the Snap Frost and pours two glasses, swirling his aggressively, as if whisking an egg, before taking a sniff.

"It definitely smells like something you'd put on a wound," he says. Then he takes a sip, swishes it around in his mouth for a moment, and spits. "Lots of alcohol, but bitter on the finish. There's like this brief hint of biting into a piece of gum for one-tenth of one-tenth of a second. That's probably the flavor."[3]

Indeed, Cîroc's offerings are potent. The flavors sit at 35 percent alcohol and Snap Frost runs at 40 percent, as vodkas are wont to. Today Cîroc, a partnership between Diddy and Diageo—the beverage giant behind brands including Guinness, Tanqueray, and Johnnie Walker—moves some two million cases per year, roughly even with Ketel One and trailing only Grey Goose (2.7 million) in the premium vodka category.[4] Cîroc has earned its share of critical acclaim as well, receiving honors like the double gold medal in the vodka category at the San Francisco World Spirits Competition and the Spirits Brand of the Year Award from wine and liquor trade publication *Market Watch*.[5]

"When I'm talking strictly vodka, it's less offensive than Tito's . . . or Belvedere, or Ketel One," Fass admits. "I can't drink those straight. I think those are disgusting."[6]

I ask what he prefers about Cîroc.

"The only advantage is texture," he says. "Vodka is watery. Vodka made from grapes, my conclusion, is not watery. It's more textured. The flavor is a gimmick. That is my professional opinion."

Fass also has a professional opinion about Cîroc's effect on Diddy.

"I understand why he's not putting out any more albums or anything," he says. "This stuff is a goddamned gold mine."

Given hip-hop's success marketing soft drinks like Sprite, alcoholic beverages were a logical next step. The trend began in the early 1990s with malt liquor St. Ides, which brought in rappers including Ice Cube, Snoop Dogg, and the Wu-Tang Clan to record commercials and extended jingles. Dr. Dre jumped on the beer bandwagon in 2002 with a Coors Light commercial that finds him on a darkened airplane, working on a beat while enjoying a cold one. The tagline: "Can't stop the flow."

Jay-Z actually preceded Diddy into the spirits business, acquiring the U.S. distribution rights for Scotland-based Armadale Vodka that same year with his Roc-A-Fella Records cofounders.

They employed a strategy similar to the one rolled out for Rocawear: feature the product in songs and videos and hope the free advertising turns into sales.[7] But Armadale never really had a chance. Jay-Z split with his partners shortly after acquiring the brand, which meant that promoting Armadale would call for sharing the spoils with his erstwhile associates; he didn't mention the vodka in any of his songs after 2003. By the time I wrote my Jay-Z biography, *Empire State of Mind,* in 2011, the United States Patent and Trademark Office had marked the brand "DEAD."[8] Jay-Z didn't bother to buy out his partners as he'd done with Rocawear. Indeed, he seems to have been thinking of a better proposition: starting something new and keeping a greater portion of the spoils for himself.

Soon Jay-Z had some extra motivation to get back into the booze business. In May 2006, Frédéric Rouzaud, the managing director of the company behind Cristal champagne, the brand historically preferred by Russian tsars — and rappers, after Branson Belchie introduced the pricey bubbly to the hip-hop world in the early 1990s — made a mistake that would cost his employer millions of dollars' worth of free advertising. A reporter from *The Economist* asked Rouzaud if the rap world's preference for Cristal had tarnished the brand's image. "What can we do?" he said. "We can't forbid people from buying it." Perhaps Rouzaud thought rappers didn't read *The Economist*. He was wrong.[9]

"That was like a slap in the face," wrote Jay-Z. "You can argue all you want about Rouzaud's statements and try to justify them or whatever, but the tone is clear…I felt like this was the bullshit I'd been dealing with forever, this kind of offhanded, patronizing disrespect for the culture of hip-hop."[10] So Jay-Z immediately issued a release stating that he'd never drink Cristal again, and that he'd banned it from his clubs as well. He temporarily changed his preference to Dom Pérignon and Krug. But in typical Jay-Z fashion, a more profitable plan was fermenting in his brain.

In the fall of 2006, Jay-Z released the video for his song "Show Me What You Got," which featured him zooming around Monte

Carlo in a Ferrari with Dale Earnhardt Jr. and then racing Danica Patrick in a Pagani Zonda roadster before joining model Jarah Mariano for a game of blackjack at a party on a private island. But the star of the video is the mysterious gold bottle of champagne that Jay-Z accepts after waving off a Cristal delivery: Armand de Brignac—introduced in the song by its nickname, Ace of Spades— a brand produced by a French company called Champagne Cattier.

"He discovered our champagne by pure coincidence in a wine shop and a few months later came to Monaco," explained Cattier's Philippe Bienvenu when I visited France while reporting *Empire State of Mind*. "He ordered a few cases that we shipped to his hotel there… We just thought that he wanted to enjoy our champagne during his stay."[11]

Bienvenu said Armand de Brignac was a dormant brand that Cattier had recently resuscitated, but he couldn't name the New York wine shop in which Jay-Z had supposedly unearthed it. I later discovered the reason for this: according to the United States Patent and Trademark Office, the Armand de Brignac name was first used for commerce in America in November 2006, meaning that Jay-Z couldn't possibly have found the champagne in a Big Apple store in time for the video shoot, which had taken place that summer. When I confronted the Cattier team about this inconsistency, a spokesperson admitted that Jay-Z had met with Sovereign Brands, Armand de Brignac's importer, and that they'd had discussions about forming some sort of relationship.[12] From my conversations with industry sources, it seemed that Jay-Z, Sovereign, and Cattier all owned a piece of Armand de Brignac by the time it became available to New York vintners.

As all this unfolded, I went to visit Branson at a champagne speakeasy he once operated in Harlem. When I told him about my discovery, he produced a gold bottle that looked eerily like Armand de Brignac, aside from a different logo and name: Antique Gold. The brand, also produced by Cattier, sold for sixty to eighty dollars and was discontinued the same year Jay-Z's champagne arrived.

"Armand de Brignac—this product already existed," Branson told me for *Empire State of Mind*. "They attached Jay-Z to it."[13]

The fact that Armand de Brignac was essentially an old Cattier brand revived at a fivefold markup was one of the key revelations from my first book. Jay-Z didn't comment on the disclosure, but six months after the book's release, branding guru Steve Stoute—a longtime friend and business partner of Jay-Z—confirmed that the rapper had "invested in his own line, Ace of Spades, made by Champagne Cattier."[14] Then, in 2014, Jay-Z and Sovereign issued a press release saying that the rapper had bought out the importer's interest in Armand de Brignac. In reality, Jay-Z was either increasing the size of his equity stake or simply acknowledging something that had happened long ago. He still garnered a raft of gee-whiz headlines marveling that he'd decided to buy his favorite champagne, with scant mention of his existing interest in the brand.

Armand de Brignac, meanwhile, expanded from its initial gilded offering to five variants, all bottled in similarly ostentatious fashion: a chromed-out blanc de blancs, a glimmering pink rosé, a ruby-red demi-sec, and a gunmetal-gray blanc de noirs; all were at least several hundred dollars per bottle. Well-heeled customers have been popping with impunity: according to Eric Schmidt, director of alcohol research at Beverage Marketing Corporation, the brand moved an estimated five thousand cases in 2009, surging to twenty-five thousand by 2015; in the high-margin champagne business, the latter figure likely translates to roughly $30 million in profit on $90 million in revenue.[15]

The brand has wowed a selection of wine critics as well. Armand de Brignac's flagship variant topped Cristal and Dom Pérignon in a 2010 blind tasting held by *Fine Champagne* magazine, and the blanc de noirs did the same in 2016.[16] But skeptics remain, including Fass, who still prefers Cristal and can't understand why consumers don't feel the same way.[17] "They went from a great champagne— granted, owned by a racist asshole—to a shitty champagne owned by Jay-Z that's more expensive," he says. "That doesn't make any sense to me. It obviously wasn't about the quality."[18]

Regardless of one's opinion on the taste of Armand de Brignac, it's clear that marketing served as a major ingredient in its success—and the way that Jay-Z promoted the brand represented something of a change in his own conspicuous consumption. Just as he featured the exotic Pagani Zonda instead of a better-known Bentley or Rolls-Royce in the "Show Me What You Got" video, Jay-Z displayed Armand de Brignac in lieu of Dom Pérignon or the newly forbidden Cristal. Sure, he had financial incentive to do this, but he also had a new philosophy to broadcast: *I'm so rich that you've never even heard of the products I consume.* Armand de Brignac and subsequent offerings were positioned to tempt fans with a taste of that lifestyle.

By this point, Jay-Z had really ascended to a different level than that of his audience and even other A-list entertainers. As the 2008 presidential race heated up, he and Beyoncé campaigned for Barack Obama, who showed mutual admiration by referencing Jay-Z's "Dirt off Your Shoulder" during the primaries when asked how he felt about recent jabs thrown by Hillary Clinton in the Democratic primaries. After Obama's boundary-breaking election, Jay-Z and Beyoncé performed at the inauguration in early 2009 and soon became frequent visitors to the White House; in a matter of years, Jay-Z's Roc-A-Fella cofounders had been replaced in his inner circle by heads of state and billionaires.[19]

"I guess Obama took this [hope] thing already," Jay-Z told Warren Buffett and Steve Forbes in a 2010 interview. "But...I hope to inspire."[20]

"Jay is teaching in a lot bigger classroom than I'll ever teach in," Buffett added. "They're going to learn from somebody. For a young person growing up, he's the guy to learn from."

Jay-Z wasn't the only hip-hop mogul to embrace Obama in the lead-up to the historical presidential election of 2008. Diddy did it his way: by periodically broadcasting off-the-cuff YouTube missives that he dubbed the "Diddy Obama Blog."

"Due to the social revolution, things started to change," Diddy once told me. "I started to be able to connect with people from around the world. I started to see different things...that inspired me. And I was just like, 'Your journey is not done. You have a mission. You have to be able to share your experiences with people that are coming behind you.' "[21]

In Diddy's vlog—which typically opened with the mogul spinning in a circle in his front yard, holding a camera to his face— he'd offer his thoughts on current affairs, such as Sarah Palin being named the Republican vice presidential candidate in 2008 ("You are bugging the fuck out, John McCain," Diddy explained). He also gave himself a new nickname: Cîroc Obama.[22]

The moniker reflected an agreement he'd struck with Diageo's Cîroc, then a four-year-old grape-based vodka line moving a mediocre forty thousand cases per year, hawked only by unremarkable ambassadors, like former NFL player Earl Little,[23] who were paid flat fees to appear with the bottles. Diddy marked a clear improvement. "We were observant of the idea [that] at one point he was selling more clothes than Ralph Lauren," says Stephen Rust, Diageo's president of new business and reserve brands. "Which was really the impetus of beginning to think ... *Together with him, could we do something different with this brand?*"[24] Diddy had also offered a preview of his beverage-peddling abilities with frequent brand mentions, perhaps most notably while teaming with Busta Rhymes for "Pass the Courvoisier, Part II," which helped boost sales of the cognac by 4.5 percent in the first quarter of 2002.[25]

Because of Cîroc's prior lukewarm performance, Diageo had little to lose, and Diddy and his team were able to negotiate an incredible deal. In my reporting over the years, I've learned that he splits profits from the brand with Diageo. Though the deal does not involve an actual equity stake, it functions like one; if Cîroc were ever sold, Diddy would share evenly in the proceeds. Says his lawyer Kenny Meiselas: "We made him a true participant in the success of the vodka."[26]

It is unlikely that Diageo would move a key brand out of its stable—"I would characterize us as buyers, not sellers," says Rust[27]—but the ceiling for Cîroc is quite high. For instance, the late liquor baron Sidney Frank built Grey Goose into the world's top premium vodka by pricing it ten dollars above Absolut, giving his beverage away at charity galas, and placing bottles in limos that transported glitterati to the Academy Awards. He sold his brand to Bacardí for $2.3 billion in 2004.[28]

Diddy dove into Cîroc with his trademark tenacity. In addition to using YouTube, he was an early adopter of Twitter and, eventually, Instagram, all of which served as platforms for him to spout inspirational quotes alongside advertisements for Cîroc and other products. Millions followed him to catch a glimpse of his high-flying existence—itself an aspirational brand he'd been building since his days as a party promoter in the early 1990s. His lifestyle translated into compelling wealth porn in the visually driven social media world—and he made Cîroc an integral part of his image.

One of his first moves after inking his deal with Diageo: defining his focus as "the art of celebration." He told Rust that he was going to make Cîroc the official vodka of New Year's Eve—and said it again in one of his first commercials for the brand, while seated between gorgeous women and consuming the beverage. Another ad depicted him arriving in Las Vegas on a private jet with a cadre of sharply dressed compatriots and then partying until daybreak, with Frank Sinatra's "Luck Be a Lady" providing the soundtrack.

"It's not about who you know, it's not about the consumers who recognize you," says Rust. "It's really about, how can you engage consumers in a way that they want to be part of the journey that you're on? That's what I think Sean Combs has done extraordinarily...He brings consumers along [on] the journey with him."[29]

It was the opposite of the air of exclusivity that Jay-Z had culti-vated for Armand de Brignac, and it paid off almost immediately. In 2008, Cîroc's first full year with Diddy on board, the brand moved 250,000 cases, up from 100,000 cases the year before, and the number soared to 340,000 in 2009.[30] Says Rust: "When we first did the deal, we imagined that in a few years' time, if we had even doubled the business...we would have been wildly successful."[31]

Interestingly, some argue that Cîroc isn't even technically vodka because it's made from grapes instead of the customary potatoes or cereal grains. Beverage Marketing Corporation's Schmidt points out that in the eighteen American "control states"—the ones in which the sale of booze is most heavily regulated by the government—many classify Cîroc's flavors as part of the "cordials and liqueur" cat-egory. "Look at the actual definition of vodka," adds Fass. "It does not say vodka can be made from these three things. It says vodka can be made from these two things."[32] Roberto Rogness, NPR com-mentator and general manager of Santa Monica's Wine Expo, dis-agrees. "The definition is 'odorless, colorless rectified alcohol diluted to sale proof,'" he says. "Lots of leeway there!"[33] Rust's take: "Does it matter?"[34]

As a wine expert, Fass knows a thing or two about grapes, including the ugni blanc variety (also known as Trebbiano) at the heart of Cîroc. The brand's bottles identify these as "fine French grapes," but Fass tends to disagree. "It's the cheapest fucking grape you can get...There's not a shittier white grape," he says, and then pulls back a bit. "I mean, it's not bad like a fart." Fass estimates that the price per ton of an extremely high-end grape that would go into a costly Pinot Noir from Burgundy could be as much as 1,000 to 2,000 percent more than a ton of ugni blanc. He figures the raw cost of a bottle of Cîroc is somewhere in the seven-to-ten-dollar range, meaning there's a roughly threefold markup to wholesale. "The marketing is genius," he says.[35]

The term "fine French grapes" is certainly a subjective one, but wine experts generally agree that ugni blanc doesn't exactly fit that description. Due to its high levels of acidity, it doesn't become as sugary while it ripens, meaning that animals are less likely to eat it. Yields tend to be high, and cost is low. Ugni blanc grapes are still pricier than traditional vodka ingredients, though. "Off one acre of land, you'd definitely be able to make more vodka for far less money by growing a grain than you would by growing grapes," says former *Wine Spectator* editor Eric Arnold. "However, if Cîroc tastes better than other vodkas, the higher price might very well be justified given the greater expense of cultivating the primary ingredient."[36]

One of Diddy's crucial contributions to Cîroc was persuasively articulating an argument that the brand's brass had been trying to make for years: that grapes are simply sexier than potatoes.[37] "One of his favorite things [to say] is, 'If you can have a vodka that comes from a history of wine-making, why would you do that versus the history of coming from potatoes?'" says Rust. "That's Sean."[38] It's almost a Steve Jobs move: just as the Apple founder gained a reputation for creating products that consumers didn't even know they wanted, Diddy somehow managed to convince people that they had wanted vodka made from grapes, not potatoes, all along.

The same could be said of flavored vodka. Cîroc's Diddy-fueled success allowed it to expand beyond Snap Frost, starting with Coconut and Red Berry in 2010. That year, Cîroc's sales doubled to eight hundred thousand cases.[39] Diddy involved himself in every stage, from tasting early runs to picking the colors used on the front of the bottles and the words on the back. He managed to convey exactly what he wanted while tasting an early iteration of Peach, which debuted in 2011. "I want a cool peach that comes out of a basket on the back of a pickup truck," he explained in one meeting. (In the booze business, "cool" means you can't really taste the alcohol; "hot" means the opposite.) "You bite into it and it's a little bit sharp, it's a little bit tart, and then it gives you that full peach flavor, but it's a little bit cool; it's not hot."[40]

Diddy's involvement extended all the way to the point of sale.

He would personally ask bartenders at swank locales like Soho House why the Cîroc wasn't on the top shelf—and made sure it ended up there.[41] "It's not just about running commercials, or putting up banners, or having signage at a festival," Diddy told me in Austin. "It's about actually being in the trenches."[42]

More flavors followed—Amaretto (2013), Pineapple (2014), Apple (2015), and Mango (2016)—and Cîroc's sales went to 1,350,000 cases in 2011 and 2,000,000 in 2012, peaking at 2,100,000 in 2014.[43] Diddy's overall annual earnings surged in lockstep, from $30 million in 2010 to $60 million in 2014, per my estimates for *Forbes*. By that point, Cîroc was his largest income stream, and nonmusical ventures represented more than three-quarters of his haul. Diddy's talent for monetizing his reputation as a party promoter had proved considerably more profitable than his musical output.

"Sean was everything from [billboards] in Times Square in a tuxedo to jet planes to the house in the Hamptons to the White Party," says Rust. "He was leading a lifestyle that Cîroc nicely fit into . . . Sean was able to drive this brand in an extraordinary way."[44]

In the wake of Jay-Z and Diddy's success in the booze business, numerous hip-hop copycats emerged. Ludacris served up Conjure cognac in 2010, Pharrell Williams brought his Qream liqueur to market in 2011, Timbaland released sparkling spirit LeSutra in 2012, and Nicki Minaj launched Myx Moscato in 2013, to name a few. Rather than rival Jay-Z and Diddy's products, these brands took aim at different categories—or even tried to complement their predecessors.

"It's not a hard liquor, but it could be mixed with Cîroc," Timbaland told me of LeSutra right before its debut. "Men will wanna spike it up. Me, I'm not a heavy, heavy drinker; it's perfect for me. I can walk around all day and get a buzz. It'll boost me up for the meeting and not make me feel like I'm slurring."[45]

The results of some of these collaborations make one wonder if meetings should have been accompanied by a shot of sobriety. Though many of the agreements mimicked Jay-Z and Diddy's moves, guaranteeing rappers equity or a profit share — perhaps most notably Minaj's Myx, which moved 220,000 units in 2015 and 300,000 the following year[46] — most have had much shorter shelf lives. LeSutra still exists, though Timbaland is no longer featured in its online marketing materials; same goes for Ludacris and his Conjure cognac. Pharrell filed a $5 million lawsuit against Diageo when the company pulled the plug on Qream after just two years.

The latter venture turned out to be similar in structure to a typical record deal, with Pharrell getting an advance against future royalties up front in exchange for being the face of the brand and making a set amount of public appearances on its behalf. He would receive additional cash only upon earning out — something that never happened, his team alleged, because the beverage giant didn't properly promote Pharrell's peach-flavored liqueur. According to the 2013 suit, Diageo "shrugged its proverbial shoulders and said there was inventory out in the field."[47] (Pharrell agreed to drop his complaint later that year.) There was indeed plenty of competition in the market — from Diageo's own Cîroc Peach, among others. At the end of the day, though, Qream and its ilk failed because the beverages weren't a seamless part of their ambassadors' lifestyles in the way that Cîroc was for Diddy.[48]

Meanwhile, Jay-Z busied himself rarifying his own lifestyle even further. He helped protégé-turned-superstar Kanye West establish an entire hypermaterialistic subgenre of hip-hop — luxury rap — whose apotheosis came in the form of *Watch the Throne,* an album they released jointly in 2011. The lyrics to "Otis" feature West dubbing himself the "Hermès of verses" and Jay-Z issuing a "new watch alert" for Hublot, a Swiss brand that sells five-figure timepieces. Again, he was plugging a European luxury goods provider that most of his listeners had probably never heard of. And again, he stood to benefit financially: Hublot chief Jean-Claude Biver told me when the song hit that he and Jay-Z were close to inking an official agreement. "It's only a matter of time," Biver said.[49]

Sure enough, Hublot and Jay-Z partnered up in 2013 and released the Classic Fusion Shawn Carter, a limited-run watch available in black ceramic (250 pieces at $18,300 apiece) and gold (100 at $33,700). Unveiled in collaboration with Barneys New York, 25 percent of all sales went to Jay-Z's Shawn Carter Foundation, a charity that offers college scholarships to needy kids. Did Jay-Z pick up an equity stake in Hublot along the way? "The brand doesn't comment on their investors," a spokesperson said.[50]

Watch the Throne earned platinum certification and went on to capture four Grammy Awards. When Jay-Z arrived to pick up his hardware at the 2013 ceremony in Los Angeles, he came prepared with a plan to take the next step in the monetization of luxury rap. Decked out in a velvet tuxedo, he produced a bottle of D'Ussé cognac and proceeded to pour several ounces into his golden gramophone, taking sips as the cameras rolled.

This was Jay-Z's latest venture, a partnership with beverage giant Bacardí with aspirations to chase category leader Hennessy, just as Diddy had signed on with Diageo to create a spirit capable of competing with Grey Goose; indeed, Jay-Z's D'Ussé deal resembled Diddy's Cîroc agreement.[51] The Grammy stunt sparked a wave of coverage that included a reasonably positive review from the *Wall Street Journal:* "While this may not be a cognac for the cognoscenti, it's definitely an easy and enjoyable sip."[52]

The stories neglected to mention a fascinating connection between Jay-Z and Diddy: just like Cîroc, D'Ussé is made from ugni blanc grapes—one of a handful of varieties whose inclusion is necessary to earn the "cognac" designation. Labels aside, the process of making cognac lends itself to heavy use of cheap grapes. Finer types tend to be more difficult to grow, and low yields drive up costs. Cognac is distilled, so much of the flavor from a pricier grape would be lost along the way; during the aging process, additional material evaporates (the "angel's share"). Says wine expert Arnold: "Using a higher-end grape would really be a waste of money."[53]

Because there's such an abundant supply of ugni blanc, costs are low, and there's not the same risk of fluctuating yields and prices that could befall a champagne like Armand de Brignac. In other words, Jay-Z's involvement with D'Ussé served as an effort to both expand and hedge his alcoholic beverage portfolio.

"As long as the world doesn't run out of grapes, which I don't see happening ever…this is a good business to get into," says Fass. "Any business where you can just keep turning the shit out for the rest of your life is a good business."[54]

An hour before midnight on a fall Tuesday in 2014, I walked through the door of Cedar Lake, an airplane hangar–esque event space on Manhattan's West Side, to get my first glimpse of the latest addition to Diddy's beverage portfolio. Inside, several hundred people sipped cocktails over the din of the sound system as an acrobat contorted herself while sliding up and down a long piece of ribbon hanging from the ceiling. Across the room, a lithe young woman stood motionless in front of the VIP area, naked save for a head-to-toe coat of body paint and a garment that was more a suggestion than an actual pair of underwear.

But the main attraction of the night was the brand behind the logo projected onto the wall: an ornate letter *D,* not unlike the logo of Major League Baseball's Detroit Tigers. The *D* stood for Diddy's new DeLeón tequila, a tumbler of which appeared in front of my face as the sound system's bass rattled the oversize ice cube inside. I placed the drink on a nearby chrome-plated table, and when I picked it up to take another sip, a server materialized and polished the surface. At around midnight, Swizz Beatz waltzed in, and then Naomi Campbell.[55]

The atmosphere reflected Diddy's outsize ambitions for DeLeón, which he acquired in partnership with Diageo that same year. DeLeón's variants sell for $35 to $850 per bottle, making it a "sipping" tequila, unlike Sammy Hagar's Cabo Wabo. (The rocker sold 80 percent of the brand to beverage giant Gruppo Campari for $80 million in 2007.)[56] Diddy aimed to build something bigger. Says Meiselas: "He could have easily just started a new tequila, but he wanted to grow DeLeón the same way that he grew Cîroc."[57]

Spirits entrepreneur Brent Hocking originally launched the libation in 2009, naming it after León, the Mexican town of its origin. He aged the tequila in wine barrels instead of jacking it up with artificial flavors, as many competitors did, and the results showed when his Diamante edition won the World Beverage Competition in Geneva two years in a row. For three consecutive years starting in 2011, DeLeón took home spirit of the year honors from luxury goods bible *Robb Report*.[58]

When Diddy initially approached Diageo about a tequila joint venture, the beverage giant had some reservations. "Sean, is it better for you just to focus on one brand?" Rust asked. Diddy's typically outrageous response: "It's like, after Spielberg made a movie, [having] somebody saying, 'You can't have another movie.' I want another movie."[59]

Rust couldn't help but admire the mogul's moxie. Diageo agreed to buy DeLeón with Diddy, and soon he was running a brainstorming session with one hundred of the beverage giant's employees, figuring out how to relaunch the brand. Just as he'd done with Cîroc, he fixated on everything from the feel of the bottle to the font of the logo, making sure he knew exactly who handled every aspect of the product. "It was like watching a general at work with his army," says Rust. "I called my boss and I said, 'Well, he just took over the company. He's got everybody working for him.'"

For Diddy, DeLeón also represented a way to insulate his liquor portfolio from potentially unfavorable industry trends. Toward the beginning of his Diageo run, Diddy's new Cîroc variants—along with flavored vodkas from Pinnacle and others—helped drive the entire vodka category to a growth rate of 5 to 6 percent annually. But after peaking at 2.1 million cases in 2014, Cîroc dipped to about 2 million the following year, according to beverage analyst Schmidt. Though he believes it's a billion-dollar brand, it's hard to get bigger in a category whose growth has plateaued. Tequila is a different story. DeLeón moved an estimated ten thousand cases in 2014 and doubled that number in 2015, its first full year with Diddy on board. Says Schmidt: "Tequila's growing faster than vodka."[60]

Diddy believed he could grow the brand by focusing on the same "art of celebration" he had brought to Cîroc — a notion evident at Cedar Lake. At about half past midnight, the DJ began to repeat a proclamation: "Puff Daddy is in the house." This continued for twenty minutes before Diddy finally appeared, decked out in a black fedora, sunglasses, and a dark fur coat that combined to make him look like a very fashionable porcupine. He grabbed a microphone, and the crowd noise faded to a murmur.

"There's no 'I' in 'team,'" he said, before thanking dozens of friends and colleagues. "There's a new tequila in town, and you are here for the first part of our history as we launch, as we raise our glasses to health, to love, to happiness, and to DeLeón!"[61]

Fass and I have nearly made it through all eight Cîroc variants, and though I've tried to take his lead and spit out each sip as I taste it, I've indulged a bit, which has made his commentary all the more entertaining.

Fass was quite displeased with Green Apple ("so candied and so sugary and so awful"), somewhat mystified by Red Berry ("That does not exist in nature…What the fuck is a red berry?"), heartened by Coconut ("The coconut would be really nice to mix"), and unsurprised by Pineapple ("It tastes like pineapple juice spiked with vodka").

The most colorful reactions were reserved for Peach ("like a peach truck crashed with an Absolut truck and all of a sudden you're passing by the accident and this is what you smell") and Mango, which Fass seemed to like a lot more ("It's not cough syrup mango, it's not dumb mango, it's like polished mango...like mango went into a nightclub").

Now we're down to the last variant—Cîroc Amaretto—whose name technically suggests a drink-flavored drink.

"That's like Courvoisier-flavored vodka," says Fass wryly, before offering a hint of optimism. "This could be the best. That's why I saved it for last—because you can't fuck up hazelnut. You know? Just like you can't fuck up fried calamari. It's just one of those things."[62]

Fass takes a whiff.

"It smells almost like...Italian Christmas cake."

"Kind of like a marzipan," I offer.

"Totally marzipan," he says, taking a sip. "Marzipan. Oh, God. Fucking marzipan. Fuck marzipan, seriously. Like, yes, I want to eat candy that looks like a fucking hot dog. Who came up with that? And it's not even good candy."[63]

We move on to the final beverage of the night: D'Ussé. The bottle is designed like an upside-down water tower: fat on the bottom, curving up into a thin cylinder. The front is dominated by a gold double-barred cross of Lorraine, the centuries-old French symbol used as an emblem of resistance during World War II.

"Despite the Cattier debacle, I have high hopes for this, although I'm looking at the bottle right now and my hopes have just gone down," says Fass, prying open the vessel. "It smells really fucking fruity. That's the fruitiest cognac I've ever smelled in my life... Usually cognac smells like alcohol."[64]

He takes a sip.

"Caramel and spice," he says. "And lots of alcohol."

Fass sighs.

"All this shit is awful," he explains. "I've had cognac that's been buried at the bottom of the fucking sea since eighteen seventy-five... I've had the most expensive liquor on earth, and the whole thing's a fucking con, dude, in my humble opinion."

Though our tasting hasn't instilled an appreciation of hard liquor in Fass, it has highlighted more threads that weave through the stories of Jay-Z and Diddy, two men who, despite their differences, have the same first name and last initial, the same hometown, the same birth year — and the same preference for partnering with beverage giants to make spirits from ugni blanc grapes.

"They are businessmen, and you want to have the lowest possible cost, and you want to make the highest possible profit, and they both have figured it out in their own way," says Fass. "That is the bottom line. Because at the end of the day, any person that has half a fucking palate understands that liquor is designed to get you drunk as quickly as possible. Period."

CHAPTER 10

Sound Investments

There might not be a single soul on the planet who understands the link between hip-hop, Hollywood, and Silicon Valley better than Troy Carter. In addition to working with this book's three kings in various capacities throughout his decades-long career, he has managed Lady Gaga, John Legend, Meghan Trainor, and many others. The list of startups he's invested in personally or through his company, Atom Factory, includes Uber, Dropbox, and Spotify.

I pull up to Carter's office, located on a nondescript stretch of pavement in Culver City, just north of Los Angeles International Airport. The building more closely resembles a refrigerator tipped on its side than the office of an entertainment industry power player: the structure's color palette is composed entirely of chilly shades of gray, and there are no windows visible. But once the ponderous doors groan open, Carter's headquarters comes to life.

An anteroom features plush couches, soft lighting, and a fish tank the size of a movie theater screen. Through a door is Carter's inner sanctum, where skylights illuminate two floors arranged like a Moroccan souk, with walkways encircling an interior courtyard. The decor is dominated by warm wood floors, sumptuous leather sofas, and accoutrements Carter has accumulated: MTV Video Music Awards moon men, won by Gaga and others, gleam on shelves alongside pictures of Carter with dignitaries including Barack Obama. On one wall hangs a saxophone that once belonged to Bill Clinton—a gift from Legend.

But one of Carter's favorite artifacts is a picture that's about a quarter of a century old. In the photo, he sits on a folding chair in an orange T-shirt, his slight stature magnified by the two men on either side of him: to his right, Notorious B.I.G., clad in baggy pants and a black Mecca brand T-shirt, and to his left, Diddy, bare-chested and wearing athletic shorts, a black beret, and black-and-white Adidas shoes with Nike socks. "I never noticed that until Heavy D pointed it out," Carter says of Diddy's clashing footwear.[1]

The photo was taken at the Philadelphia Civic Center; Carter promoted half a dozen Biggie and Diddy concerts in the area during the mid-1990s. The relationship didn't exactly start off on the right foot: the first time Carter booked Biggie, the rapper stayed late in New York filming a music video, and by the time he got to Philly, it was too late to play the show. Rather than give in to bitterness, though, Carter asked Biggie and Diddy to refund his costs, which they did—$15,000 to $20,000—and they decided to go out on the town. Though Carter already had a decent gig as a local promoter, his keen sense for promising startups caused him to ask Diddy for a job at Bad Boy ("His pretty good thing was better than my pretty good thing"). Diddy offered him an unpaid internship on the spot ("Free labor!" says Carter, who accepted)—and then asked Carter to arrange an introduction between himself and a bartender who'd caught his eye.

"That was my first interaction with Puff," says Carter. "I got him the girl from behind the bar...I started my internship with them a few weeks later."

Carter began commuting between Philadelphia and New York, and was immediately impressed with his new boss, who would frequently party until three o'clock in the morning and still be the first person in the office the next day. At the same time, Diddy navigated the different worlds inhabited by his artists, who mostly

came from the streets, and his Arista mentor, Clive Davis, a deni-
zen of New York society circles.

In the years that followed, Carter became an artist manager and
ended up working with Jay-Z at Roc-A-Fella and Dr. Dre at Aftermath on various projects. His interactions with all three kings
remind him in hindsight that, although they had very different
personalities and methods, they were all doing the same funda-
mental thing: running hip-hop-focused startups long before the
term "startup" was popularized by today's Silicon Valley elite.

"None of us had MBAs, none of us came from business backgrounds," Carter tells me. "None of us went to college or anything
like that. We were all building these companies off of instinct."

Indeed, hip-hop's top organizations were born out of a combination of gut feel and necessity. Diddy, Dre, Jay-Z, and their ilk
founded record companies because at first they couldn't get deals
with major labels; they launched their own clothing and liquor
lines because mainstream brands wouldn't meet their compensation requirements for endorsements.

"We were forced to start these record labels out of trunks of cars
and distribute music like that," says Carter. "It's been this thing of
forced entrepreneurship that turned into a significant amount of
equity in these businesses."

It's only natural that, after hip-hop's top moguls learned how to
start their own businesses, they began to leverage their fame as a
way to invest in promising companies started by other people — yet
another means of monetizing their celebrity.

In the early 2000s, 50 Cent became the first rapper to grab a chunk
of equity in something that could be classified as a startup created
by someone else — Vitaminwater parent Glacéau — but Jay-Z and
Diddy turned down a potentially bigger investment opportunity at
around the same time: Boost Mobile.

The cellular prepaid provider was founded in Australia in 1999 by the trio of Peter Adderton, Paul O'Neill, and Mike McSherry. Boost operated as a mobile virtual network operator (MVNO) that would provide a branded front end to be used with other companies' towers and networks. Boost took its name from a term that Aussie surfers use to describe cresting a wave; its founders initially geared much of its marketing toward extreme-sports enthusiasts.[2]

Though prepaid cell phones enjoyed great popularity overseas at this point in time, they hadn't yet made a major splash stateside. Mobile provider Nextel wanted to experiment with the model but faced one major problem. "Prepaid in the U.S. was seen as a very lowbrow, credit-challenged service," says McSherry. "Nextel was hesitant to associate its brand with prepaid."

So McSherry and his colleagues convinced Nextel to try out prepaid with a Boost-branded joint venture in the United States. The partnership—one-third owned by Boost and two-thirds by Nextel—was launched in 2002; in its first year, Boost activated more phones in California than the rest of Nextel did. The prepaid offering popped with young people in urban areas. Boost found an eager audience for Nextel's push-to-talk feature—rumored to be untraceable by police—which the company had previously marketed to limo drivers and construction workers. The brand lured new customers by offering unlimited walkie-talkie messaging for one dollar per day.[3]

At the same time, Boost cofounder Adderton sensed an opportunity to push the brand deeper into the hip-hop world. He reached out to a number of big names in 2002, including Jay-Z and Diddy, to see if they'd be interested in partnering with Boost as investors and brand ambassadors. Diddy seemed particularly interested and agreed to meet with Adderton and his team.[4]

"He talked for over an hour; we said nothing," the Boost cofounder recalls. "He said he knew the market we were going after, and [that] he was the key to let us in, almost like a godfather."[5]

Adderton asked what it would take to get a deal done.

"Two Gs," Diddy said.

Thinking that Diddy meant $2,000, an elated Adderton quickly offered to throw in a small amount of equity to seal the deal. Diddy laughed.

"Two Gulfstream jets," he explained.

That was just a starting point. As talks progressed, it became clear that Diddy wanted his very own mobile brand — Sean John Wireless, or some such — perhaps in the form of a joint venture, as Boost had initially done with Nextel. Adderton was attempting to get Diddy, along with Jay-Z in a separate deal, to become a shareholder in the Boost brand. He tried to explain that setting up a stand-alone wireless service wasn't as easy as it sounded; there were customer service, billing, and retail considerations to be dealt with. But neither king budged.

"They wouldn't listen," says Adderton. "But they knew, as I did, that in the future the mobile phone was going to be the conduit to the youth market... They just didn't know how to connect the dots."[6]

It was certainly a missed opportunity. In August 2003, Nextel paid somewhere between $50 and $100 million to buy out Boost's one-third share of the joint venture; by December, Boost had gained its millionth customer.[7]

Boost hired Coca-Cola's Darryl Cobbin the following year to be vice president of marketing, figuring he might be able to replicate the success he'd had with Sprite with the help of hip-hop. The genre had expanded beyond its traditional footholds: Percy "Master P" Miller's No Limit label and Bryan "Birdman" Williams's Cash Money put Louisiana on the map, while Houston specialized in a syrupy subgenre and Atlanta launched Outkast and others to superstardom. So Cobbin decided to bring on three artists from different regions of the country — Ludacris from the South, Kanye West from the Midwest, and the Game from the West Coast — to put together the song "Where You At?" The track, which appeared on a West mixtape and was distributed by regional DJs, featured all three rappers shouting out the song's title, which also happened to be Boost's tagline.[8]

Cobbin took another crack at partnering with Jay-Z and Diddy. ("Dre was still mostly known as a seminal producer," says Cobbin. "Frankly, we missed on that one.") He was willing to have them launch their own lines of phones within the Boost brand, a compromise of sorts after the prior negotiation. He offered a cut of revenue for every cell phone and every mobile plan sold—and a taste of the broader Boost brand via individual joint ventures with each impresario. But Cobbin wanted Jay-Z and Diddy to actually pay for the equity they were set to receive. They'd get a discount, to be sure, but they had to put in more than "sweat equity." They didn't bite.[9]

"I'm a skin-in-the-game businessperson," says Cobbin. "I don't like going into business with people if I feel like they don't have skin in the game... They were willing to bring none of that to the table."

For Jay-Z, at least, there may have been another sticking point developing, one that hadn't been in play so much a couple of years earlier. Cobbin remembers John Meneilly, Jay-Z's consigliere at the time, expressing concerns about associating the rapper with a brand like Boost—whose no-contract offerings still felt like the cellular equivalent of a check-cashing joint—at a time when Jay-Z was beginning to flirt with exclusive, expensive products like Armand de Brignac.[10]

"Michelangelo has a quote," says Cobbin. "I'm not going to get it right, but he said when he looks at a piece of stone, he sees the image already in the stone, and his job is to chip away the excess. I think that's Jay... You can't go fast when you're chipping marble. You fuck up the whole thing. I think that's what he's now doing: he's taking his time, tap by tap by tap, to build his masterpiece."[11]

Jay-Z may have been playing the long game, but he missed out on a bonanza in the short term—again. In 2006, Sprint merged with Nextel in a $36 billion deal.[12] Though the Nextel brand has been discontinued, Boost lives on, clocking annual revenues north of $3 billion within Sprint.[13] Diddy and Jay-Z could have been sharing in those spoils.

"A cut of a monthly subscription? Are you kidding me? They didn't fully understand that," says Cobbin. "I think it was a loss on both sides."[14]

Jay-Z, however, would find other ways to tie up with Sprint later on.

The first rapper to regularly invest in the sort of startups lionized in Aaron Sorkin's *The Social Network* and HBO's *Silicon Valley* was someone who otherwise lagged behind the three kings in the business department: Nas.

The Queens-born rapper's career had gotten a boost after he signed to Jay-Z's Def Jam, earning his first number one album of the new millennium with *Hip-Hop Is Dead* in 2006. But each of his ensuing albums sold fewer copies than the last. Things weren't going well in his personal life either: Nas split with his wife, the singer Kelis—known for her 2003 hit, "Milkshake" ("Damn right, it's better than yours"). Soon he had to cough up $25,000 per month in alimony and child support. Financial trouble followed, with the IRS slapping him with a $2.5 million lien in 2009 and another $3 million in 2010.[15]

Enter Anthony Saleh, a bright young electrical engineering grad who wanted to work in the music business. He convinced Nas that he could help sort out his affairs, and eventually became his manager. One of Saleh's first moves was scoring seven-figure endorsement deals with two brands that resonated with the rapper: Hennessy (whose praises Nas sang on the first track of *Illmatic*) and Sprite (he had done an "Obey Your Thirst" spot in 1997). But Saleh knew there were greater rewards to be reaped outside the realm of traditional brand deals. Social media had emerged as a key cog in artists' careers. Having a virtual presence grew particularly important as traditional media outlets floundered, their reach often outpaced by individual celebrity Twitter accounts. At the same time, new platforms were looking for ways to gain followers and mindshare. Having famous investors represented a shortcut of sorts.[16]

Saleh linked up with Troy Carter; when the latter launched Atom Factory in 2010, they teamed to scour the country for start-ups that might be interested in taking on celebrity investors. (This was already happening in other corners of the entertainment business, starting most notably with Ashton Kutcher, a hands-on investor who now runs his own venture fund with partner Guy Oseary. Less business-focused acts like Justin Bieber jumped into the fray with the help of savvy managers.)

Initially, Saleh and Nas aimed to get stakes in businesses in exchange for the benefit of association and promotion. By 2011, though, the sweat equity model was starting to shift, and startups were beginning to require that celebrity investors have skin in the game.[17] Saleh didn't mind: "The quality of people we were meeting were much higher from folks that were like, 'We want money, and fuck the sweat equity.'"[18]

Their first big hit was with a company created by a trio of Yale graduates. Initially called Rap Exegesis, then Rap Genius, and now simply Genius, the Brooklyn-based outfit got its start as a site for crowd-sourced hip-hop lyrics and explanations of what rappers meant by their rhymes. In 2011, after a turn in startup incubator Y-Combinator, the Genius cofounders—Ilan Zechory, Tom Lehman, and Mahbod Moghadam—met Carter, who immediately appreciated the company's potential as a tool for artists to tell their stories.

Carter quickly invested and made an introduction to Saleh, who brought in Nas for a demonstration. The rapper clicked around the site, looking at annotations of his lyrics, and turned to the cofounders. "'This could be bigger than Twitter,'" Zechory recalls him saying. Nas and Saleh made "a substantial angel investment" shortly thereafter; they didn't receive a special discount, but they knew they had a chance to get in early on a company that the average investor couldn't.[19] "It wasn't about the amount that I put in," Nas told me in early 2012. "It was about me caring about this thing, the asset."[20]

Nas became the first of thousands of Genius's "verified" acts, which entailed getting a badge on his profile, annotating his own songs, and uploading video explanations. The pages he interacted with tended to get much more traffic than other offerings; the day his verified profile went live, the buzz around Nas's appearance on the site caused it to crash.[21]

The technical difficulties didn't end up hurting: in 2012, venture capital firm Andreessen Horowitz plowed $15 million into the company. When I interviewed the firm's cofounder Ben Horowitz at the time and asked why he'd taken the plunge, he explained that he and his partners were hoping to turn the site into more than a place to explore rap lyrics. "We think they have a real shot at building the Internet Talmud," he told me; indeed, the site now hosts explanations of literature, law, and news in addition to music.[22]

Encouraged by their early success, Nas and Saleh continued to expand their portfolio. Nas liked the Fancy, a site dedicated to sharing images of unique—and expensive—products ("I can order some real cool shit on there," Nas explained).[23] Saleh, working with Carter, took a more sophisticated approach and scored stakes in Lyft and Dropbox, helping the rapper diversify along the way.[24]

Saleh and Nas eventually formed an entity to encapsulate their investments, naming it after the infamous New York housing project where Nas grew up. QueensBridge Venture Partners employs several people to help scout deals, often investing in tandem with bigger funds like Silicon Valley legend Ron Conway's SV Angel (to buy into mattress industry disruptor Casper) and early Facebook investor Accel Partners (to nab a piece of ticket search engine Seat-Geek). This approach gives Nas and Saleh a bit more assurance that they're moving in the right direction even when plowing money into companies outside their comfort zone. The method contrasts with that of artists like Bieber who mostly invest in apps they use.

"Nas is fortysomething years old," says Saleh. "He is going to look at the world differently. If he only invested in apps he played with, he'd have no investments... The point is to push forward innovation, and that necessarily has nothing to do with you sometimes."[25]

QueensBridge has now invested in over one hundred startups in total. Saleh wouldn't reveal the return on investment that he and Nas have achieved, saying only, "We made money." But they certainly seem to be doing well on their earliest big bet. In 2014, Genius raised another $40 million in a round led by billionaire Dan Gilbert, the owner of the Cleveland Cavaliers. At the same time, Pharrell Williams invested through a fund that he's a part of; Eminem also poured some of his own money into Genius the following year.[26]

Genius is worth considerably more than when Nas and Saleh first invested — "Only God and capitalism can tell us how much," explains Zechory, who nevertheless confirms that his company's value is "definitely many times more" than it was in 2011. But it's still early.

"As an angel investor, you expect a decade of waiting," adds Zechory. "The companies that Nas and Anthony have invested in... are doing very well now, but haven't sold or had IPOs. Give it a few years. Nas invested in Genius five and a half years ago. That's still a relatively short period of time in the life of a company."

As Nas racked up myriad startup stakes, Diddy took a more methodical approach, quietly amassing pieces of a select few companies. In 2011, he became acquainted with alkaline water Aquahydrate — not the sort of startup staffed by engineers in jeans and hoodies, but a company that met the definition more broadly[27] — while living up to his role as Cîroc's celebrator in chief.

Diddy ran into Mark Wahlberg at a boxing match one evening in Las Vegas. The actor was clutching a clear blue bottle, and

Diddy asked what it was. Wahlberg introduced him to Aquahydrate, the bottled water he'd stumbled upon while training for his 2010 movie *The Fighter*.[28] ("I started to really feel the difference in my recovery time," Wahlberg said. "I thought, *Well, the only thing it could be is the water*.")[29] So the actor had a couple of bottles sent to Diddy's hotel room, and the two parted ways.

"I went out that night, had a Vegas night," Diddy explained. "I woke up, had a Vegas morning. I drank two of the bottles, and it was the best-tasting water that I've tasted. It really, honestly, helped me recover. I saw [Mark] again. I'm just like, 'Hey, if you're doing something with that water, I want to be involved in it.'"[30]

According to Diddy, it wasn't just a fortuitous coincidence, but a chance for him to get into a line of business that he'd been dreaming about for many years. He especially gravitated toward the idea that, unlike 50 Cent's Vitaminwater, Aquahydrate was not a sugary product. And unlike his own Cîroc, it wasn't an alcoholic beverage. It was a simple, healthy drink, theoretically good for consumers if not for their wallets (at $2.19 per 33.8-ounce bottle, Aquahydrate is several times the price of milk or gasoline on a drop-by-drop basis).

It's worth noting the science behind alkaline water is a bit murky. The Mayo Clinic says that, despite studies suggesting its health benefits, "further investigation is needed" to determine if it's truly better than regular water.[31] Diddy seems to have already made up his mind on the matter. "If I test your body and your pH balance, and you're full of acid, it's a great chance that you need to... get your body leveled out."[32] This is the same sort of logic he applied to vodka. Just as grapes are sexier than potatoes, bottled water with an alkaline pH — the opposite of acidic — *sounds* like something you'd rather put in your body than the alternative, regardless of the science behind it.

Diddy soon organized a meeting with his billionaire pal (and Sean John investor) Ron Burkle and Wahlberg. The latter had gotten to know Aquahydrate's management team and felt that the business was in "rough shape." So Diddy, Burkle, and Wahlberg invested $10 million in the company and received a controlling stake. According to Wahlberg, they put "sweat and cash" into the business, meaning they likely got a discount from the original owners, who kept a smaller stake, thinking its value would rise significantly with an infusion of fame.[33]

Perhaps most important was the retail expertise brought to the table by Burkle, who'd made his fortune in the supermarket business. Aquahydrate soon appeared on shelves at stores including grocery giants Kroger and Walmart, two companies with which Burkle had done business. Along with Diddy and Wahlberg, he helped hire a new chief executive: Hal Kravitz, a veteran of Coca-Cola's Glacéau division. But Diddy bristled at comparisons to Formula 50.

"I didn't get into this to do what anybody else did," he said. "I'm definitely a fan of what 50 Cent and Vitaminwater and Smartwater and a lot of the other brands have been able to do, but I didn't get into this to follow in the footsteps and just do what somebody else has done. I want to go in whatever path we have for ourselves."[34]

Wahlberg was impressed with Diddy's level of involvement with the product: as he does with Cîroc and DeLeón, he poured himself into the details, down to the design of the bottle. "He's relentless, he's brilliant when it comes to marketing," Wahlberg explained. "He also has a very competitive edge, too. When he sees me creating deals with GNC because of my relationship with them, he's automatically trying to outdo me [and] bring as much to the table as possible."[35]

Though Aquahydrate does not release sales figures, company executives claim that it's the country's fastest-growing water brand; today, it's available at all Rite Aid outlets, 900 Target stores, and all 2,700-plus Speedway supermarket locations. For Diddy, it all goes back to Cîroc and that Vegas night. "It's the perfect combination to my spirit empire," he told me of Aquahydrate. "Because anybody that celebrates knows that water is key . . . I'm doing my best to start this boutique consumer products empire. I have a lot of work ahead of me."[36]

It frequently takes a decade or more to see if a company will prove to be a success, but losers often reveal themselves much more quickly — and hip-hop acts have had their fair share of those in the venture capital world. Jay-Z alone has quietly had plenty of failures: Viddy, an Instagram-for-videos service that counted the rapper among its shareholders, closed down in 2014.[37] (It's worth noting the startup seems to have been giving away stakes to celebrities rather than selling them.)[38] He also invested in cosmetics company Carol's Daughter, which was bought out of bankruptcy by L'Oréal in 2014.[39]

After successfully plowing cash into Uber, Jay-Z has shown a particular penchant for investing in companies aiming to be a sort of Uber for private jets, with varying results thus far. He reportedly picked up a piece of a company called BlackJet; it went under in May 2016. Months later, he joined members of the Saudi royal family in backing JetSmarter, a Fort Lauderdale–based company that has raised a reported $157 million. Its 6,500-plus customers pay $15,000 for their first year of membership, and $11,500 per year after that, to book seats on private jets' "empty legs" (in other words, flights in which a plane heads back to its home base after dropping off passengers without picking up any new ones).[40]

Then there are his nightlife brands. In addition to investing in a range of bars and restaurants (the Spotted Pig and the Rusty Knot in Manhattan's West Village), Jay-Z famously purchased a chunk of the NBA's Nets once estimated at 1.5 percent.[41] The *New York Daily News* reported he paid $1 million for his stake[42] — quite a bargain considering the team's value sat somewhere in the neighborhood of $300 million at the time. (Others have since asserted that he received face value: one-third of 1 percent.)[43] This may have been an example of a purchase price paid with a combination of cash and sweat, or simply a case of a celebrity using his name to get in on a good deal closed to the outside world. Regardless, he did put in his share of sweat, becoming the face of the franchise when the Nets were still languishing in New Jersey. When Russian billionaire Mikhail Prokhorov bought 80 percent of the team for $300 million in 2009, Jay-Z's stake shrank to one-fifteenth of 1 percent, though he picked up one-fifth of 1 percent of the Barclays Center itself along the way; it is unclear if he took cash off the table at the same time.[44]

Jay-Z also helped spearhead the team's 2012 move to Brooklyn, appearing at events like the arena's ceremonial ground-breaking, despite some protests over the ambitious construction project and the gentrification it might bring. As the Barclays Center rose on the same Atlantic Yards site that Walter O'Malley had once eyed for the Dodgers, Jay-Z reaffirmed his support for the basketball team in verse. "I jack, I rob, I sin — aw man, I'm Jackie Robinson / 'cept when I run base, I dodge the pen / Lucky me, luckily, they didn't get me / Now when I bring the Nets, I'm the black Branch Rickey,"[45] he rapped on the Kanye West–produced "Brooklyn (Go Hard)." (The song, which also featured indie darling Santigold, debuted on the soundtrack for the Diddy-produced Biggie biopic *Notorious*.)

Once the Barclays Center was completed, Jay-Z christened the Nets' billion-dollar home with a string of eight sold-out shows, drawing more than 120,000 fans and grossing $7.4 million.[46] He negotiated the placement of a satellite location of his 40/40 Club and a Rocawear store in the building. Jay-Z's initial investment soared: once ensconced in Brooklyn, the Nets' value vaulted to $530 million.[47] But within a year of the arena's opening, Jay-Z made a startling move: he dumped his equity in both the team and the arena, selling the former to Nets coach Jason Kidd for $500,000 and collecting $1.5 million for his stadium stake.[48] Jay-Z did this to remove any conflicts of interest that might have prevented him from becoming a sports agent at the head of a new venture: Roc Nation Sports (more on this in chapter 12).

Jay-Z's growing experience as an investor seems to have spurred him to look for new ways to plow money into promising young companies. Shortly before this book went to press, he announced a startup incubator, Arrive, along with plans to launch a venture fund. Structured as a partnership between Roc Nation, seed-stage investment firm Primary Venture Partners, and publicly traded holding company GlassBridge, Arrive should give Jay-Z access to the sort of war chest needed to take the next step in the startup world.

"Jay is somebody who takes large risks and makes big bets, and day to day shows up at the office, and has opinions," says Genius cofounder Zechory. "He's not just sort of throwing his name on it."[49]

And now, more than a decade after putting an end to his beef with his chief rival, Jay-Z seems set to battle Nas not for the King of New York title, but for Silicon Valley supremacy.

Aside from Beats, Dre's most notable tech investment happened as part of his headlining gig at the Coachella music festival in 2012. That year, he brought a host of old friends—including Snoop Dogg, Eminem, and 50 Cent—to the stage in front of a crowd estimated at a hundred thousand. But the star of the show was Tupac Shakur, in the form of a Dre-funded hologram-like illusion that moved and sounded so much like the late rapper that some wondered if he'd never died.

The virtual resurrection might not have happened if it wasn't for Beats. Concert promoter Goldenvoice, a subsidiary of live-music giant AEG, had just expanded the festival to two weekends but didn't yet have a headliner for the second. As the date approached, Jimmy Iovine caught wind of the situation and invited Dre and Coachella founder Paul Tollett to his home in Holmby Hills. By this point, Dre hadn't toured in ages, so he didn't have a traditional agent or manager to handle the negotiation—Iovine took care of that (and didn't charge a commission).[50]

"Jimmy helped convince him, and that's how that happened," says Randy Phillips, AEG's chief at the time. "He's a branding genius. I'm sure he thought it would only make Dre hotter, which made Beats hotter...That was his motivation, other than he thought it would be a great piece of entertainment."

Phillips couldn't reveal the precise dollar amount Dre received for his set but confirmed that it was "into the multiple millions." For Dre, though, the performance fee wasn't a major motivation. "Dre's such a perfectionist," says Phillips. "He really wanted it to be something that no one's ever done before." In fact, given what Dre paid to develop the hologram, Phillips believes that the superproducer simply broke even on the show.

It may be hard to understand how a performance could be so pricey to stage, but there were quite a few moving parts. The details of Shakur's image were crafted by Digital Domain, the Hollywood effects house behind Brad Pitt's reverse-aging character in *The Curious Case of Benjamin Button,* and the image itself was brought to life with an old trick used in theater. An overhead projector splashed the image of Shakur onto a tilted piece of glass on the floor, which reflected it up through a Mylar screen to create the illusion of a three-dimensional human.[51]

Dre spent both cash and time tweaking the ersatz Shakur with its creators; on top of that, he shelled out to bring living guests to the Southern California desert. Interestingly, Dre had wanted the release of his long-rumored album *Detox* to coincide with the groundbreaking Coachella moment; according to a ghostwriter who worked with him at around the same time, he had—and still has—"hundreds" of completed tracks in his vault. But Dre couldn't identify an album's worth that satisfied him. So he shelved *Detox,* it seems, for good.

One could say that Dre did bring new music with him—in the

form of Kendrick Lamar. Dre had taken the up-and-coming Compton rapper under his wing, opening doors for Lamar after Top Dawg Entertainment, the independent label he'd gotten his start with, signed up with Interscope/Aftermath. While recording his major label debut with Dre, Lamar immediately identified something that the producer, now infinitely wiser and more circumspect than he'd been in his reckless 1990s days, brought to the table: leadership.

"That's probably one of the best qualities you can have when you have these young kids all around you in the studios, trying to create," Lamar told me at the end of an interview for a 2015 *Forbes* story. "When you have leadership, you have people that actually genuinely care about you and your well-being and your growth, not only in the industry, but as a person."[52] Lamar's manager, Dave Free, added anecdotes about Dre giving his young charge instructions both vocal ("You should be more aggressive here...Pronounce the word this way") and strategic (to make songs eternal, "you should never say dates").[53]

The tutelage paid off, lyrically and financially: Lamar made his Coachella debut in 2012, performing "The Recipe" with Dre. The song was the first single on Lamar's album *Good Kid, M.A.A.D. City,* which would go on to earn platinum certification and Grammy nominations for Best New Artist, Best Rap Performance, Best Rap Album, and Album of the Year. Though he didn't win any in his first go-around, Lamar picked up six golden gramophones for his subsequent album, *To Pimp a Butterfly.*

The Coachella performance by Dre and his guests—living and otherwise—was the highlight of the festival, prompting Phillips to try to coax Dr. Dre into doing a world tour. The superproducer declined. When Phillips encountered Dre sitting one row behind him at a staging of *The Book of Mormon* in Los Angeles in 2014, he figured he had to give it one last shot. Dre knew what Phillips wanted even before he opened his mouth.

"Oh no," said Dre with a chuckle. "Not you again."[54]

Phillips pestered Dre throughout the evening, but no matter how much money he offered, the Beats cofounder turned him down.

"He would have gotten a hundred, a hundred and fifty million dollars guaranteed for a world tour," says Phillips with a shrug. "He doesn't need the money."

As Troy Carter and I wind down our conversation in Culver City, we touch on the reason Dre doesn't need any more money: Beats, which is probably hip-hop's most successful startup thus far, and its corporate parent, Apple, which arguably holds the same distinction in the tech world.

I point out a paradox in the companies' intertwined history: that Apple probably wouldn't have purchased Beats, a headphones-and-streaming company, if Steve Jobs had still been around in 2014, because the Apple founder didn't believe that streaming would work.

"I had that conversation with Steve," Carter begins.[55]

"What did he say?" I ask.

" 'People don't want streaming. They want to own their own music, and streaming will never work.' "

"When was this? In what context?"

"The year before he passed away…I was at Apple having a meeting with him. We got into a debate around streaming: 'People want to own music; they don't want to stream it.' "

Carter pauses.

"If you look at the history of Apple, he didn't do that many acquisitions," he says. "He was more of a builder than an acquirer."

In the end, Carter believes that Jobs's successor, Tim Cook, did the Beats deal due to a combination of factors: first, to bring a billion-dollar headphone business into Apple's fold; second, to get Iovine and Dre—and their music industry connections—under the tech giant's umbrella; and third, to acquire the functioning skeleton of a promising music streaming service.

"As you're projecting out, and you're looking at being able to compete with Spotify, what the future of the business looks like, being able to have insiders…Apple can't do that [alone]," says Carter. "Dre's and Jimmy's competence, and being able to bring them into a team, is fantastic as you're doing deals with the music business and you see this change in landscape."

Dre's Beats Music, and the Apple Music behemoth it developed into, gave him the biggest foothold in the streaming space among all three kings. As was the case with so many business categories, though, the others managed to get into the sector in their own lucrative ways — even if it meant going quite literally to the ends of the earth in search of promising leads.

CHAPTER 11

Ice in the Winter

By the fall of 2015, the Barclays Center was barely three years old, but it already felt like the House That Jay Built. And though there were others who played a larger role in the Nets' move to downtown Brooklyn, Jay-Z became the individual most closely associated with the arena that transformed the urban fabric of a vast swath of his hometown — for better or worse — from a nondescript neighborhood by the train tracks into a bustling commercial hub.

Though he sold his pieces of the team and its arena in 2013, he did so only after securing a branch of his 40/40 Club and a cozy relationship with the venue's management, as well as a brick-and-mortar Rocawear store on-site. So when Jay-Z took the stage on October 20 at the charity concert to celebrate "one million people and counting"[1] using his streaming service, Tidal — whose parent company he acquired earlier in the year for $56 million — the building whose glowing neon innards he gazed up at was more of a personal clubhouse than an 18,000-seat arena.

A look around the Barclays Center during the show, dubbed Tidal X, yields confirmation: in the rafters, a banner bearing Jay-Z's name boasts of his eight sold-out shows alongside the retired numbers of basketball legends Julius Erving and Jason Kidd, and down on the floor, ads for D'Ussé wrap the VIP section in front of the stage. A handful of the hottest young names in all genres of music take the stage, from Nick Jonas to Thomas Rhett to Meek Mill, ahead of planned sets by Jay-Z, Nicki Minaj, Beyoncé, and — the rarest treat of all — Prince.[2]

As the show's headline portion begins, Jay-Z struts out, decked in black save for the gold chain carrying his cognac's logo. "I want to thank every single person here tonight...We raised a lot of money," he says matter-of-factly, as if reading from a teleprompter. "We're also having a good time." Then he pauses, allowing the synths behind him to soar ominously through his silence, eliciting some additional whoops from the crowd.

"Right now, though — I said *right now, though*," he continues, his tone suddenly aggressive. "Don't *fuck* with me. Brooklyn, make some motherfucking noise!"[3]

Backed by a full band, he proceeds to launch into his set, bumping the audience into new levels of hysteria with "U Don't Know." As he glowers out across a sea of hands forming his Roc-A-Fella triangle logo with thumbs and forefingers, he delivers a line that's long been one of his trademarks — but this time, it seems clearly aimed at the many observers, mostly outside the Barclays Center, who've been expressing doubts that his fledgling service can make a dent in the vast streaming market.

"I will not lose," he shrieks, his voice crackling with passion. "Ever!"

Jay-Z's theatrics at the Tidal X concert may have been a bit over-the-top, but they were nothing compared to the live-streamed launch event he arranged in March 2015, shortly after acquiring the company. A cast of music's top acts were introduced as fellow artist-owners, standing shoulder to shoulder: Usher, Rihanna, Nicki Minaj, Madonna, Deadmau5, Kanye West, Jay-Z, J. Cole, Calvin

Harris, Chris Martin, Jason Aldean, Jack White, Daft Punk, Beyoncé, Arcade Fire, and Alicia Keys (Lil Wayne, Indochine, and Damian Marley were later added to the roster).

Keys gave an impassioned declaration to open the proceedings. The members of Daft Punk stood expressionless in their chrome helmets. Chris Martin and Calvin Harris tuned in remotely, their faces appearing split screen on a large monitor in the center of the stage. And then everyone came up and signed a sheet of paper to seal the deal; perhaps in the spirit of consummation, Madonna suggestively draped her leg across a table while scrawling her name. Each artist owned a piece of the company — estimates ranged from 3 percent per act (according to *Billboard*) to 1 percent (a source who asked not to be named) to somewhere in between (Aldean). "It's a couple percent, or whatever it was, for us to initially come on and sort of help to launch it," the country star told me a few months later. "Any other artist that comes in . . . they have a stake in it, too."[4]

Although nobody seems willing to say whether the acts made any cash payment for their equity stakes, it appears that committing to offer exclusive material to the service was their main contribution. That would have made sense for Jay-Z even if he'd given each act a 3 percent stake for free. Given Tidal's $56 million valuation, that translates to $1.68 million per act, about half what Apple is thought to have offered the likes of Drake for exclusive-release windows on Apple Music at around the same time.

Yet even as Jay-Z celebrated Tidal "going platinum" at his Barclays Center show, reports began to trickle out that things were looking less rosy behind the scenes. The company lost double-digit millions in its first full year under Jay-Z's ownership, running through three CEOs along the way. Tidal's employees and investors — with the partial exception of Aldean — were tight-lipped about the company's financial situation. After multiple inquiries went unanswered by Tidal's press department, I decided to head to Oslo, home to the company's headquarters. A handful of people agreed in advance to talk to me, including Scandinavian hip-hop pioneer Tommy Tee, former employees of Tidal and its corporate parent, and a couple of Norwegian journalists who've been covering the service for years. Perhaps dropping by Tidal head-quarters unannounced could also yield some useful information.[5]

I arrived in Oslo—a city nestled among fjords and forests, where the winter sun rises at 9 a.m. and scoots slowly along the horizon for about seven hours before disappearing again—and immediately began to notice something odd: most Norwegians I encountered had never heard of Tidal. The trend spanned people from all walks of life, from local music industry operatives to coffee shop attendants; even a bartender at the hotel where Jay-Z stays when he's in town hadn't heard of the streaming service. It was all very strange for a company that described itself, even before Jay-Z's takeover, as "an innovative media technology company at the fore-front of the ongoing redefinition of music consumption in the modern digital world."[6]

More knew of WiMP, Tidal's unfortunately named sister ser-vice, but barely. Tommy Tee confirmed that Tidal and, before that, WiMP had long been sort of like Spotify's little brother. "They never really got a foothold in the market," he told me.[7] At the end of my first night in town, I met up with Kjetil Saeter and Markus Tobiassen, journalists working on a story about Tidal for the coun-try's top business daily, *Dagens Naeringsliv*. Over several rounds of beer, they painted a picture of a desperate, money-losing company; both wondered aloud how long Jay-Z would be willing to pour cash into an unprofitable enterprise.

The next day, I trudged down to Tidal's offices in central Oslo to see what I could glean. I walked into the nondescript five-story office building and made my way to the second floor, where a sign covered the entire wall, emblazoned with Tidal's logo. While the office was far from packed—no security guard, no receptionist—it didn't really seem like a company in crisis either. With its open layout and Pearl Jam posters, it just felt like a typical startup. Even-tually, a woman dressed all in black walked by, and I introduced myself. She turned out to be Tidal's French language curator[8] and asked if I was being helped; I shook my head. She apologized, saying that someone named Louise usually manned the front desk.[9]

A blonde woman appeared and suggested that I set up an interview with someone through the press contact listed on Tidal's website; I informed her that I had already tried this. Then she said that Louise might be in a better position to help me. Did Louise have an email address I could try? I asked. Nope. The blonde woman went and fetched a tall guy named Erik sporting a gray beard and a rather unwelcoming disposition.

By this point, Tidal employees were starting to notice the scene brewing by the door. I introduced myself, and Erik informed me that there were really only tech people at this particular office. (A bit of fishing on LinkedIn reveals that Erik's title is senior vice president of customer experience—not exactly an entry-level IT job—and that he's based in New York; one would think an SVP could speak knowledgeably about his company regardless.) When I asked if he or one of these tech people might be able to simply talk to me about Tidal past and present, I again received a flat denial.

I clearly wasn't welcome, and there weren't any answers forthcoming, so I bade the group of onlookers *ha det* and walked out the door. If there was intrigue afoot, it didn't seem as though anyone at Tidal wanted to tell me about it—or anything at all, for that matter. I would have to find answers elsewhere.

Jay-Z may have purchased his very own streaming service in 2015, but Diddy had actually invested in one several years earlier—after getting a nudge from a Harvard alum named D. A. Wallach in 2011.[10]

Wallach graduated in 2007, one class behind Facebook founder Mark Zuckerberg, and his first job after college was serving as lead singer of indie pop band Chester French. The group's demo was discovered by Pharrell Williams, Kanye West, and Jermaine Dupri almost simultaneously, leading to a deal with Williams's Star Trak imprint at Interscope.[11] After three years of recording and touring, Wallach took a role as artist in residence for Spotify in 2011 as the service made its U.S. debut.[12]

Swedish entrepreneur Daniel Ek founded the company in 2006, and in 2008 it expanded across much of Europe. Spotify quickly proved itself a viable alternative to piracy: for ten dollars per month, consumers could have essentially unlimited access to a vast buffet of music encompassing most major acts and albums. One-third of the population of Sweden signed up, and soon the company accounted for half of all music consumption there. Billionaires Sean Parker and Li Ka-shing joined a $50 million round that valued the company at $250 million; during the summer of Spotify's U.S. launch, venture capital firms including Accel and Kleiner Perkins poured in another $100 million to bump Spotify's valuation to $1 billion.[13]

At the same time, Wallach set about recruiting artists to invest some of their own money into the service. It was a savvy move for Spotify, which needed musicians to buy into its model — figuratively more than literally — and offering them a chance to own a piece of the future of their industry was so compelling that they piled in without demanding a celebrity discount. "They were investing alongside other institutional investors and venture capital firms," says Wallach. "By that time, it was attractive enough to them that we were just allowing them to invest."[14]

One of the first artists Wallach contacted was Diddy, whom he knew from his Chester French days. (In 2010, the band released the madcap Vegas anthem "Cîroc Star" with Diddy, who rapped, "Half a billion stashed, I'm ready / Buy the bar, that's petty / I buy the whole company.") After a meeting in New York, Diddy invested an undisclosed sum in Spotify. Wallach also persuaded Justin Bieber's manager, Scooter Braun, of the streaming service's merits; Braun and Bieber put up money as well. Perhaps Wallach's biggest coup: Troy Carter, who was managing Lady Gaga at the time. He not only invested but eventually joined Spotify as global head of creative services.

Since 2011, Spotify has blossomed. Though its path to long-term profitability is complicated by the whims of the music streaming business—its operating loss ballooned to $189 million even as revenue surged 45 percent to $1.2 billion in 2014—its valuation sat at $8.5 billion when this book went to press. Those who invested in 2011, such as Diddy, likely had their stakes diluted as new money came in, but their investments are now worth many times what they initially poured into the company. Those returns could grow even more impressive in the public markets.[15]

All of this comes as little surprise to Wallach. "Artists understand media and communications as well as anyone," he says. "I don't know why some random [venture capitalist] should have a better intuitive understanding."[16]

Indeed, with more than sixty million paying subscribers by 2017, Spotify had emerged as the king of interactive streaming. But Dr. Dre's new employer had an eye on the throne. Apple Music, launched a year after the Beats acquisition, was the tech giant's attempt to win. In addition to an essentially unlimited catalog of songs, the service contained elements sourced from Beats Music, which Apple shuttered in late 2015, much to the dismay of its three hundred thousand or so U.S. subscribers, who'd grown fond of its curated playlists.[17]

Apple Music attempted to distinguish itself from Spotify and others by ramping up the human element, starting with Beats 1, a twenty-four-hour worldwide live virtual radio station available only to subscribers. The flagship channel featured three DJs, all of them well-known on their own turf: Julie Adenuga (United Kingdom), Ebro Darden (United States), and Zane Lowe (United Kingdom, via New Zealand).

Perhaps even more important were Apple Music's celebrity

broadcasts, like Elton John's Rocket Hour and Dre's own offering, the Pharmacy, in which A-list artists brought their favorite music, new and old, to eager audiences. Apple Music now boasts dozens of similar shows, with hosts including Drake, Pharrell Williams, DJ Khaled, Mary J. Blige, Mike D of the Beastie Boys, and Corey Taylor of Slipknot.

Today, Apple Music has more than thirty million subscribers, each paying $9.99 per month. There is no free tier, unlike with Spotify, which has a similarly expansive catalog. To lure users away from its rivals, Apple has been banking on content like the aforementioned shows, as well as albums by the likes of Drake and Dr. Dre, both of whom made recent works available exclusively on the service before expanding their availability to other platforms. A desire to broaden that strategy may have been the impetus behind rumors of an Apple buyout of Tidal in mid-2016, but the year came and went without a deal.

Though I couldn't get any current Tidal employees to talk during my trip to Norway, I was able to gain a better understanding of the company through interviews with former employees and executives in Oslo. They all offered valuable insights that informed the writing of this chapter, though most refused to go on record, citing fear of legal action. One who didn't mind talking openly was Gunnar Sellaeg, the CEO of Tidal's parent company, Aspiro, from 2006 to 2012, before Jay-Z came into the picture.[18]

Sellaeg took me through the company's murky history over lunch. Aspiro was founded by a trio of Swedish entrepreneurs in 1998, initially focusing on mobile business services (using text messages to book plane flights, for example).[19] It wasn't particularly successful at first, but the company found a profitable focus—mobile ringtones—and reorganized itself with that in mind. By 2004, all that was left of the original Aspiro was the name and shareholder structure. After a public offering, Schibsted, arguably the most powerful media conglomerate in Norway, took a 40 percent interest. Sellaeg, who had been working as the head of Schibsted's media divisions, became Aspiro's CEO in 2006; by that point, it was one of the largest ringtone companies in the world. When that business began to falter a couple of years later, Sellaeg led the company on a quest to find promising new income streams.[20]

In Sellaeg's mind, if Aspiro could tap into an unlimited buffet of music to use for ringtone downloads, surely there was a way to build a database of millions of songs that could be accessed directly from mobile phones and computers. His team put together a prototype, giving it the working name WiMP (wireless music player). The word did not have a negative connotation in Scandinavia, and Sellaeg figured they could always rebrand it if they ever wanted to expand to the United States. When Spotify launched in Sweden, though, it almost immediately became the dominant player in the space. "It led us to take a different route," says Sellaeg. "We wanted to become the service for music lovers."

Aspiro rolled out WiMP in Scandinavia and northern Europe, offering the high-quality sound favored by audiophiles. The company curated songs for users and tried to feature local artists; it also prioritized paying higher royalty rates than other services. "They were always giving three times as much, as far as royalties," says rapper and label owner Tommy Tee. "So they were always valuable to us as artists and me as an independent label."[21]

WiMP soon grew to five hundred thousand active users, but it still hadn't bothered to change its name. That didn't seem to hurt its appeal, at least in Scandinavia, as the company struck a $15 million partnership with Norwegian telecom giant Telenor to provide content; subsequently, the latter's subsidiary, cable provider Canal Digital, made WiMP available to hundreds of thousands of its customers, who could stream music from their televisions or sign up to get access on their phones. Sellaeg left Aspiro in 2012 to join Telenor, eventually becoming its chief of product.[22]

At Aspiro, new CEO Andy Chen oversaw the creation of the Tidal brand—essentially identical to WiMP but with a name more appealing to English-speaking audiences—and launched it as a $19.99-per-month hi-fi-only service in the United States and the United Kingdom. (Chen did not respond to a request for comment in time to be interviewed for this book.) The focus on audio quality wasn't only about appealing to audiophiles: observers point out that securing the rights to only the hi-fi versions of music catalogs is cheaper than tacking on the regular-quality editions as well.[23]

Labels recognize that most consumers don't want to pay $19.99 per month for hi-fi streaming, so they are less stingy with those rights than when licensing their catalogs for $9.99-per-month regular-quality subscriptions. Spotify gained rights to both, along with permission to operate a free tier, only after negotiating for years—and forking over 15 to 20 percent of itself to the major labels, a stake worth north of $1 billion today. (The move upset musicians on whose backs the service was built, as there was no initial provision to compensate acts with any of that equity; Tidal later touted its artist-centric ownership structure as a fairer alternative.[24])

In the fourth quarter of 2014, Aspiro's sales increased 8 percent to roughly $8 million, but the company declared a net loss of $4 million. Though hemorrhaging cash is not terribly unusual for a streaming service, it can be problematic if there's no war chest upon which to fall back. Aspiro's quarterly report indicated that the company didn't have enough cash to make it through the year, let alone strike huge new deals with major labels. In addition, the vast majority of Aspiro's 500,000 subscribers came from WiMP, many through the Canal Digital arrangement. Tidal had just 12,000 subscribers, which explains why nobody in Oslo appeared to know what it was when I asked.[25]

Enter Jay-Z. One of the rapper's lieutenants had caught wind of Aspiro's struggles and brought the company to his attention. Someone in Aspiro's Oslo office got a call in late 2014 from a party expressing interest on behalf of an anonymous big-name U.S. investor who wanted to keep a low profile for the time being. Says journalist Saeter: "Someone told us that they thought it was Donald Trump."[26]

In the waning days of 2014, Jay-Z materialized from the shadows with a $56 million offer for the company through an entity dubbed Project Panther Bidco. The number represented a premium of roughly 60 percent over Aspiro's share price at the time, and its investors enthusiastically accepted. Several months later, Jay-Z and his cast of high-profile artist-owners officially relaunched the service.[27]

His logic for buying the company was clear. Tidal's hi-fi strategy would never allow it to achieve large-scale growth; most consumers can't tell the difference between hi-fi and regular streaming and would rather save ten dollars per month by signing up for the lesser version. Jay-Z knew he needed to get the rights to the latter. That appears to be why he took on artist-owners diverse not only in genre but in label affiliation: Universal (Kanye West, Madonna, Rihanna), Sony (Beyoncé, Daft Punk, Alicia Keys), Warner (Coldplay, Jack White), and indie (Arcade Fire, Jason Aldean). Music companies want to keep their superstars happy.

"I would assume that the record labels would listen much more to Jay-Z and his friends than to me and my friends," says Sellaeg. "If I was a label, I would listen more to them."[28]

Sure enough, almost as soon as Jay-Z announced his roster of artist-owners, he got the major label clearances needed to expand beyond hi-fi—seemingly without giving up any equity to the labels—and rolled out regular-quality service with an essentially unlimited menu of songs for $9.99 per month, just like Spotify (but without the option of a free tier). "It's sort of taking the power back, putting it back in our hands, instead of [labels saying], 'This is what we're going to do,'" Aldean told me. "Now it's us going, 'No, no, this is what we're going to do, because this is the way it should be.'"[29]

Tidal made good on its exclusive-release strategy in 2016. Rihanna launched her new album, *Anti,* in late January, making it available for streaming only on Tidal for its first week. In mid-February,

West released what turned out to be a rough draft of *The Life of Pablo* (as in Picasso) exclusively on Tidal. The album underwent several subsequent tweaks to lyrics and beats, with West calling it "a living, breathing, changing creative expression" and declaring that the record would "never be on Apple." (By the end of March, he'd changed his mind.) Tidal reported that *The Life of Pablo* had garnered 400 million streams in two weeks and 250 million in its first ten days, topping Spotify's most popular album at that point (Justin Bieber's *Purpose*).[30]

In April, Beyoncé launched *Lemonade* on Tidal, and for several days it wasn't available for download anywhere else. (At press time, the album could be streamed on Tidal, but not Apple Music or Spotify—same as much of Jay-Z's discography.) Even as reports emerged that Tidal's annual loss had widened to $28 million in Jay-Z's first full year as the company's owner, brighter news followed in the form of subscriber numbers: 4.2 million, according to several outlets.[31]

During my trip to Norway, however, Saeter and Tobiassen released their exhaustively reported story in *Dagens Naeringsliv,* revealing that Tidal had drastically inflated its numbers and let inaccurate reports go unchallenged. The real total, Saeter and Tobiassen said, was closer to 850,000. There were irregularities galore. Apparently, 170,000 subscribers appeared overnight after Jay-Z tweeted that his company had hit the one million mark ahead of the Tidal X show in late 2015; this seems to have been accomplished by reactivating dormant Canal Digital accounts.[32]

As the writers had suggested it would, their story painted a picture of a company on the brink of insolvency desperate to be seen as successful, with day-to-day operations guided to a surprising extent by Jay-Z's 40/40 Club partner Desiree Perez. (Perez also boasts a hefty résumé when it comes to distribution—of illegal drugs, not legal music—during the 1990s.)[33] On my way home from Norway, I picked up a physical copy of the report at the airport; the story, which came out the day of Donald Trump's inauguration, was stillborn in the stateside press cycle. But its findings were quite damning, down to the print headline, a classic Jay-Z lyric turned back on the rapper and his dubious subscriber count: "Men lie, women lie, numbers don't."

Is it possible that Tidal could so thoroughly torture its numbers that the larger figures could technically be true? Maybe. In statements by the company, often filtered through the press, it's often unclear whether the totals reflect commonly used metrics, like active monthly users, or measures that would naturally be much larger, like total user count. Even Jay-Z's aforementioned tweet was ambiguous: "1,000,000 people and counting." By early 2017, perhaps it's possible that Tidal had signed up 4.2 million users in its entire history, with the help of those Canal Digital subscriptions and myriad free trials. But if that's the total being touted, it's a hollow number. The only thing that really matters is the number of active subscriptions; free trials and canceled subscriptions obviously don't generate any cash.

Tidal did threaten legal action against its former owners in April 2016, claiming that the service's actual subscriber count vastly trailed the half-million total stated at the time of the acquisition. But even if it turned out that Tidal and WiMP had zero subscribers at the time, it still wouldn't account for the difference between 850,000 and 4.2 million.[34] Those who were at the company before Jay-Z took over are adamant that there weren't any discrepancies with user numbers on their watch; as a publicly traded company, they were held to rigorous standards. "We just counted those who were actually active," says Sellaeg. "I see there are different ways of doing that now."[35]

In the end, it didn't really matter if Tidal was plumping up its figures. On January 23, thirty-six hours after I returned from Norway, the company put out a press release announcing that Sprint had purchased a 33 percent stake in Tidal. *Billboard* reported the investment at $200 million, valuing Jay-Z's company at $600 million, more than ten times what he paid for it. He and his two dozen artist-owners would stay on, with plans to dole out more exclusives to Sprint's forty-five million customers—including Jay-Z's *4:44,* released shortly after the deal's announcement. The company also pledged to dedicate $75 million annually to artist initiatives and releases. Added Jay-Z in a statement: "Sprint shares our view of revolutionizing the creative industry."[36]

The quote was classic anodyne press release material, but the message couldn't have been clearer: Jay-Z had pulled off the same feat he'd achieved with Rocawear, convincing a multibillion-dollar company in search of cool points to cough up a nine-figure sum for a generic product upon which he'd sprinkled his stardust. The Tidal move also smacked of his Armand de Brignac strategy. Once again, he had purchased a generic European consumer product that Americans hadn't heard of, dressed it up, and peddled it as a high-end specialty item. As he bragged in the song "U Don't Know," he could sell ice in the winter, fire in hell, water to a well— and with Tidal, he had done it again.

"Make some noise for everybody that touched the stage tonight," says Jay-Z, returning to the Tidal X microphone after an interlude that featured Nicki Minaj performing with a squadron of dancers clad in black hosiery and Beyoncé fronting a rival crew dressed all in pink. "Nicki Minaj, Usher, Nas, Lil Wayne, Rick Ross, Meek Mill, Hit-Boy, Thomas Rhett...Nick Jonas. If I forget one person, it'll be really fucking bad."[37]

He rattles off a few more names, omitting only Prince, who hasn't yet taken the stage.

"Before we go," he continues, "I want New York City to sing this song so loud they can hear us all the way in Timbuktu...It's your turn to perform."

At that point, with the audience possibly expecting "Little Red

Corvette" or "When Doves Cry," the voice of Frank Sinatra blares out across the arena, suddenly turning an autumn evening in Brooklyn into a summer night at Yankee Stadium.

"It's up to you, New York, Ne-ew *York!*" croons the chairman — and then, about ten seconds later, the song stops abruptly. After a moment of near-total silence, the bass booms through Barclays with Jay-Z's own Big Apple anthem, "Empire State of Mind," eliciting wild whoops from the crowd. "I like that. I like that!" he screams, before launching into his first verse. "Yeah I'm out that Brooklyn, now I'm down in Tribeca, right next to De Niro, but I'll be hood forever / I'm the new Sinatra, and since I made it here, I can make it anywhere..."

It's clear that the night is about to be over, and indeed, the house lights at Barclays go back on seconds after Jay-Z completes his final chorus. Prince, the night's biggest attraction — who had publicly declared his allegiance to Tidal months earlier by making it the only service authorized to stream his catalog — is nowhere to be found.

Aside from the authors of a few barbs on Twitter that night, it seemed that everyone had been blinded by the star power of the acts who did show up. *Billboard* later described the event as "an all-star gathering that played as eclectic and seamless as a carefully curated playlist," neglecting to mention the absence of Prince.[38] The closest thing to an announcement of Prince's removal from the lineup seemed to be an email sent to Tidal subscribers at 7:38 p.m. the night of the show — long after most attendees were well on their way to Brooklyn — that touted the concert's headliners but included no mention of Prince. Tragically, the Purple One passed away several months later; his music remained on Tidal exclusively, tied up in legal wrangling between Jay-Z and the singer's estate, until a few weeks after Sprint invested.

Sprint's eventual investment gave Jay-Z not only a lifeline but a war chest to fund such battles while continuing to expand Tidal's reach. The infusion probably won't be the last move for the streaming service. Now connected to Sprint's forty-five million customers, Tidal has the sort of audience that might make it an appealing buyout target for competitors Spotify and Apple, or even another tech giant like Google or Amazon looking to make a splash in streaming.

In the meantime, Jay-Z's connection to the mobile phone industry has come full circle. Though he missed a chance to get in on Boost Mobile at the turn of the new millennium, he finds himself under the same umbrella — Sprint — and worth hundreds of millions more on paper. Now that's a Jay-Z–style boost.

CHAPTER 12

State of the Art

Somewhere along the two-mile stretch between the Hudson River and Crispy Crust Pizza — the Englewood, New Jersey, slice joint where Sylvia Robinson formed the Sugarhill Gang — sits the home of Kasseem "Swizz Beatz" Dean. The Bronx-born beatmaker, now in his late thirties, continued Charlie Stettler's unlikely Switzerland–U.S. hip-hop connection by taking his name from the European sneaker brand K-Swiss, and was once dubbed the best hip-hop producer of all time by Kanye West. Over the course of his decades-long career, he's worked with Diddy, Dre, and particularly Jay-Z; he's also a crucial conduit linking hip-hop's graffiti heritage to the world of fine art.

Swizz has a fittingly immodest home, a several-dozen-room mansion that he and wife Alicia Keys purchased from Eddie Murphy for about $15 million in 2012, after they'd grown weary of paparazzi attention at their SoHo pad. They have decidedly different decorative taste from that of the aforementioned comedian. Though Swizz left Murphy's basement movie theater intact, complete with its light-bulb-framed posters for *Coming to America* and *The Nutty Professor,* he peppered the upstairs with prized pieces from what he calls the Dean Collection, including works by Andy Warhol, Damien Hirst, and, of course, Jean-Michel Basquiat.

Swizz also ripped up Murphy's basketball court, sunk the floor down a meter or so, and built a gallery big enough to hold, on one wall, a Kehinde Wiley painting the size of the broad side of a shipping container and, right next to it, a forty-foot-tall wooden Mickey Mouse–looking creature crafted by the artist Kaws.

"One of his biggest sculptures that he's done," Swizz muses as we settle into a pair of Eames chairs covered in graffiti. "See how shiny it is?"[1]

"Do you have to wax it?" I inquire.

"You gotta keep it greased up."

"How often?"

"Every couple of months."

"I guess it would get dusty."

"Yeah," he sighs. "This is a project in itself."

Giant wooden mice aside, Swizz's main focus these days is his gig as Bacardí's global creative director, a remarkable career move that grew out of his No Commission art fair, which allows artists to keep all the cash generated from the sale of their work instead of having to fork over half of the total to a gallery. The beverage giant came on as a sponsor for the first iteration, held at Miami's Art Basel in 2015, and agreed to Swizz's conditions.

"This is not a logo contest," Swizz explained to the company's brass. "This is something where the artist should be free, and they should have their work breathe and live on its own without somebody trying to stamp their logo on it just because they're partnering with the event."

Bacardí's executives were knocked out by that sort of approach to marketing, and within a few months they signed him to an incentive-laden, multiyear, multimillion-dollar deal to join the company— which does $5 billion in annual revenue—as an executive. Two months in, Bacardí chief Mike Dolan was even more impressed by Swizz than he thought he'd be.

"You're not going to get many celebrities who will go to meetings from eight in the morning through dinner and listen to endless presentations," he told me. "I want the creativity that he can bring to this, and across the various brands that we've got, and [for him to] help us think out of the box."[2]

It's amazing to think that, just a decade after Cristal famously dismissed rappers as unwanted customers, one of the world's biggest beverage companies decided to place a beatmaker from the Bronx in charge of a two-hundred-brand portfolio that includes Grey Goose vodka, Dewar's Scotch, and Bacardí rum. But hip-hop keeps reinventing itself. When getting paid to appear in a commercial wasn't enough, 50 Cent took equity in Vitaminwater's parent company. Then Diddy reached new financial heights by earning the trust of Diageo and hawking Cîroc through new media and old. Today, Swizz marks the latest step in the evolution, quietly and discreetly pulling strings from the executive suite.

"They are aware me and Puff are friends," says Swizz of his Bacardí bosses. "I'm not downplaying any of that. I am going to go hard. I am going to be competitive. [But] we do two different things."[3]

Swizz may boast one of hip-hop's finest art collections, but perhaps the strangest development in the connection between the two worlds came from the Wu-Tang Clan. In late 2013, I first learned about this link through a missive sent from a suspicious-looking email address touting a project too strange to be fiction.

The sender, a Morocco-based producer named Tarik "Cilvaringz" Azzougarh, said that he had spent the past six years collaborating with the Wu-Tang Clan to create a secret album. The recording process was so clandestine that the Wu-Tang members didn't even have access to the full digital drafts of the songs to which they had contributed; they laid down their vocals over bare-bones beats and sent them to Cilvaringz for completion. He told me the album sat in a vault in Marrakech — where it would remain until the group sold the lone existing copy to a single buyer.[4]

I followed up with Cilvaringz and asked him to put me in touch with Wu-Tang ringleader Robert "RZA" Diggs to verify that this was, in fact, a real project with the group's buy-in. "The idea that music is art has been something we advocated for years," RZA explained, speaking of his inspiration for *Once Upon a Time in Shaolin.* "And yet [music] doesn't receive the same treatment as [fine] art…especially nowadays, when it's been devalued and diminished to almost the point that it has to be given away for free."[5]

His argument centered on the notion that the culprit wasn't just music piracy. Streaming services, traditional albums, and terrestrial radio play all had something to do with the perceived devaluation. In the view of RZA and Cilvaringz, music had been falling from its perch among the fine arts for centuries. Long ago, Leonardo was supported by the wealthy Medici family in Renaissance Italy as he crafted classic works of visual art, just as European royalty hired Mozart, and the archduke of Austria underwrote Beethoven's work. Today, though, the prices paid for the most expensive paintings are often orders of magnitude larger than the biggest record advances. Wu-Tang hoped that a one-of-a-kind album might just begin to change that paradigm, or at least call attention to it, and make the group some extra cash along the way.

After I broke the news in March 2014, the story quickly snowballed. First came music publications like *Billboard* and *Rolling Stone,* and then mainstream outlets from the *Wall Street Journal* to the *Los Angeles Times.* Eventually, papers from as far away as New Zealand weighed in. The reaction veered from skepticism (*Is this an elaborate publicity stunt?*) to admiration (*It's about time for music to be valued properly!*) to shock (*Rappers care about fine art?*) to fan outrage (*Wu-Tang is being greedy by not letting the world hear its work!*). A few weeks later, Cilvaringz offered to play me part of the secret album if I visited him in Marrakech. *Forbes* leapt at the opportunity to send me to be the first civilian to listen to the record.[6]

Once I arrived in Morocco, Cilvaringz took me to see the lone copy of *Once Upon a Time in Shaolin,* housed in a safe in a suite at the Royal Mansour, a hotel popular with monarchs and billionaires.

The physical album, a simple CD, was ensconced in a one-of-a-kind silver-and-nickel box hand-engraved by British-Moroccan artist Yahya, whom I met as well. ("It's either genius or madness," he told me of the endeavor.[7]) The music Cilvaringz played me lived up to the promise of its grandiose casing: urgent, hard-edged hip-hop punctuated by the soundtrack of life in New York — some rather startling fire engine horns, for example — and the trenchant sort of rhymes that have been displaced by meandering triplets in recent rap.

"It's a conceptual record where you're trying to go back to ninety-three [to] ninety-seven, that glorious time," Cilvaringz told me. "You're trying to get [Wu-Tang] into an aggressive mode, and the beats are aggressive."[8]

In early 2015, Wu-Tang tapped upstart auction house Paddle8, which had previously peddled the work of artists including Damien Hirst and Jeff Koons, to sell the album. Despite the crush of interest in *Once Upon a Time in Shaolin,* no buyer immediately emerged. Part of the problem may have been the restrictions placed on reproduction. A record label might well have purchased the album for $5 million or so — an amount that a premier act might receive for an advance — with the goal of releasing it for mass consumption. But Wu-Tang's insistence that the record remain hidden made the economics tricky. Though there were discussions of playing the album for fans at a series of tightly secured museum exhibits, the group eventually insisted that any potential buyer agree to not release the record publicly for at least eighty-eight years.[9]

Many months later, Wu-Tang found a buyer: baby-faced pharma bad boy Martin Shkreli, who agreed to pay $2 million for the record. After the deal was announced, though, the group started to feel some blowback over its choice of buyer. The centimillionaire Shkreli had earned the ire of a vast swath of people — including both Hillary Clinton and Donald Trump, remarkably — for jacking up the price of a drug often used to treat infections in AIDS patients by several thousand times. (Earlier in 2015, the BBC had dubbed Shkreli "the most hated man in America.")

RZA publicly reacted to the feedback by claiming that the deal had been agreed upon in May, before the extent of Shkreli's unpopular dealings came to light, and pledged to donate a large chunk of the proceeds to charity. The album's buyer didn't take kindly to the response. "I fucking make money," he told the site HipHopDX. "What do you think I do, make cookies? No, motherfucker. I sell drugs."[10]

Hip-hop had come full circle. Many of its most celebrated practitioners—including members of Wu-Tang—had not only sold drugs at one point or another but openly and repeatedly bragged about it in verse. Now RZA was trashing the buyer of the group's latest record for doing the same. No matter: at the end of the day, Wu-Tang had at least partially achieved its goal of putting music back into the fine arts conversation.

"I'm staring at a Picasso in my living room right now that's no different from the Wu-Tang box except it's about twenty times more expensive," said Shkreli at the end of 2015, before ending up in jail for fraud charges. "It is what it is."

Diddy, meanwhile, continued to find new ways to place hip-hop in the living rooms of additional scores of American families, bringing his Revolt network to fifty million people between cable, Web, and mobile.

"I saw a wide-open lane to kind of create the CNN of music, the ESPN of music, to follow our artists that we love in such a journalistic and passionate way that ESPN follows Kobe or LeBron or Serena," Diddy told me in 2014. "That's the same way that we'll follow anybody from Chance the Rapper to Jay-Z to me."[11]

Revolt has a long way to go before it reaches the status of the aforementioned networks, but it has still helped boost Diddy's fortune, which ballooned from $475 million in 2011 to $820 million in 2017. Perhaps more interesting is the culture at Revolt, particularly in the context of Diddy's earlier entrepreneurial ventures. In the 1990s, Diddy would berate superiors on a regular basis; in the 2000s, he sent underlings on arduous cheesecake expeditions. Yet on a 2014 reporting trip to Revolt's headquarters, I found his new employees painting a different picture.

"When I worked at the other office, it was so different, because it was just everybody working toward what Mr. Diddy wanted," explained Tiesha LeShore, who started out as an assistant for the mogul years ago before taking a role with Revolt. "[Now] he seems to be more interested in supporting what everyone is doing. He sees the value and he makes sure your supervisors know that you are valuable. It's amazing to see that difference."[12]

Added Diddy, in a separate conversation: "I don't think I was having enough dialogue with the people who believed in my dream enough to come and work with me. So I was like, 'I want to become a better boss, I want to become a better leader.' . . . You should treat people how you would treat yourself."[13]

Dr. Dre has been undergoing similar revelations of late. He and his Beats cofounder teamed up to donate $70 million to the University of Southern California in 2013, creating the Jimmy Iovine and Andre Young Academy for Arts, Technology, and the Business of Innovation. The four-year undergrad program brought students a curriculum packed with one-on-one mentoring from professors and entertainment industry legends alike, welcoming its first class of twenty-five students in 2014.[14]

It seemed to be a penance of sorts, at least for Dre. "I made some fucking horrible mistakes in my life," he told *Rolling Stone* in 2015, shortly before N.W.A. biopic *Straight Outta Compton* made its debut.[15] At around the same time, Dre released his long-awaited third studio album, *Compton*. It won praise from critics (the often harsh Pitchfork called it "charged up, nimble, and relevant"[16]) but earned only gold certification, the first time one of Dre's solo albums didn't go multiplatinum.

It didn't really matter, though. The film — coproduced by Dre, Ice Cube, and a handful of others — went on to gross north of $160 million domestically, on par with mainstream blockbusters of that year like *Fifty Shades of Grey* and *The SpongeBob Movie: Sponge Out of Water. Rolling Stone* called *Straight Outta Compton* "an electrifying piece of hip-hop history that speaks urgently to right now."[17] Photographer Jonathan Mannion remembers seeing Dre speak at the premiere. "He was just like, 'Yo, yo, thank you all for fucking being here, man,'" says Mannion. "There were f-bombs...He hasn't changed and become something that he isn't."[18]

Back on the East Coast, in a fitting bit of poetic justice, Robert Moses's beloved Shea Stadium fell to the wrecking ball in 2009, just one year before Jay-Z helped break ground on the Barclays Center. In 2013, Jay-Z ditched his Nets stake in order to launch Roc Nation Sports — and became a professional agent representing NFL stars from Dez Bryant to Ndamukong Suh and NBA players like Kevin Durant, who signed a two-year, $54 million deal with the Golden State Warriors in 2016. Jay-Z and his firm capture 3 to 5 percent of such deals.

In baseball, the agent's cut tends to be toward the higher end of that spectrum, as Jay-Z and his team knew when signing up MLB stars Yoenis Céspedes and Robinson Canó. The rapper snagged the latter away from Scott Boras, and then lured the superagent into a war of words by taunting him with a rap lyric: "Scott Boras, you over, baby / Robinson Canó, you coming with me." (The line was delivered in "Crown," on Jay-Z's 2013 album, *Magna Carta...Holy Grail,* which went platinum before it even came out: he had convinced Samsung to pay him $5 million for one million copies to give to its customers.) Boras made the mistake of clapping back. "If Steven Spielberg walked into USC Medical Center," he blustered, "and said, 'I want to do neurosurgery,' they don't give him a scalpel."

Boras had fallen into Jay-Z's trap, elevating the rapper to his own level by calling attention to him; soon ESPN had dubbed the Boras–Jay-Z dynamic "baseball's fascinating new rivalry."[19]

Nobody thought Canó wanted to leave the Yankees, or that the wealthy Bronx Bombers would let their best player walk. After the 2013 season, the team reportedly offered the slugger $170 million over seven years; he declined, and despite industry-wide doubts that he could get a better deal, Jay-Z's firm eventually landed him a ten-year, $240 million pact with the Seattle Mariners. (Though the average annual value of the Yankees' offer was slightly higher, the salary Canó got for his age thirty-eight to forty seasons — beyond the end of a typical baseball player's career — made the Mariners' deal far better for him.)[20]

It wasn't even clear if the deal had been negotiated by Jay-Z himself or by his partners at CAA's sports division. But he proved that he had no problem helping hometown players leave the Big Apple for bigger bucks. Perhaps because of this, he managed to extract a four-year, $110 million deal for New York Mets outfielder Yoenis Céspedes to stay with the team after the 2016 season. And more athletes keep signing up, flattered by the attention from Jay-Z. "It's a family. You gotta feel special when they're asking you to join them," said NBA player Willie Cauley-Stein. "It's so exclusive."[21]

Meanwhile, Jay-Z has continued to sign recording artists to his Roc Nation management division, which now includes Rihanna, Big Sean, Grimes, J. Cole, Korn, Santigold, and Shakira. The corporate reception has been quite positive. Though Live Nation is traded on the New York Stock Exchange, it doesn't break out Roc Nation's performance in its reports. But Iconix, another publicly traded company, did leave a fascinating financial Easter egg in its 2014 year-end rundown: the company, which had acquired Rocawear nearly a decade earlier, paid $32 million for a minority interest in Jay-Z's Marcy Media LLC — the holding company containing his half of Roc Nation — to effectively pick up a 5 percent piece of Roc Nation.[22] The deal placed a theoretical value of $640 million on Jay-Z's company, though that number may include other assets contained beneath the opaque Marcy Media umbrella. At any rate, the move gave Jay-Z a big cash infusion that he likely plowed right into his Tidal acquisition, which happened at around the same time.

Jay-Z has continued to ink new acts, adding DJ Khaled in 2016 and, in early 2017, longtime rival Fat Joe, after appearing on a remix of the Bronx rapper's hit "All the Way Up": "Twenty-one Grammys that I use for D'Ussé cups / I'm on the penthouse floor, call your way up." It's a description of his current reality. Jay-Z is a near-billionaire father of three who continues to rap about his lifestyle, even if it's not remotely relatable to certain audiences. "We've never seen the maturation of hip-hop in this sort of way," he told *Forbes*. "But, you know, people that listen to hip-hop when they're eighteen listen to it when they're twenty-eight. It's just that the voices of hip-hop are not speaking directly to them anymore. Or weren't. They're speaking to an eighteen-year-old. I'm not going to do that anymore. I'm just going to make the music I love to make, and I'm going to mature with my music."[23]

And yet in some areas, hip-hop still isn't afforded proper respect. Former Def Jam chief Kevin Liles recalls a recent meeting with an auto executive. "The guy says, 'Our brand has been devalued by hip-hop music because the truck was never built to be [rapped about],'" Liles recalls. "I said, 'What you're really saying is that all of the hundreds of millions of dollars that you made, you didn't want that?'... We're still fighting the battle."[24]

Hip-hop has encountered similar pushback in Hollywood. (In a sign that the coastal feud of the 1990s is a distant memory, or was never really coastal to begin with, most of hip-hop's big names are now based in Los Angeles, including Diddy, Dre, and Jay-Z.) Though there have been some examples of massively successful films and television shows influenced by hip-hop—*Straight Outta Compton* and *Empire,* to name a pair—there's a tendency to check boxes and move on. "I take the meetings," says Russell Simmons. What does he hear? "'We already have an *Empire*...Why do we need [another]?' Well, you had *E.R.,* and how many fucking hospital shows did you have? It's almost like they can play one rap record at a time on the radio. It's like that a little bit in Hollywood. We still do one at a time."[25]

Yet some of hip-hop's biggest stars are already optimistically planning their curtain calls. Wiz Khalifa and Snoop Dogg like the idea of following in the footsteps of Celine Dion and Elton John. "Snoop was telling me, like, 'Man, we're going to be the first rappers to retire and do Vegas, like, seven nights a week,'" Wiz told me. "Hip-hop is going to be a mainstream thing right now. And it's something that brings people from all over. Jay-Z's going to be sixty, but that means all his fans are going to be that age, too... They're always going to show up, and they're always going to put their kids onto it."[26]

Many of hip-hop's earliest pioneers are already approaching senior citizen status, and they aren't exactly pulling in six figures per night at the Colosseum in Sin City. A quick glance at touring database Pollstar finds the disgraced Bambaataa — whose Bronx River housing project is now surrounded by bus stops wrapped in Sprite ads featuring Tupac Shakur, Missy Elliott, and J. Cole — grossing just $3,000 per show; Herc, Caz, and Starski don't even play enough to register.

"Why go into a young party of today and be a failure to them, or have them feel like you failed at something you've been doing for forty years?" Starski asked me. "I don't want to walk away feeling like a failure, so I stay in my lane. I stay in my crowd. I stay under my umbrella for my own security, and my own feeling, and my own sanity. That's where I feel safe at."[27]

Yet there are signs of hope. In the middle of my interview with Starski, he called up Kurtis Blow, and the two of them discussed plans to perform on a cruise together. Flash was hired as a producer for the Netflix miniseries *The Get Down,* a Baz Luhrmann–produced spectacle based on the early days of hip-hop. In the six months following the show's August 2016 launch, Grandmaster Flash played a dozen shows from Brooklyn to Australia, putting him on pace to spin more in a twelve-month span than he did in the first decade of the new millennium.

Even the landmarks of the movement's birth are getting their due. In 2007, with the support of Herc and his sister — as well as New York senator Chuck Schumer — 1520 Sedgwick was deemed eligible for listing in the National Register of Historic Places.[28] Plans are also in the works for the Universal Hip Hop Museum, scheduled to open in 2022. The latest designs call for a mixed-use development nestled between Yankee Stadium and the Harlem River.[29] "Hip-hop is about peace, love, unity, and having fun," says Grandwizzard Theodore. "When we put out this hip-hop museum, all the myths and all the misconceptions that a lot of these parents got about rap and hip-hop — you can take them to the museum."[30]

In the meantime, Grandmaster Caz, Kurtis Blow, and a host of other pioneers lead visitors from all over the world on bus excursions through the cradle of hip-hop via Bronx-focused Hush Tours.[31] (Blow is even taking a page out of the three kings' book: he told me he was trying to put together a streaming service of his own.[32]) Caz has moved on in the aftermath of having his lyrics cribbed for "Rapper's Delight," though he never really reconciled with the Sugarhill Gang's Big Bank Hank, who died of cancer in 2014.

"He never looked back," says Caz. "Not to say thank you, not to say, 'Here's a few dollars.' Nothing." But Caz recently scored the first platinum hit of his four-decade career, thanks to an unlikely ally: Macklemore. The Seattle-born white rapper of "Thrift Shop" fame recruited Caz, Kool Moe Dee, and Melle Mel to appear on "Downtown," which went platinum in 2016. "The people that have benefited from [hip-hop] and came out on top, and was in a position to do something like Macklemore did, never did," says Caz. "So how do I feel about Macklemore? I love him to death."[33]

Grandwizzard Theodore, who says he now plays about a hundred shows per year, also takes a kind view toward the latest generation of rappers. He appreciates Jay-Z's contribution to the cause with his 2001 line about exacting revenge on label executives for what they did to the Cold Crush Brothers. He also cites Diddy, Biggie, LL Cool J, Public Enemy, and the Wu-Tang Clan as acts that showed respect to the founding fathers. "They actually look us in the eye and be like, 'Thank you, thank you guys for all the blood, sweat, and tears that you guys put into this art form, this culture,'" he says. "They say, 'I wouldn't be who I am today if it wasn't for you guys. Thank you.' That's basically all I need."[34]

Fab 5 Freddy continues to make art, displaying and selling his work at exhibitions across the country; he even starred in an Acura commercial in 2015. The spot features a woman cruising down the highway, blithely belting "Rapture"—including the classic line "Fab 5 Freddy told me everybody's fly"—and inadvertently calling Fab, who sits in a conference room with a group of puzzled executives. "They came with this idea to see if I would want to be in the commercial," says Fab. "We worked it all out...They have a *Billboard* chart for commercials and it was in the top five."[35]

At the same time, Fab's old friend Basquiat is enjoying ever-greater postmortem success. He's continually name-checked by the likes of Jay-Z, who in "Picasso Baby" compares his home—with its "Basquiat in the kitchen corner"—to the Louvre and the Tate Modern. Today the artist's works hang everywhere from France to Japan in some of the world's finest museums, just as he would have hoped. "I wanted to be a star," Basquiat explained in 1985. "Not a gallery mascot."[36]

That wish came true—and then some. In 2017, a Japanese billionaire bought Basquiat's 1982 work *Untitled* for $110.5 million, the sixth-highest total of any work ever sold at auction and the highest price paid for a piece by any American artist.[37]

In August 2016, Swizz held his second No Commission art fair, this time taking it to the borough that he, and hip-hop, calls home. The

Bacardí-backed event brought the work of artists from all over the world to the Port Morris section of the South Bronx, where their work was seen by "billionaires, millionaires, thousand-aires, zero-naires," according to Swizz, who appeared along with creative types from Kehinde Wiley to A$AP Rocky. Individual pieces sold for prices ranging from $50 to $270,000—almost $1 million in total—as thousands of onlookers participated in the extravaganza.

"I'm bringing Basel to the Bronx," Swizz tells me. "The kids that live around here, the people that live around here, should be able to see things that they might not be able to afford to get on a flight to go see."[38]

Yet Swizz still got flak from a few protesters for selecting a venue owned by Keith Rubenstein, a developer accused of trying to gentrify the borough and exoticize its heritage. Swizz scoffs at the accusations. "I'm from the Bronx. I lived twelve blocks from this place," he says. "The space was the best space that fit the event. I'm not the landlord. I don't own the property. I'm not a developer. Why are you protesting this again?"

It was a fascinating outcome of hip-hop's journey: the brainchild of the Bronx grows up, expands into the rest of New York, takes over the rest of the world, turns into a multibillion-dollar industry, and comes home to find itself so changed as to be unrecognizable to some. But Swizz took the time to hear out the activists and eventually assuaged some of their concerns, partly by agreeing to launch a fair for Bronx artists exclusively.

Overall, the feedback for No Commission was positive. Store owners in the community wrote letters to Swizz, thanking him for boosting their sales by as much as 200 percent in some cases. A$AP Rocky called the event "the greatest art fair in the world."[39] Needless to say, Swizz's new colleagues at Bacardí were quite pleased as well. "A lot of people came up to me and congratulated us for supporting it," says Bacardí chief Dolan. "It was really Swizz's instinct that, 'Hey, this is the right thing to do. This is the right place to do it.'"[40]

Swizz is quick to credit the three kings as an inspiration for himself and others to keep pushing boundaries. "They let people know that they can make it big other than [in] music," he says, growing philosophical as we wind down our interview in the cavernous cool of his in-home art gallery. "Puff is just the ultra hustler. He always had a gift."

He notes the same for Jay-Z, marveling at the mogul's vision for companies like Tidal and Roc Nation (the latter was launched as part of Jay-Z's landmark ten-year, $150 million Live Nation deal signed in 2008; in 2017, he topped himself, inking a $200 million decade-long pact with the concert giant). "We always complain about, 'We don't own this, we don't own that,'" explains Swizz. "Here he is, this man who owns *that*."

And the producer from Compton who found a way to sell speakers as though they were sneakers? "Dre did it—changed the electronic industry and headphones," says Swizz.

He smiles.

"I think that it just shows that the sky is not the limit: it's just a view," Swizz concludes, gazing upward. "There are billions of galaxies out there."[41]

Kings, Queens, Presidents, and Precedents

On May 12, 2009, Michelle and Barack Obama held an evening of spoken-word performance—and transformed the White House into a launching pad for hip-hop. That night, Lin-Manuel Miranda debuted *The Hamilton Mixtape,* which later blasted off to Broadway and circled the globe as the smash musical *Hamilton.* The Obamas would go on to host hip-hop royalty from Jay-Z to Nicki Minaj to Kendrick Lamar, becoming the sort of cultural gatekeepers America had never before seen in a first family.

"It's not even about a kid from Compton going to the White House," Lamar told me in 2017. "It's really about *Barack* letting urban kids walk inside that building."[1]

On November 9, 2016, hip-hop woke up to a different sort of White House metamorphosis. Donald Trump's upset victory over Hillary Clinton—for whom Jay-Z and Beyoncé, among other entertainment-world luminaries, had campaigned—augured the end of spoken-word evenings for at least four years. And although many of the divisive issues that have since come to the forefront of the national conversation aren't new, they had long seemed dormant to many. In any case, Trump's platform, with its calls to build walls and slash corporate taxes, was as far from the pillars of hip-hop as could be. One of his few attempts to woo black voters was the tone-deaf "Plan for Urban Renewal," which coupled a Robert Moses–esque title with proposed tax incentives aimed at luring foreign investment to "blighted American neighborhoods."[2]

Hip-hop has perhaps unsurprisingly been at the forefront of the pushback against the administration, from YG's "Fuck Donald Trump" to the more diplomatic efforts of *Hamilton*. When Mike Pence attended the musical in New York in November 2016, actor Brandon Victor Dixon read a speech collaboratively written by *Hamilton*'s creator, director, producer, and cast exhorting the vice president–elect to "uphold our American values and to work on behalf of all of us." Though Pence handled the situation with relative grace, Trump raged against the musical's "very rude" cast on Twitter and demanded an apology.[3]

"There's this rhetoric about being grateful and happy that you're getting paid for your art," said Okieriete Onaodowan, an original cast member who played President James Madison and Hercules Mulligan that night, in an interview with me a year later. "We are told to put our own stuff aside, but doesn't everyone have a job they should just shut up and do? Shouldn't the president just shut up and lead?"[4]

Hip-hop has been closely tied to Obama for a decade, but there are also connections to Trump in its past — even for the three kings. In the 1990s, Dre was one of many who paid verbal homage to him as a sort of wealth deity; Diddy and Jay-Z schmoozed with him in the Hamptons. And Trump has been rightfully slammed for some of the same things for which certain hip-hop figures have been criticized: namely, peddling overpriced junk, stiffing contractors, being a terrible role model for kids, and using language too crude for television. Perhaps most alarming are the casual boasts of sexually assaulting women, laid bare in the *Access Hollywood* tapes and underscored by a dozen or so actual accusations. Hip-hop's virtues have been diluted by a still-too-prevalent tendency to demean women; the world heard a disturbing echo of this when Russell Simmons stepped down from running his businesses in late 2017 after several allegations of sexual assault (which he, like Trump, denied).

The stories of Simmons and other disgraced legends like Afrika Bambaataa serve as an important indicator of the work that hip-hop still has left to do. As diverse and inclusive as it is in some ways, the genre historically has exhibited various types of prejudice, most notably in the form of misogyny and homophobia. And despite the contributions of women from Sylvia Robinson to Debbie Harry to Minaj, there's still a tendency to pit female stars against one another in a battle for a single seat at the table. If there are three kings, there should be room for more than one queen. As hip-hop lurches forward, its leaders need to find ways to empower those who've built their identities on the movement—even if they don't necessarily look, sound, or act like its founding fathers and most profitable practitioners.

"Hip-hop is more than a genre," twentysomething British rapper Simbiatu "Little Simz" Ajikawo, the daughter of Nigerian immigrants, told me in 2016. "It's the only time I'm one hundred percent me."[5]

To my eye—which admittedly comes with inherent limitations of lived experience—hip-hop has lately shown new signs of progress when it comes to including a more representative sampling of voices, thanks to acts from Simz to Cardi B to Frank Ocean to Young M.A. And the three kings have made various efforts to build a bigger tent. While Diddy and Dre have bankrolled schools, Jay-Z used his 2017 album, *4:44,* as a vehicle for social commentary, from pushing the thought-provoking treatise "The Story of O.J." to supporting his mother coming out as a lesbian on "Smile" to envisioning a more female-focused future in the Ava DuVernay–directed video for "Family Feud"—and tackling issues from marital transgressions to mass incarceration at the same time.

Diddy, Dr. Dre, Jay-Z, and their peers will have to continue to move in this sort of direction if hip-hop is to keep inspiring and cultivating its next generation of royalty. I, for one, am betting they will.

Zack O'Malley Greenburg
New York, January 2018

Acknowledgments

On a lazy afternoon during the summer of 2015, I was walking through my godmother's living room, trying to think of ways to frame a book proposal I'd been kicking around, when my eyes landed on a copy of Walter Isaacson's *The Innovators*. Seeing the excellent tome, which presents the history of invention through the lives of great thinkers from Ada Lovelace to Steve Jobs, flicked on a lightbulb in my head.

Hip-hop was enjoying one of its periodic high points thanks to the popularity of *Hamilton, Empire, Straight Outta Compton,* and other works. Though there had been books written about the genre, none had taken the sort of "great thinkers" approach I had in mind—a combination of history, biography, and blueprint— and I became certain that it was time for a history of the business of hip-hop told through the lens of its three most prosperous practitioners. I'm deeply grateful to my agent, William Clark, for understanding my vision; to my editor, John Parsley, for immediately grasping the idea behind this book and elegantly refining it; and to Gaby Mongelli, Phil Marino, Ben Allen, and the rest of the team at Little, Brown and Hachette Livre for seeing it through. And a big thanks to the Mosses for providing the setting for my eureka moment.

Every nonfiction book needs great sources, and I was lucky to have more than a hundred of those—too many to list here; you can see most of their names in the notes section. I'm also eternally grateful to those whose contributions aren't cited in the text but who pointed me toward helpful data, documents, and sources, especially Eric DiNicola at PrivCo, Liv Buli at Pandora, and Sue Radlauer at *Forbes*.

On that note, I owe a thank-you to my colleagues at the aforementioned business bible. Some of them helped me get my start covering the business of music, media, and entertainment (Lea Goldman, Neil Weinberg, Dan Bigman), while others gave me the flexibility that allowed me to write this book (Lewis D'Vorkin, Randall Lane, Mike Noer, Mark Coatney) while holding down a day job at a place packed with inspiring coworkers (Natalie Robehmed, Maddie Berg, Hayley Cuccinello, Paul Anderson, and many others). No mention of *Forbes* would be complete without shouting out my pals on the softball team, which will hopefully be gearing up for a successful NYMSL championship run shortly after this book goes to press.

Thanks to all the other friends who kept me sane—Vicky Schussler, Nathan Griffith, Dan Kato, Mike Seplowitz, and Emily Misch, with some help from YouTube and karaoke—and even the ones who drove me nuts (the K&B C and his commissionees). Peter Schwartz and Mike Safir made sure I got out at least once a month to enjoy myself in style; Charlie Warner and Julia Bradford kept me infused with youthful spirit. Choppy, "H," Madeline Kerner, and David Korngold were super supportive "downtown" New York neighbors, as were Daniela, Josh, and Rafa Davis across town, and Zoe Blacksin uptown.

I'm super grateful for the excellent company and generous hospitality I received in California (from Matt Lachman, Jon Bruner, Bethany Kerner, Nicole Villeneuve, and Andrew Cedotal), as well as positive vibes from other friends around the globe (Jon Bittner, Rebecca Blum, Dan Adler, Sam Allard, Mallory Hellman, Kelly Reid, Marcus Leonard, Lara Berlin, Kartikeya Singh, Aranya Berlin Singh, Ezra Markowitz, Melissa Ocana, and Avi Ray Markowitz Ocana, to name a few) and from family (the La Roccos, Pecks, O'Malleys, and Greenburgs). A special thank-you to the Seymours for their friendship (and salubrious summertime writing perch). Among early readers, Cherie Hu was instrumental in helping me fact-check this book, and I hope she remembers me once she has taken over the music industry (any day now). Nick Messitte continues to be a great friend and an invaluably incisive critic. And Fab, you are the king of crowns — your striking cover art and fantastic foreword were the perfect finishing touches for the book.

I'll always be thankful to my parents: to Suzanne O'Malley, for sending encouragement from Texas; to Dan Greenburg, for being such a fine example as a writer and a human; and to Judith Greenburg, for being the most ruthlessly wonderful — and wonderfully ruthless — first draft editor I could ask for (and then some). I so wish this book could have been read by my aunt Naomi, my cousin Andrew, and my grandparents, particularly my grandma Irma, who passed while I was writing it. (She was a late hip-hop convert: toward the end of her life she told me and my cousins that she liked Kanye's music.) Also gone far too soon: my mother-in-law, Terry Fixel, a paragon of wit and tenacity.

Last but certainly not least is my marvelous wife, Dr. Danielle La Rocco. She weathered an unbelievably shitty 2016 with her usual humor and grace, while giving great feedback on the book and sometimes also surprising me during late-night writing sessions with cheese deliveries. Danielle: There may be three kings, but you are my queen.

Giving Back

For my last book, *Michael Jackson, Inc.*, I decided I'd borrow an idea from 50 Cent — and give away a free meal to someone in need via the United Nations' World Food Programme for every book sold. (The rapper did the same for every sale of his Street King energy shot.) Though I love the idea of per-unit donations, I wanted to do something a little different for this book.

So for each hardcover copy this book sells (as determined by Nielsen BookScan), I'll donate a meal-equivalent sum to the American Civil Liberties Union Foundation. The ACLU's work is more important now than ever, as individuals around the country — and the world — are finding that their freedoms, too often taken for granted, are coming under attack.

Among the most vulnerable people are those in communities like the ones from which Diddy, Dr. Dre, and Jay-Z hail, as well as hardworking immigrants like my own ancestors (we get the job done!). For nearly one hundred years, the ACLU has been there to stand up for these populations and others, preserving the liberties guaranteed by the U.S. Constitution.

The ACLU speaks truth to power and promotes individual freedom — I can't think of anything more hip-hop than that — and I'm proud to share a portion of the proceeds from this book with such a stellar organization.

Cast of Characters

The history of hip-hop is packed with a dizzying array of characters, so I've assembled a dramatis personae to help readers make sense of the maze of names, particularly dense in the book's early chapters. I interviewed roughly 80 percent of the people listed below (and many others on background or off the record) for this book. Most are crucial to the history of hip-hop, or at least to the lives of its three kings. Some are experts in nonmusical fields whom I interviewed due to their knowledge of the sectors in which Diddy, Dre, and Jay-Z are or were involved.

Shawn "Jay-Z" Carter Rapper, multifaceted mogul, husband of Beyoncé; Brooklyn native

Sean "Diddy" Combs Performer, serial entrepreneur, beverage mogul; Harlem born, Mount Vernon raised

Andre "Dr. Dre" Young Superproducer and rapper, cofounder of Beats; born and raised in Los Angeles

Sal Abbatiello Head honcho of legendary Bronx nightclub the Disco Fever

Peter Adderton, Mike McSherry, Paul O'Neill Australian cofounders of Boost Mobile

Cast of Characters

Eric Arnold Former *Wine Spectator* editor, author of *First Big Crush*

Tarik "Cilvaringz" Azzougarh Morocco-based producer of secret Wu-Tang album

Afrika Bambaataa DJ, cofounder of hip-hop; disgraced after sex abuse allegations

Branson "Branson B" Belchie Harlem entrepreneur; hip-hop's sommelier

Michael "MC Serch" Berrin Emcee of 3rd Bass, automotive consultant

Philippe Bienvenu Employee of Cattier, the company behind Jay-Z's champagne

Briant "B-High" Biggs Jay-Z's cousin and confidant

Jean-Claude Biver Chief of high-end watchmaker Hublot, a Jay-Z favorite

Mary J. Blige Queen of hip-hop soul, early Diddy protégé

Gary Bongiovanni President and editor in chief of touring data outfit Pollstar

Richard Branson Billionaire founder of Virgin (Records, Airlines, Galactic, etc.)

Fred "Fab 5 Freddy" Brathwaite Hip-hop pioneer, artist, *Yo! MTV Raps* host

Calvin "Snoop Doggy Dogg" Broadus Seminal West Coat rapper, protégé of Dr. Dre

Rocky Bucano Bronx-born DJ, mastermind behind the Universal Hip-Hop Museum

Kareem "Biggs" Burke Roc-A-Fella Records cofounder with Jay-Z and Damon Dash

Jonathan "Jaz-O" Burks Golden age Brooklyn rapper, Marcy mentor to Jay-Z

Clive "DJ Kool Herc" Campbell DJ, cofounder of hip-hop; 1520 Sedgwick party host

Troy Carter Rap veteran, venture capitalist, Spotify exec, former manager of Lady Gaga

Cast of Characters

Darryl Cobbin Exec at Coca-Cola's Sprite, Boost Mobile, others; hip-hop evangelist

Lyor Cohen Early Def Jam employee, Run-D.M.C.'s road manager, music executive

Salvador Contes High school classmate of Jay-Z

Joe Conzo The photographer who took hip-hop's baby pictures

Tracy "D.O.C." Curry Texas-born West Coast rapper, longtime friend of Dre

Damon Dash Roc-A-Fella Records cofounder with Jay-Z and Kareem Burke

Donald David Veteran entertainment attorney, sushi aficionado

Kasseem "Swizz Beatz" Dean Artist, entrepreneur, art collector, Bacardí exec

Robert "RZA" Diggs Ringleader of the Wu-Tang Clan (and its secret album)

Mike Dolan CEO of Bacardí who hired Swizz Beatz as an executive

Brian Dunn Former CEO of Best Buy, early supporter of Beats

Lyle Fass Wine and spirits expert; entrepreneur, sneaker head

Fat Boys One of the first hip-hop groups to enjoy mainstream success; managed by Charles Stettler

Curtis "Grandmaster Caz" Fisher Pioneering Bronx emcee, uncredited ghostwriter

Rodolfo "DJ Clark Kent" Franklin Brooklyn DJ/producer, early Jay-Z booster

Dave Free Manager and longtime friend of Kendrick Lamar

David Gest Attorney who worked on 1520 Sedgwick historical registry application

Tyrese Gibson Actor, singer, and friend of Dr. Dre; near-billionaire bean spiller

Verna Griffin Dr. Dre's mom, author of *Long Road Outta Compton*

Benjamin "Macklemore" Haggerty Rapper half of duo Macklemore and Ryan Lewis

Cast of Characters

Antonio "Big Daddy Kane" Hardy Golden age rapper, booster of Jay-Z and Tupac

Andre Harrell Veteran record exec, Diddy's first boss; now works for Diddy

Jerry Heller Late manager of N.W.A.; frequent rap villain

Brent Hocking Serial spirits entrepreneur, original founder of DeLeón tequila

Jimmy Iovine Cofounder of Interscope and Beats, longtime friend of Dr. Dre

DeHaven Irby Marcy Houses alum, drug-dealing mentor and friend of Jay-Z

Curtis "50 Cent" Jackson III Rapper, entrepreneur, Vitaminwater shiller; fourth king?

O'Shea "Ice Cube" Jackson Rapper, actor, original member of N.W.A.

Nasir "Nas" Jones Rapper, venture capitalist, pal turned enemy turned pal of Jay-Z

Craig Kallman Record collector, DJ, chief executive of Atlantic Records

Marion "Suge" Knight Cofounder of Death Row; intimidator, ruiner of hip-hop fun

Beyoncé Knowles International icon, superstar singer, entrepreneur, wife of Jay-Z

Rob LaFranco Former *Forbes* reporter, Diddy whisperer

Kendrick Lamar Compton-bred millennial hip-hop star, protégé of Dr. Dre

Noel Lee Founder of Monster Cable, the company behind early Beats headphones

Chris Lighty Late manager of 50 Cent and several other hip-hop acts

Kevin Liles Former president, Def Jam; cofounder, 300 Entertainment; artist manager

Theodore "Grandwizzard Theodore" Livingston Bronx DJ, inventor of the scratch

Cast of Characters

Craig Mack "Flava in Ya Ear" rapper who got his start on Diddy's Bad Boy label

Jonathan Mannion Photographer of Jay-Z's *Reasonable Doubt* cover and much more

Christopher "DJ Premier" Martin Legendary hip-hop producer for Jay-Z and others

Marshall "Eminem" Mathers Rapper, top-selling act of 2000s, protégé of Dr. Dre

Kenny Meiselas Diddy's longtime attorney

Eddie "Scorpio" Morris Emcee, member of Grandmaster Flash and the Furious Five

Dillard Morrison Jr. Son of legendary Harlem gangster "Red" Dillard Morrison Sr.

Kevin Morrow Longtime Los Angeles concert promoter

Tracy "Ice-T" Morrow Gangsta rap pioneer, actor, record label founder

Timothy "Timbaland" Mosley Superproducer, entrepreneur, occasional rapper

Dwight "Heavy D" Myers Rapper, Mount Vernon resident, early mentor to Diddy

Jalal "Lightnin' Rod" Nuriddin Protorapper known for *Hustlers Convention* spoken-word album

Shaquille O'Neal NBA Hall of Famer, occasional rapper

Rohan Oza Marketing guru starting at Coca-Cola/Sprite; Vitaminwater mastermind

Lawrence "KRS-One" Parker Old-school rapper, activist, Bronx native

Randy Phillips CEO of concert outfit LiveStyle, former head of Live Nation rival AEG

Darnell Robinson Grandson of Sugar Hill Records founders Sylvia and Joe Robinson

Joe Robinson Cofounder of Sugar Hill Records; more than a studio gangster

Cast of Characters

Leland Robinson Son of Sugar Hill Records founders Sylvia and Joe Robinson

Sylvia Robinson Cofounder of Sugar Hill Records, architect of "Rapper's Delight"

Roberto Rogness Spirits aficionado, general manager of Santa Monica's Wine Expo

Jessica Rosenblum New York party promoter, early associate of Diddy

Stephen Rust Diageo's president of new business and reserve brands; Cîroc fan

Joseph "Grandmaster Flash" Saddler DJ, hip-hop cofounder

Kjetil Saeter and Markus Tobiassen Norwegian journalists closely following Tidal

Anthony Saleh Venture capitalist, manager of Nas

Eric Schmidt Director of Alcohol Research at Beverage Marketing Corporation

Gunnar Sellaeg Telenor executive, former CEO of Tidal parent Aspiro

Tupac Shakur Rapper, actor, poet; Death Row partisan; star gone too soon

Todd "Too Short" Shaw California hip-hop pioneer

Tom Silverman Early hip-hop aficionado, founder of Tommy Boy records

Earl "DMX" Simmons Rapper, actor, Yonkers native, pit bull enthusiast; Def Jam value booster

Russell Simmons Disgraced cofounder of Def Jam, Phat Farm; the original hip-hop entrepreneur

James "LL Cool J" Smith Early Def Jam rapper; actor, Grammy host

Kevin "Lovebug Starski" Smith Early emcee/DJ, "Rapper's Delight" inspiration

Charles Stettler Swiss-born manager of the Fat Boys; early monetizer of hip-hop

Rob Stone Cofounder, *The Fader* and Cornerstone; former EMI and Arista employee

Steve Stoute Marketing guru, Translation CEO, friend and business associate of Jay-Z

Edward "Eddie Cheeba" Sturgis DJ, contemporary of Lovebug Starski and DJ Hollywood

Sugarhill Gang Early rap group—Henry "Big Bank Hank" Jackson, Guy "Master Gee" O'Brien, and Michael "Wonder Mike" Wright—that recorded "Rapper's Delight"

Tommy "Tommy Tee" Flaaten Godfather of Scandinavian hip-hop; label owner

Sebastian Telfair Highly touted point guard who played on Jay-Z's Rucker Park team

Cameron "Wiz Khalifa" Thomaz Pittsburgh-bred rapper; marijuana enthusiast

Touré Mononymous author, journalist, thinker, hip-hop head

Kurt "Kurtis Blow" Walker First rapper to land a major label record deal

Christopher "Notorious B.I.G." Wallace Legendary lyricist, keystone Bad Boy act

Voletta Wallace Mother of Notorious B.I.G.; reluctant fan of hip-hop

D. A. Wallach Venture capitalist, musician, college acquaintance of Mark Zuckerberg

Alonzo Williams Front man of World Class Wreckin' Cru; early Dr. Dre employer

Bruce Williams Former right-hand man to Dr. Dre

Pharrell Williams Hip-hop star, producer, fashionista; *Star Trek* enthusiast

Chenise Wilson Goddaughter of Branson Belchie, early associate of Diddy

Eric "Eazy-E" Wright Founding member of N.W.A.; chief of Ruthless Records

Cast of Characters

Wu-Tang Clan Seminal Staten Island hip-hip group; secret-album purveyor

Walter Yetnikoff Longtime head of CBS Records; music industry character; agent of music video desegregation

Ilan Zechory Cofounder of Genius, the "Internet Talmud" first known as Rap Genius

Notes

This book contains insights culled from over one hundred personal interviews, augmented on occasion by secondary reference material. The bulk of the information I've gathered comes directly from primary sources (including the three kings, though Diddy, Dre, and Jay-Z didn't grant me new interviews for this book); the vast majority of information was gleaned through original interviews that I conducted from 2015 to 2017 with those most familiar with the rise of the titular trio and hip-hop itself. Here's a chapter-by-chapter accounting of the origins of the details packed into *Three Kings*.

Introduction

1. Dr. Dre and Tyrese Gibson, self-recorded video, location unknown, May 2014.
2. Author's note: Diddy would be Michelangelo, Dre would be Donatello, Jay-Z would be Raphael.
3. Diddy, interview by author, Austin, Texas, March 2014.
4. Fab 5 Freddy, electronic message to author, February 2017.
5. Russell Simmons, interview by author, New York, New York, April 2016.
6. Craig Kallman, interview by author, New York, New York, January 2016.
7. Noel Lee, interview by author, New York, New York, May 2016.
8. Richard Branson, interview by author, New York, New York, September 2011.
9. Stephen Rust, telephone interview by author, January 2017.
10. Jay-Z, conversation with author, Philadelphia, Pennsylvania, September 2012. Author's note: This quote was originally published in my story "Jay-Z's Review of the Book I Wrote About Him," *Forbes,* September 6, 2012, http://www.forbes.com/sites/zackomalleygreenburg/2012/09/06/jay-zs-review-of-the-book-i-wrote-about-him/.

Notes

11. Diddy, interview by author, Austin, Texas, March 2014.
12. Author's note: I discovered Dre's NDA habit while seeking interviews for this book.
13. Grandwizzard Theodore, interview by author, Bronx, New York, August 2016.
14. Grandmaster Caz, interview by author, Bronx, New York, August 2016.
15. Troy Carter, interview by author, Los Angeles, California, November 2015.
16. Jay-Z, interview with Steve Forbes and Warren Buffett, September 2010. Transcript: http://www.forbes.com/forbes/2010/1011/rich-list-10-omaha-warren-buffett -jay-z-steve-forbes-summit-interview.html.
17. Tommy Tee, interview by author, Oslo, Norway, January 2017.
18. Kevin Liles, interview by author, New York, New York, October 2015.
19. Rob Stone, interview by author, New York, New York, November 2015.

Chapter I: The Originators

1. Lovebug Starski, interview by author, New York, New York, January 2016.
2. Lightnin' Rod, telephone conversation with author, August 2016.
3. Lovebug Starski, interview by author, New York, New York, January 2016.
4. Author's note: Shea Stadium was torn down several decades later to make room for a Citi Field parking lot.
5. Robert Caro, *The Power Broker,* Random House, New York (1974), p. 6.
6. District Six Museum, visit by author, Cape Town, South Africa, September 2016.
7. Robert Caro, *The Power Broker,* Random House, New York (1974), p. 20.
8. Jeff Chang, *Can't Stop Won't Stop,* Picador, New York (2005), pp. 72–76.
9. Tom Silverman, interview by author, New York, New York, October 2015.
10. David Gest, telephone interview by author, January 2017.
11. Disaster Center via FBI UCS Annual Crime Reports, "New York Crime Rates 1960–2015," http://www.disastercenter.com/crime/nycrime.htm.
12. Grandmaster Caz, interview by author, Bronx, New York, August 2016.
13. Afrika Bambaataa, interview by author, New York, New York, June 2009.
14. Dan Rys, "Afrika Bambaataa Sexual Abuse Allegations," *Billboard,* May 10, 2016, http://www.billboard.com/articles/columns/hip-hop/7364592/afrika-bambaataa -abuse-allegations.
15. Grandwizzard Theodore, interview by author, Bronx, New York, August 2016.
16. Grandmaster Caz, interview by author, Bronx, New York, August 2016.
17. Tom Silverman, interview by author, New York, New York, October 2015.
18. Grandwizzard Theodore, interview by author, Bronx, New York, August 2016.

Notes

19. Branson Belchie, interview by author, New York, New York, October 2015.

20. Jayson Rodriguez, "Real 'American Gangster' Frank Lucas Talks About Hanging with Diddy's Dad," MTV News, November 6, 2007, http://www.mtv.com/news/1573648/real-american-gangster-frank-lucas-talks-about-hanging-with-diddys-dad-possible-sequel/.

21. Diddy, "Confessions," Revolt TV, October 2013, https://www.youtube.com/watch?v=S9HNZwUiuM8.

22. Dillard Morrison Jr., interview by author, New York, New York, October 2015.

23. Diddy, interview by author, Austin, Texas, March 2014.

24. Ibid.

25. Dan Charnas, *The Big Payback,* New American Library, New York (2010), p. 459.

26. Diddy, interview by author, Austin, Texas, March 2014.

27. Lovebug Starski, interview by author, New York, New York, January 2016.

28. Michael Wilson, "Relics of the Bygone (and the Illegal)," *New York Times,* March 22, 2013, http://www.nytimes.com/2013/03/23/nyregion/numbers-runner-a-rarity-is-arrested-in-harlem.html.

29. Tom Silverman, interview by author, New York, New York, October 2015.

30. Grandmaster Caz, interview by author, Bronx, New York, August 2016.

31. Lovebug Starski, interview by author, New York, New York, January 2016.

32. Leland Robinson, interview by author, Edgewater, New Jersey, November 2015.

33. Darnell Robinson, interview by author, Edgewater, New Jersey, November 2015.

34. Lovebug Starski, interview by author, New York, New York, January 2016.

35. Leland Robinson, interview by author, Edgewater, New Jersey, November 2015.

36. Lovebug Starski, interview by author, New York, New York, January 2016.

37. Sean Michaels, "Sylvia Robinson, 'Mother of Hip-Hop,' Dies Aged Seventy-Five," *The Guardian,* September 30, 2011, http://www.theguardian.com/music/2011/sep/30/sylvia-robinson-dies-aged-76.

38. Grandmaster Caz, interview by author, Bronx, New York, August 2016.

39. Lovebug Starski, interview by author, New York, New York, January 2016.

40. Nelson George, *The Death of Rhythm and Blues,* Pantheon Books (1988), p. 191.

41. Leland Robinson, interview by author, Edgewater, New Jersey, November 2015.

42. Grandmaster Caz, interview by author, Bronx, New York, August 2016.

43. Lovebug Starski, interview by author, New York, New York, January 2016.

44. Jay-Z, *Decoded,* Spiegel and Grau, New York (2010), p. 4.

Notes

45. Michael D'Antonio, *Forever Blue*, Riverhead Books, New York (2009), pp. 239–240.

46. Demographia, "City of New York and Boroughs: Population and Population Density from 1790," http://www.demographia.com/dm-nyc.htm.

47. Michael D'Antonio, *Forever Blue*, Riverhead Books, New York (2009), p. 137.

48. Jay-Z, *Decoded*, Spiegel and Grau, New York (2010), p. 13.

49. DJ Clark Kent, interview by author, Brooklyn, New York, January 2010.

50. B-High, interview for Jay-Z retrospective *RD 20*, Tidal, June 2016.

51. Jay-Z, interview with Steve Forbes and Warren Buffett, September 2010. Transcript: http://www.forbes.com/forbes/2010/1011/rich-list-10-omaha-warren-buffett-jay-z-steve-forbes-summit-interview.html.

52. Jonathan "Jaz-O" Burks, telephone interview by author, May 2010.

53. Sal Abbatiello, interview by author, Scarsdale, New York, January 2016.

54. Author's note: Starski says he was rapping with Cowboy, one of the wordsmiths of Grandmaster Flash and the Furious Five, when he first developed the term "hip-hop."

55. Sal Abbatiello, interview by author, Scarsdale, New York, January 2016.

56. Russell Simmons, interview by author, New York, New York, April 2016.

57. Verna Griffin, *Long Road Outta Compton*, Da Capo Press, Philadelphia (2008), pp. 47–49.

58. Thomas Pynchon, *The Crying of Lot 49*, Bantam Books, New York (1966), p. 12.

59. Douglas S. Massey and Nancy A. Denton, *American Apartheid: Segregation and the Making of the Underclass*, Harvard University Press, Cambridge, Massachusetts (1993), p. 54.

60. Mike Davis, *City of Quartz*, Verso, London (1990), pp. 161–162.

61. Ibid., p. 7.

62. Dr. Dre, "Intro," *Compton*, Aftermath/Interscope Records, August 7, 2015.

63. Alonzo Williams, telephone interview by author, January 2016.

64. Verna Griffin, *Long Road Outta Compton*, Da Capo Press, Philadelphia (2008), pp. 111, 116.

65. Ibid., pp. 125–127.

66. Alonzo Williams, telephone interview by author, January 2016.

67. *Rolling Stone* staff, "N.W.A. Tell All," *Rolling Stone*, August 12, 2015, http://www.rollingstone.com/music/news/n-w-a-tell-all-inside-the-original-gangstas-rolling-stone-cover-story-20150812.

68. Verna Griffin, *Long Road Outta Compton*, Da Capo Press, Philadelphia (2008), p. 131.

69. Lovebug Starski, interview by author, New York, New York, January 2016.

70. DJ Kool Herc and Lovebug Starski, telephone conversation observed by author, New York, New York, January 2016.

71. Lovebug Starski, interview by author, New York, New York, January 2016.

Chapter 2: Writing on the Wall

1. Fab 5 Freddy, interview by author, New York, New York, January 2016.

2. Joe Conzo, interview by author, New York, New York, January 2016.

3. Fab 5 Freddy, interview by author, New York, New York, January 2016.

4. Author's note: Debbie Harry actually flipped Fab's original nickname, but he didn't mind. "It was Fred Fab 5, then Debbie called me Fab 5 Freddy [in "Rapture"]," he told me. "I decided, wow, you know, I'm going to rock with that."

5. Fab 5 Freddy, interview by author, New York, New York, January 2016.

6. Vincent Canby, "*Wild Style,* Rapping, and Painting Graffiti," *New York Times,* March 18, 1983, http://www.nytimes.com/movie/review?res=9C0DE0DA103 BF93BA25750C0A965948260.

7. Russell Simmons, interview by author, New York, New York, April 2016.

8. Ibid.

9. Tom Silverman, interview by author, New York, New York, October 2015.

10. Scorpio, telephone interview by author, November 2015.

11. Leland Robinson, interview by author, Edgewater, New Jersey, November 2015.

12. Scorpio, telephone interview by author, November 2015.

13. Harry Allen, "Time Bomb," *Vibe,* December 1994, pp. 71–72.

14. Fab 5 Freddy, electronic message to author, January 2017.

15. Nelson George, *Hip-Hop America,* Penguin Books, New York (1998), p. 40.

16. Jay-Z, *Decoded,* Spiegel and Grau, New York (2010), p. 12.

17. Jaz-O, telephone interview by author, May 2010.

18. DeHaven Irby, interview by author, Brooklyn, New York, January 2010.

19. Jay-Z, *Decoded,* Spiegel and Grau, New York (2010), p. 15.

20. Jaz-O, telephone interview by author, May 2010.

21. MC Serch, telephone interview by author, December 2009.

22. Jaz-O, telephone interview by author, May 2010.

23. Jay-Z, *Decoded,* Spiegel and Grau, New York (2010), p. 18.

24. Charles Stettler, interview by author, New York, New York, November 2015.

25. Russell Simmons, interview by author, New York, New York, April 2016.

26. Charles Stettler, interview by author, New York, New York, November 2015.

27. Alonzo Williams, telephone interview by author, January 2016.

28. Author's note: While performing with the Cru, Dre occasionally donned a white sequined doctor's outfit. I am told that real doctors don't do this.

Notes

29. Alonzo Williams, telephone interview by author, January 2016.

30. Jerry Heller, *Ruthless,* Simon Spotlight Entertainment, New York (2006), p. 55.

31. Alonzo Williams, telephone interview by author, January 2016.

32. Jerry Heller, *Ruthless,* Simon Spotlight Entertainment, New York (2006), p. 75.

33. Ibid., pp. 104–106.

34. Kendrick Lamar, "Return of the Riot Squad," *Billboard,* August 22, 2015.

35. *Newsweek* staff, "Number One with a Bullet," *Newsweek,* June 30, 1991, http://www.newsweek.com/number-one-bullet-204074.

36. Jonathan Gold, "Rolling in Compton with Snoop and Dre," republished in *Rolling Stone,* October 29, 2010, http://www.rollingstone.com/music/news/rolling-in-compton-with-snoop-and-dre-20101029.

37. Ben Westhoff, *Original Gangstas,* Hachette Books, New York (2016), p. 86.

38. Frank Owen, "Hanging Tough," *Spin,* April 1990, p, 32.

39. Ronald J. Ostrow, "Casual Drug Users Should Be Shot, Gates Says," *Los Angeles Times,* September 6, 1990, http://articles.latimes.com/1990-09-06/news/mn-983_1_casual-drug-users.

40. Milt Ahlerich, FBI letter to Priority Records, August 1, 1989.

41. Julie Hinds, "The Famous 1989 Detroit Concert by N.W.A., Then and Now," *Detroit Free Press,* August 13, 2015, http://www.freep.com/story/entertainment/movies/2015/08/13/straight-outta-compton-movie-detroit-ice-cube-joe-louis-arena/31496317/.

42. Steve Hochman, "Compton Rappers Versus the Letter of the Law," *Los Angeles Times,* October 5, 1989, http://articles.latimes.com/1989-10-05/entertainment/ca-1046_1_law-enforcement/.

43. Frank Owen, "Hanging Tough," *Spin,* April 1990, p. 32.

44. Alonzo Williams, telephone interview by author, January 2016.

45. Rob Stone, interview by author, New York, New York, November 2015.

46. Russell Simmons, electronic message to author, July 2013.

47. Russell Simmons, interview by author, New York, New York, April 2016.

48. Ibid.

49. Author's note: "LL Cool J" is short for "Ladies love cool James," which is a lot cooler than his real name: James Todd Smith.

50. MC Serch, interview by author, New York, New York, November 2015.

51. Tom Silverman, interview by author, New York, New York, October 2015.

52. MC Serch, interview by author, New York, New York, November 2015.

53. Walter Yetnikoff, interview by author, New York, New York, March 2013.

54. Dr. Dre, interview with Fab 5 Freddy, *Yo! MTV Raps,* 1991, https://youtu.be/aRDBBO1Z4g0?list=PLiy6fM6jYdYHVXo76SuXVQFcfKT6TaZ_B.

55. Fab 5 Freddy, interview by author, Brooklyn, New York, January 2013; electronic message to author, February 2017.

56. MC Serch, interview by author, New York, New York, November 2015.

57. Diddy, interview by author, Austin, Texas, March 2014.

58. Chenise Wilson, interview by author, New York, New York, October 2015.

59. Jessica Rosenblum, interview by author, New York, New York, April 2016.

60. Author's note: For a party promoter, going to clubs probably still counts as work, depending on how "freaky" they are.

61. Jessica Rosenblum, interview by author, New York, New York, April 2016.

62. Scott Poulson-Bryant, "Puff Daddy," *Vibe,* February 1993, p. 90.

63. Jessica Rosenblum, interview by author, New York, New York, April 2016.

64. Fab 5 Freddy, interview by author, New York, New York, January 2016.

Chapter 3: Bad Boys

1. Branson Belchie, interview by author, New York, New York, October 2015.

2. Kenny Meiselas, interview by author, New York, New York, November 2016.

3. Mary J. Blige, monologue at concert observed by author, Brooklyn, New York, May 2016.

4. Kenny Meiselas, interview by author, New York, New York, November 2016.

5. Jessica Rosenblum, interview by author, New York, New York, April 2016.

6. Chenise Wilson, interview by author, New York, New York, October 2015.

7. Robert D. McFadden, "Stampede at City College," *New York Times,* December 30, 1991, http://www.nytimes.com/1991/12/30/nyregion/stampede-at-city -college-inquiries-begin-over-city-college-deaths.html.

8. Chenise Wilson, interview by author, New York, New York, October 2015.

9. Fab 5 Freddy, interview by author, New York, New York, January 2016.

10. DJ Clark Kent, interview by author, Brooklyn, New York, January 2010.

11. Branson Belchie, interview by author, New York, New York, October 2015.

12. Too Short, interview by author, Los Angeles, California, December 2016.

13. Chenise Wilson, interview by author, New York, New York, October 2015.

14. MC Serch, interview by author, New York, New York, November 2015.

15. Lucas G., "The Complete List of Platinum Hip-Hop Albums by Year," DJ Booth, October 20, 2015, http://djbooth.net/news/entry/2015-10-20-platinum-hip-hop -albums-year-breakdown.

16. Dan Charnas, *The Big Payback,* New American Library, New York (2010), p. 558.

17. Gary Bongiovanni, telephone interview by author, October 2015.

18. Kevin Morrow, telephone interview by author, October 2015.

19. Milton Mollen, "A Failure of Responsibility," report to Mayor David N. Dinkins on the December 28, 1991, tragedy at City College of New York, January 1992.

20. John Sullivan, "Rap Producer Testifies on Fatal Stampede at City College," *New York Times,* March 24, 1998, http://www.nytimes.com/1998/03/24/nyregion/rap-producer-testifies-on-fatal-stampede-at-city-college.html.

21. Kenny Meiselas, interview by author, New York, New York, November 2016.

22. Diddy, monologue at concert observed by author, Brooklyn, New York, May 2016.

23. Kenny Meiselas, interview by author, New York, New York, November 2016.

24. Rob Stone, interview by author, New York, New York, November 2015.

25. Branson Belchie, interview by author, New York, New York, October 2015.

26. Stephen Holden, "*Billboard*'s New Charts Roil the Record Industry," *New York Times,* June 22, 1991, http://www.nytimes.com/1991/06/22/arts/billboard-s-new-charts-roil-the-record-industry.html.

27. Jerry Heller, *Ruthless,* Simon Spotlight Entertainment, New York (2006), p. 23.

28. Verna Griffin, *Long Road Outta Compton,* Da Capo Press, Philadelphia (2008), p. 161.

29. Jeff Rosenthal, "Suge Knight's Run-ins with the Law: A Timeline," February 5, 2015, *Vulture,* http://www.vulture.com/2015/02/suge-knights-run-ins-with-the-law-a-timeline.html.

30. Jerry Heller, *Ruthless,* Simon Spotlight Entertainment, New York (2006), p. 16.

31. Electronic message from author to Knight's attorney Thaddeus Culpepper, October 30, 2016; phone message left by author for Knight's attorney Stephen Schwartz, November 1, 2016.

32. Amanda Silverman, electronic message to author, September 2016.

33. VH1, "Dr. Dre," *Behind the Music,* November 21, 1999.

34. Natalie Weiner, "Dee Barnes, Michel'le Respond to Dr. Dre's Apology for Beating Women," *Billboard,* August 25, 2015, http://www.billboard.com/articles/columns/the-juice/6677544/dr-dre-apology-dee-barnes-michelle.

35. Dr. Dre and Death Row, agreement with Interscope, Los Angeles, California, November 1, 1992.

36. Ben Westhoff, *Original Gangstas,* Hachette Books, New York (2016), pp. 188–194, 229.

37. David Fricke, "Jimmy Iovine: The Man with the Magic Ears," *Rolling Stone,* April 12, 2012, http://www.rollingstone.com/music/news/jimmy-iovine-the-man-with-the-magic-ears-20120412.

38. Ibid.

Notes

39. Jonathan Gold, "The Rap's Flat, but Ya Can't Beat the Beat," *Los Angeles Times,* December 27, 1992, http://articles.latimes.com/1992-12-27/entertainment/ca-4829_1_dirty-beats.

40. Fab 5 Freddy, interview by author, New York, New York, March 2011.

41. Robert Hilburn, "The Dr.'s Always In," *Los Angeles Times,* September 23, 2007, http://www.latimes.com/local/la-me-dre23sep23-story.html.

42. Fab 5 Freddy, interview by author, New York, New York, March 2011.

43. Author's note: If you had to name one album that bridged the gap between 1980s old-school hip-hop and its glossier late-1990s cousin, 1993's *Doggystyle* might be it. For example, in "Lodi Dodi," Snoop and Dre essentially cover Slick Rick and Doug E. Fresh's 1985 song "La Di Da Di," including the line "Ricky Ricky Ricky, can't you see, somehow your words just hypnotize me," which became the underpinning for the Diddy-helmed 1997 hit "Hypnotize" by Notorious B.I.G. *Doggystyle* is also a sampling nexus of the three kings: in addition to the aforementioned Diddy pick, Jay-Z borrowed Snoop's line "He is I, and I am him" from "Who Am I?" and inserted it into his 2001 track "Jigga That Nigga." Dre, meanwhile, sampled himself sampling George Clinton when he put the "Atomic Dog" bass line he used in "Who Am I?" into Tupac's 1996 smash "Can't C Me."

44. Fab 5 Freddy, interview by author, New York, New York, March 2011.

45. Kenny Meiselas, telephone conversation with author, February 2017.

46. Author's note: In this case, "shotty" means "shotgun." Biggie is the only person I know of who kept one by his toilet.

47. Kenny Meiselas, interview by author, New York, New York, November 2016.

48. Rob Stone, interview by author, New York, New York, November 2015.

49. Kenny Meiselas, interview by author, New York, New York, November 2016.

50. Craigh Barboza, "'Ain't Nothing Shine Brighter Than That Bad Boy': The Inside Story of Hip-Hop's Most Notorious Label," *GQ,* September 8, 2014, http://www.gq.com/entertainment/celebrities/201409/bad-boy-hip-hop.

51. Tom Silverman, interview by author, New York, New York, October 2015.

52. Afrika Bambaataa, interview by author, New York, New York, June 2009.

53. Chenise Wilson, interview by author, New York, New York, October 2015.

54. Ibid.

55. Jonathan Mannion, interview by author, New York, New York, February 2016.

56. DJ Clark Kent, interview by author, Brooklyn, New York, January 2010.

57. MC Serch, telephone interview by author, December 2009.

58. MC Serch, electronic message to author, August 2010.

59. Touré, telephone interview by author, December 2009.
60. Jessica Rosenblum, interview by author, New York, New York, April 2016.
61. Branson Belchie, interview by author, New York, New York, October 2015.

Chapter 4: Studio Gangsters

1. Voletta Wallace, interview by author, Stroudsburg, Pennsylvania, August 2016.
2. Jerry Heller, *Ruthless,* Simon Spotlight Entertainment, New York (2006), p. 50.
3. Rachael Levy, "Former Coaches Portray Knight in Positive Light," *Las Vegas Sun,* September 10, 1996, https://lasvegussun.com/news/1996/sep/10/former-coaches -portray-knight-in-positive-light/.
4. Donald David, interview by author, New York, New York, January 2016.
5. Voletta Wallace, interview by author, Stroudsburg, Pennsylvania, August 2016.
6. Verna Griffin, *Long Road Outta Compton,* Da Capo Press, Philadelphia (2008), p. 165.
7. Jerry Heller, *Ruthless,* Simon Spotlight Entertainment, New York (2006), p. 125.
8. VH1, "Dr. Dre," *Behind the Music,* November 21, 1999.
9. Rob Stone, interview by author, New York, New York, November 2015.
10. Brian Ross, "When Suge Knight Left Vanilla Ice 'Very Scared,'" ABC News, November 6, 1996.
11. Rob Stone, interview by author, New York, New York, November 2015.
12. Emil Wilbekin, "The Return of the Uptown Girl," *Vibe,* February 1995, p. 42.
13. Chenise Wilson, interview by author, New York, New York, October 2015.
14. Suge Knight, acceptance speech at *Source* Awards, August 3, 1995.
15. Rob Stone, interview by author, New York, New York, November 2015.
16. Erik Barnouw, *The Golden Web: A History of Broadcasting in the United States: Volume II — 1933 to 1953,* New York: Oxford University Press, 1968.
17. Kenny Meiselas, interview by author, New York, New York, November 2016.
18. Diddy, interview on "The Breakfast Club," May 20, 2016, https://www.you tube.com/watch?v=XnwoaAD1x4A.
19. Michael Daly, "Improbable Bond," the Daily Beast, July 29, 2014, http://www .thedailybeast.com/articles/2014/07/28/tupac-shakur-s-race-killer-prison-pal -talks.html.
20. Bruce Williams, *Rollin' with Dre,* Ballantine Books, New York (2008), p. 51.
21. Jeff Weiss, interview by author, Los Angeles, California, February 2017.
22. Donald David, interview by author, New York, New York, January 2016.
23. Tayannah Lee McQuillar and Fred L. Johnson, *Tupac Shakur: The Life and Times of an American Icon,* Da Capo Press, Cambridge, Massachusetts (2010), pp. 33–34.

24. Jeff Weiss, interview by author, Los Angeles, California, February 2017.

25. Jessica Rosenblum, interview by author, New York, New York, April 2016.

26. Fab 5 Freddy, interview by author, New York, New York, March 2011.

27. Voletta Wallace, interview by author, Stroudsburg, Pennsylvania, August 2016.

28. Salvador Contes, telephone interview by author, December 2009.

29. Voletta Wallace, interview by author, Stroudsburg, Pennsylvania, August 2016.

30. Jeff Weiss and Evan McGarvey, *2pac vs. Biggie,* Voyageur Press, Minneapolis (2013), pp. 119–120.

31. Jessica Rosenblum, interview by author, New York, New York, April 2016.

32. Bruce Williams, *Rollin' with Dre,* Ballantine Books, New York (2008), pp. 60–63.

33. Author's note: Tupac insisted that "THUG LIFE" was an acronym for "the hate U give little infants fucks everyone."

34. Lawrence Crook III, "Tupac's Hummer Sells for More Than $300K," CNN, May 20, 2016, http://www.cnn.com/2016/05/20/entertainment/tupac-shakur-hummer -auction/.

35. *Vibe* staff, "Biggie and Puffy Break Their Silence," *Vibe,* September 1996, http://www.vibe.com/2012/03/biggie-puffy-break-their-silence-95-vibe-cover -story/.

36. Kevin Morrow, telephone interview by author, October 2015.

37. Fab 5 Freddy, interview by author, New York, New York, March 2011.

38. Ben Westhoff, *Original Gangstas,* Hachette Books, New York (2016), p. 313.

39. Brian Hiatt, "Fourteen Things We Learned About *Straight Outta Compton,*" *Rolling Stone,* August 13, 2015, http://www.rollingstone.com/music/news/14-things-we -learned-about-straight-outta-compton-20150813.

40. Fab 5 Freddy, interview by author, New York, New York, March 2011.

41. Author's note: Dre picked a spectacularly foolish way to get arrested. As he recalled in VH1's *Behind the Music,* he decided to test out his new $190,000 Ferrari Testarossa — by driving it, drunk, 140 miles per hour down Wilshire Boulevard. "Next thing I know," he said, "I'm surrounded."

42. Ekow Eshun, "The Rap Trap," *The Guardian,* May 26, 2000, https://www.the guardian.com/theguardian/2000/may/27/weekend7.weekend8.

43. Ben Westhoff, *Original Gangstas,* Hachette Books, New York (2016), p. 281.

44. Bruce Williams, *Rollin' with Dre,* Ballantine Books, New York (2008), pp. 66–67.

45. Leland Robinson, interview by author, Edgewater, New Jersey, November 2015.

46. Tom Silverman, interview by author, New York, New York, October 2015.

47. Ibid.

Notes

. Mark Landler, "Time Warner Seeks to Sell Stake in Gangsta Rap Label," *New York Times,* August 10, 1995, http://www.nytimes.com/1995/08/10/business/time-warner-seeks-to-sell-stake-in-gangsta-rap-label.html.

49. Bruce Williams, *Rollin' with Dre,* Ballantine Books, New York (2008), pp. 90–91.

50. Jeff Weiss, interview by author, Los Angeles, California, February 2017.

51. Ibid.

52. Author's note: The murders of Biggie and Tupac are no closer to being solved than they were twenty years ago. And with many of the key players now dead—including detective Russell Poole and suspect Orlando Anderson—there's little reason to suspect that anything will change.

53. Devon Maloney, "Meet the 'Real' Cookie Lyon," *Vanity Fair,* December 3, 2015, http://www.vanityfair.com/hollywood/2015/12/lydia-harris-death-row-cookie-lyon.

54. Orange County Register staff, "Electric Chair Is Hot Item at Death Row Records Auction," *Orange County Register,* January 25, 2009, http://www.ocregister.com/articles/death-124187-row-auction.html.

55. Jeff Rosenthal, "Suge Knight's Run-ins with the Law: A Timeline," February 5, 2015, *Vulture,* http://www.vulture.com/2015/02/suge-knights-run-ins-with-the-law-a-timeline.html.

56. Fab 5 Freddy, interview by author, New York, New York, January 2016.

57. Too Short, interview by author, Los Angeles, California, December 2016.

58. Voletta Wallace, interview by author, Stroudsburg, Pennsylvania, August 2016.

Chapter 5: Aftermath

1. Diddy, telephone interview by author, June 2013. Author's note: This quote was originally published in my story "Diddy Talks Cable Deal; Will It Make Him a Billionaire?," *Forbes,* June 20, 2013, http://www.forbes.com/sites/zackomalleygreenburg/2013/06/20/diddy-talks-cable-deal-will-it-make-him-a-billionaire/.

2. Diddy, interview by author, Austin, Texas, March 2014.

3. Kenny Meiselas, interview by author, New York, New York, November 2016.

4. RIAA staff, "No Way Out," RIAA searchable database, http://www.riaa.com/gold-platinum/.

5. Jon Pareles, "The Rap Tao of Success by Age Twenty-Six," *New York Times,* December 3, 1997, http://www.nytimes.com/1997/12/03/arts/pop-review-the-rap-tao-of-success-by-age-26.html.

6. Tom Sinclair, "I'll Be Missing You," *Entertainment Weekly,* May 30, 1997, http://www.ew.com/article/1997/05/30/ill-be-missing-you.

Notes

7. Voletta Wallace, interview by author, Stroudsburg, Pennsylvania, August 2016.

8. Rob Stone, interview by author, New York, New York, November 2015.

9. Shea Serrano, *The Rap Year Book,* Abrams Image, New York (2015), p. 128.

10. Rob LaFranco, "I Ain't Foolin' Around, I'm Building Assets," *Forbes,* March 22, 1999, https://www.forbes.com/forbes/1999/0322/6306180a.html.

11. Monique P. Yazigi, "A Night Out with: Puffy; Gettin' Jiggy wit the Jet Set," *New York Times,* August 23, 1998, http://www.nytimes.com/1998/08/23/style/a-night-out-with-puffy-gettin-jiggy-wit-the-jet-set.html.

12. Jessica Rosenblum, interview by author, New York, New York, April 2016.

13. Rob Stone, interview by author, New York, New York, November 2015.

14. Jessica Rosenblum, interview by author, New York, New York, April 2016.

15. Russell Simmons, interview by author, New York, New York, April 2016.

16. Teddy Riley, telephone conversation with author, July 2013.

17. Rob Stone, interview by author, New York, New York, November 2015.

18. Robert Hilburn, "The Dr.'s Always In," *Los Angeles Times,* September 23, 2007, http://www.latimes.com/local/la-me-dre23sep23-story.html.

19. Author's note: Eighteen times, if you include the one mention of "Shady" without "Slim" in front of it.

20. Bruce Williams, *Rollin' with Dre,* Ballantine Books, New York (2008), p. 95.

21. Rob LaFranco, interview by author, New York, New York, November 2015.

22. Rob LaFranco, "I Ain't Foolin' Around, I'm Building Assets," *Forbes,* March 22, 1999, https://www.forbes.com/forbes/1999/0322/6306180a.html.

23. Rob LaFranco, interview by author, New York, New York, November 2015.

24. B-High, interview for Jay-Z retrospective *RD 20,* Tidal, June 2016.

25. Jonathan Mannion, interview by author, New York, New York, February 2016.

26. Dan Charnas, *The Big Payback,* New American Library, New York (2010), p. 574.

27. Russell Simmons, interview by author, New York, New York, April 2016.

28. Dan Charnas, *The Big Payback,* New American Library, New York (2010), pp. 574–578.

29. Russell Simmons, interview by author, New York, New York, April 2016.

30. Craigh Barboza, "'Ain't Nothing Shine Brighter Than That Bad Boy': The Inside Story of Hip-Hop's Most Notorious Label," *GQ,* September 8, 2014, http://www.gq.com/entertainment/celebrities/201409/bad-boy-hip-hop.

31. Monte Williams, "Arrest Is Not First for Puffy Combs," *New York Times,* December 28, 1999, http://www.nytimes.com/1999/12/28/nyregion/arrest-is-not-first-for-puffy-combs.html.

32. RIAA staff, "Forever," RIAA searchable database, http://www.riaa.com/gold -platinum/.

33. Chris Yuscavage, "The Fifty Worst Rap Album Fails," *Complex,* August 25, 2011, http://www.complex.com/music/2011/08/the-50-worst-rap-album-fails3/.

34. Paul Lieberman, " 'Puff Daddy' Combs Arrested in NY," *Los Angeles Times,* December 28, 1999, http://articles.latimes.com/1999/dec/28/news/mn-48379.

35. *Billboard* staff, "New York Jury Finds 'Puff Daddy' Not Guilty," March 19, 2001, http://www.billboard.com/articles/news/80330/new-york-jury-finds-puff -daddy-not-guilty.

36. *Vogue* staff, "They Call It Puffy Love," *Vogue,* June 29, 2001, http://www .vogue.co.uk/news/2001/06/29/they-call-it-puffy-love.

37. Chenise Wilson, interview by author, New York, New York, October 2015.

38. Katherine E. Finkelstein, "Gun or No Gun, a Rap Empire Is Reeling," *New York Times,* March 12, 2001, http://www.nytimes.com/2001/03/12/nyregion/ gun-no-gun-rap-empire-reeling-even-if-combs-acquitted-lawsuits-other -fallout.html.

39. Diddy, telephone interview by author, January 2015.

40. Diddy, interview by author, Austin, Texas, March 2014.

Chapter 6: Fashion Fortunes

1. Russell Simmons, interview by author, New York, New York, April 2016.

2. Ian Fisher, "Phat City," *New York Times,* April 4, 1993, http://www.nytimes .com/1993/04/04/style/phat-city.html.

3. Russell Simmons, interview by author, New York, New York, April 2016.

4. Suzanne Rostler, "Forty Under Forty: Class of 1995," *Crain's,* October 12, 2012, http://www.crainsnewyork.com/40under40/1995/Khezrie.

5. Russell Simmons, interview by author, New York, New York, April 2016.

6. Jay-Z, *Decoded,* Spiegel and Grau, New York (2010), pp. 79–83.

7. Russell Simmons, interview by author, New York, New York, April 2016.

8. Author's note: This may have been true, but Jay-Z's eventual wife, Beyoncé, was a sheltered starlet from suburban Houston.

9. Barbara Ross, "Jay-Z Admits Guilt," *New York Daily News,* October 18, 2001, http://www.nydailynews.com/archives/news/jay-z-admits-guilt-years-probation -99-stabbing-article-1.925230.

10. Jay-Z, *Decoded,* Spiegel and Grau, New York (2010), pp. 110–111.

11. Dan Charnas, *The Big Payback,* New American Library, New York (2010), p. 592.

12. Kenny Meiselas, interview by author, New York, New York, November 2016.

Notes

13. Robin Givhan, "They Laughed When Diddy Launched a Fashion Line. Then He Changed the Industry," *Washington Post,* April 21, 2016, http://www.wash ingtonpost.com/sf/style/2016/04/21/they-laughed-when-diddy-launched -a-fashion-line-then-he-changed-the-industry/.

14. Ibid.

15. Kenny Meiselas, interview by author, New York, New York, November 2016.

16. Teri Agins, "Sean 'P. Diddy' Combs Sells Stake in Clothing Brand to Yucaipa Co.," *Wall Street Journal,* September 16, 2003, http://www.wsj.com/articles/ SB106366610215685300.

17. Kenny Meiselas, telephone interview by author, February 2017.

18. Too Short, interview by author, Los Angeles, California, December 2016.

19. Verna Griffin, *Long Road Outta Compton,* Da Capo Press, Philadelphia (2008), pp. 176–177.

20. Snoop Dogg, Web video interview with Strong Arm Steady, July 2012, http:// www.killerhiphop.com/video-snoop-dogg-discusses-jay-z-ghostwriting -still-d-r-e/.

21. Nielsen staff, the Nielsen Company 2009 Year-End Music Industry Report, January 6, 2010, http://www.businesswire.com/news/home/20100106007077/ en/2009-U.S.-Music-Purchases-2.1-2008-Music.

22. Kevin Morrow, telephone interview by author, October 2015.

23. Shaquille O'Neal, telephone interview by author, February 2015.

24. Steve Knopper, "Dr. Dre, Inc.," *Rolling Stone,* June 8, 2015, http://www.rollingstone .com/music/news/dr-dre-inc-a-brief-history-of-moguls-biggest-business-deals -20150608.

25. MC Serch, interview by author, New York, New York, November 2015.

26. Kevin Liles, interview by author, New York, New York, October 2015.

27. Jian Deleon, "Wu-Tang Forever: The History of Wu Wear," *Complex,* October 12, 2011, http://www.complex.com/style/2011/10/wu-tang-forever-the-history -of-wu-wear/.

28. Russell Simmons, interview by author, New York, New York, April 2016.

29. Tracie Rozhon, "Phat Fashions Is Being Sold to Kellwood for $140 Million," *New York Times,* January 9, 2004, http://www.nytimes.com/2004/01/09/business/ phat-fashions-is-being-sold-to-kellwood-for-140-million.html.

30. Dealbook staff, "Jay-Z Cashes In with Rocawear Deal," *New York Times,* March 6, 2007, http://dealbook.nytimes.com/2007/03/06/jay-z-cashes-in-with -200-million-rocawear-deal/.

31. Dan Charnas, "How 50 Cent Scored a Half Billion," *Washington Post,* December 19, 2010, http://www.washingtonpost.com/wp-dyn/content/article/2010/12/17/ AR2010121705271.html.

32. Russell Simmons, interview by author, New York, New York, April 2016.

33. James Covert, "Macy's and Sean John Ink Exclusive Distribution Deal," *New York Post,* May 5, 2010, http://nypost.com/2010/05/05/macys-and-sean-john-ink-exclusive-distribution-deal/.

34. Jean E. Palmieri, "Global Brands Acquires Majority Stake in Sean John," *WWD,* November 30, 2016, http://wwd.com/menswear-news/mens-retail-business/sean-combs-puffy-global-brands-sean-john-10714373/.

35. Russell Simmons, interview by author, New York, New York, April 2016.

36. Russell Simmons, interview by author, New York, New York, January 2013.

37. Russell Simmons, interview by author, New York, New York, April 2016.

Chapter 7: A Fourth King?

1. Real estate listing for 50 Poplar Hill Drive, Farmington, Connecticut 06032, Zillow.com, http://www.zillow.com/homedetails/50-Poplar-Hill-Dr-Farmington-CT-06032/2140575838_zpid/.

2. Newshub staff, "Mike Tyson Tried to Talk 50 Cent Out of Buying Mansion," Newshub, June 20, 2014, http://www.newshub.co.nz/entertainment/mike-tyson-tried-to-talk-50-cent-out-of-buying-mansion-2014062016#axzz3qOdSZKCW. Author's note: My favorite quote from this story comes from Mike Tyson, who reportedly said, "The party's over and four days later some girl comes out of one of the rooms…I'd be like, 'Where's your clothes? Who are you?'"

3. 50 Cent, interview by author, New York, New York, August 2008. Author's note: This quote was originally published in my story "The 50 Cent Machine," *Forbes,* August 18, 2008, http://www.forbes.com/2008/08/15/music-50cent-hiphop-biz-media-cz_zog_0818fifty.html.

4. 50 Cent, interview by author, New York, New York, March 2013.

5. Author's note: Jay-Z makes a habit of deliberately botching the names of his rivals in order to demean them—in this case, "50 Cent" became "50 Cents"; later, he mispronounces Nas's name, calling him "the little homie *Nazz*" on *Blueprint 2.*

6. 50 Cent, interview by author, New York, New York, July 2009.

7. Lea Goldman, "Capitalist Rap," *Forbes,* July 3, 2006, http://www.forbes.com/free_forbes/2006/0703/138.html.

8. Bruce Williams, *Rollin' with Dre,* Ballantine Books, New York (2008), pp. 44–45.

9. 50 Cent, interview by author, New York, New York, March 2013.

10. Ibid.

11. Author's note: Try to avoid referring to Sean Combs as "Puff Daddy or P. Diddy

Notes

or Diddy or whatever his name is now" (and, while you're at it, using the term "bling-bling") unless you are someone who wears fanny packs unironically.

12. Diddy, interview by author, Austin, Texas, March 2014.

13. Fab 5 Freddy, interview by author, New York, New York, March 2011.

14. Fab 5 Freddy, "Road to Morocco," *Vibe,* March 2003, p. 135.

15. Author's note: My wife, who is a doctor, read an early draft of this book. Her comment on the activities described in this paragraph: "This is the worst idea."

16. Fab 5 Freddy, interview by author, New York, New York, March 2011.

17. Author's note: Diddy was basically re-creating the video for "Been Around the World" in real life. Have you seen this video? You should see this video. It is ridiculous.

18. Fab 5 Freddy, interview by author, New York, New York, March 2011.

19. Diddy, interview by author, Austin, Texas, March 2014.

20. Darryl Cobbin, telephone interview by author, August 2016; electronic message to author, January 2017.

21. Tommy Tee, interview by author, Oslo, Norway, January 2017.

22. Rohan Oza, telephone interview by author, January 2017.

23. Ben Sisario, "Chris Lighty, Manager of Hip-Hop Stars, Dies at Forty-Four," *New York Times,* August 30, 2012, http://www.nytimes.com/2012/08/31/arts/music/chris-lighty-manager-of-hip-hop-stars-dies-at-44.html.

24. Kenny Meiselas, telephone interview by author, February 2017.

25. Chris Lighty, interview by author and Dan Adler, New York, New York, July 2009.

26. 50 Cent, interview by author, New York, New York, March 2013.

27. Steve Stoute, *The Tanning of America,* Gotham Books, New York (2011), pp. 162–163.

28. Author's note: This may be the most underwhelming performance of either rapper's career.

29. Rohan Oza, telephone interview by author, January 2017.

30. Ray Latif, "Strand Equity Acquires Minority Stake in Bai Brands," *BevNet,* June 27, 2013, http://www.bevnet.com/news/2013/strand-equity-acquires-minority-stake-in-bai-brands/.

31. Rohan Oza, telephone interview by author, January 2017.

32. Andrew Ross Sorkin and Andrew Martin, "Coca-Cola Agrees to Buy Vitaminwater," *New York Times,* May 26, 2007, http://www.nytimes.com/2007/05/26/business/26drink-web.html.

33. 50 Cent, interview by author, New York, New York, August 2008.

34. Jay-Z, *Decoded,* Spiegel and Grau, New York (2010), p. 27.

35. Fab 5 Freddy, interview by author, New York, New York, January 2016.

36. Kate Sheehy, "Jay-Z Snaps Up $4.5 Million Basquiat Painting," *New York Post,* November 20, 2013, http://nypost.com/2013/11/20/jay-z-buys-basquiat-painting-for-4-5m/.

37. Rob Stone, interview by author, New York, New York, November 2015.

38. Fab 5 Freddy, electronic message to author, January 2017.

39. Sebastian Telfair, telephone interview by author, December 2009.

40. Touré, "The Book of Jay," *Rolling Stone,* December 15, 2005, http://www.rollingstone.com/music/news/the-book-of-jay-20051215.

41. Fab 5 Freddy, interview by author, New York, New York, November 2009.

42. Craig Kallman, interview by author, New York, New York, January 2016.

43. Shaheem Reid, "Jay-Z and Nas Put Beef to Sleep in Onstage Show of Unity," MTV News, October 28, 2005, http://www.mtv.com/news/1512432/jay-z-and-nas-put-beef-to-sleep-in-onstage-show-of-unity/.

44. Common, interview by author, New York, New York, July 2014.

45. 50 Cent, interview by author, New York, New York, March 2014. Author's note: This quote was originally published in my story "Resolving 50 Cent's Headphone Dilemma," *Forbes,* March 20, 2014, http://www.forbes.com/sites/zackomalleygreenburg/2014/03/20/resolving-50-cents-headphone-dilemma/.

46. Travis Lyles, "50 Cent Is Bragging About His New Home in Africa Two Months After Filing for Bankruptcy," *Stamford Advocate,* September 9, 2015, http://www.stamfordadvocate.com/technology/businessinsider/article/50-Cent-is-bragging-about-his-new-home-in-Africa-6494740.php.

47. In Re: Curtis James Jackson III, Findings of Fact, Conclusions of Law and Order Confirming Third Amended Plan of Reorganization, the United States Bankruptcy Court for the District of Connecticut Hartford Division, Case No. 15-21233, August 2, 2016.

48. Daniel Gill, "Rapper Inflation," Bloomberg BNA, December 16, 2016, https://www.bna.com/rapper-inflation-50-n73014448724/.

Chapter 8: The Beats Generation

1. Noel Lee, interview by author, New York, New York, May 2016.

2. Author's note: I like to eat cheese—especially, it seems, while doing interviews.

3. Noel Lee, interview by author, New York, New York, May 2016.

4. Jimmy Iovine, opening remarks at Beats reception, New York, New York, October 2011. Author's note: This quote was originally published in my story "HTC Hasn't Forgotten About Dr. Dre," *Forbes,* October 12, 2011, http://www

.forbes.com/sites/zackomalleygreenburg/2011/10/12/htc-hasnt-forgotten
-about-dr-dre-or-jimmy-or-monster/.

5. Noel Lee, interview by author, New York, New York, May 2016; electronic message to author, January 2017.

6. Burt Helm, "How Dr. Dre's Headphones Company Became a Billion-Dollar Business," *Inc.,* May 2014, http://www.inc.com/audacious-companies/burt-helm/beats.html.

7. Antony Bruno, "Beats by Dre: The Secrets Behind a Headphone Empire," *Billboard,* November 19, 2010, http://www.billboard.com/articles/news/950594/beats-by-dre-the-secrets-behind-a-headphone-empire.

8. Noel Lee, interview by author, New York, New York, May 2016.

9. Brian Dunn, telephone interview by author, December 2016.

10. Noel Lee, interview by author, New York, New York, May 2016.

11. Brian Dunn, telephone interview by author, December 2016.

12. Jeff Leeds, "Jay-Z to Quit His Day Job as President of Def Jam," *New York Times,* December 25, 2007, http://www.nytimes.com/2007/12/25/business/25music.html.

13. Jay-Z, interview with Steve Forbes and Warren Buffett, September 2010. Transcript: http://www.forbes.com/forbes/2010/1011/rich-list-10-omaha-warren-buffett-jay-z-steve-forbes-summit-interview.html.

14. Jennifer Garcia and Mike Fleeman, "Source: Beyoncé and Jay-Z Are Married," *People,* April 4, 2008, http://people.com/celebrity/source-beyonc-and-jay-z-are-married/.

15. Jeff Leeds, "In Rapper's Deal, a New Model for Music Business," *New York Times,* April 3, 2008, http://www.nytimes.com/2008/04/03/arts/music/03jayz.html.

16. Ray Waddell, "It's a Hard Roc Life," *Hollywood Reporter,* May 5, 2008, http://www.hollywoodreporter.com/news/a-hard-roc-life-jay-110862.

17. Jay-Z, interview with Steve Forbes and Warren Buffett, September 2010. Transcript: http://www.forbes.com/forbes/2010/1011/rich-list-10-omaha-warren-buffett-jay-z-steve-forbes-summit-interview.html.

18. NPG Records, Inc., and NPG Music Publishing LLC Versus Roc Nation LLC and Aspiro AB, United States District Court, District of Minnesota, Case No. 16-cv-03909-JRT-FLN, January 9, 2017.

19. Ray Waddell, "U2 Signs Twelve-Year Deal with Live Nation," *Billboard,* March 31, 2008, http://www.billboard.com/articles/news/1046023/u2-signs-12-year-deal-with-live-nation.

20. Gary Bongiovanni, telephone interview by author, October 2015.

21. Randy Phillips, interview by author, Los Angeles, California, February 2016. (The article in question: Steve Knopper, "Live Nation Strikes Deal with Jay-Z, U2," *Rolling Stone,* May 1, 2008, pp. 11–12.)

22. Randy Phillips, interview by author, Los Angeles, California, December 2016.

23. Gary Bongiovanni, electronic message to author, February 2017; Pollstar Pro, "Artist Tour History Report," 2007 to 2017, courtesy of Bongiovanni.

24. Kevin Morrow, telephone interview by author, October 2015.

25. Randy Phillips, interview by author, Los Angeles, California, February 2016.

26. Noel Lee, interview by author, New York, New York, May 2016.

27. Antony Bruno, "Beats by Dre: The Secrets Behind a Headphone Empire," *Billboard,* November 19, 2010, http://www.billboard.com/articles/news/950594/beats-by-dre-the-secrets-behind-a-headphone-empire.

28. PrivCo staff, "Beats Electronics Financials and KPIs," accessed January 5, 2017, www.PrivCo.com (account needed for log-in).

29. BusinessWire staff, "Timbaland Joins 50 Cent and SMS Audio as Investor Partner," BusinessWire, January 3, 2013, http://www.businesswire.com/news/home/20130103005697/en/Timbaland-Joins-50-Cent-SMS-Audio%E2%84%A2-Investor.

30. Hannah Karp, "Apple's New Beat: What Steve Jobs and Dr. Dre Have in Common," *Wall Street Journal,* June 6, 2014, http://www.wsj.com/articles/apples-new-beat-what-steve-jobs-and-dr-dre-have-in-common-1402080817.

31. Noel Lee, interview by author, New York, New York, May 2016.

32. Brian Dunn, telephone interview by author, December 2016.

33. Jimmy Iovine, opening remarks at Beats reception, New York, New York, October 2011.

34. MC Serch, interview by author, New York, New York, November 2015.

35. PrivCo staff, "Beats Electronics Financials and KPIs," accessed January 5, 2017, www.PrivCo.com (account needed for log-in).

36. Noel Lee, interview by author, New York, New York, May 2016.

37. Ingrid Lunden, "MOG Went for a Song," TechCrunch, July 3, 2012, https://techcrunch.com/2012/07/03/mog-went-for-a-song-htc-says-beats-paid-only-14m-for-the-music-streaming-service/.

38. Beats staff, "Beats Electronics Announces Independent Funding for Music Service," press release, March 6, 2013, accessed via Engadget, https://www.engadget.com/2013/03/06/beats-apple-streaming-rumor/.

39. Ibid.

40. Noel Lee, interview by author, New York, New York, May 2016; timeline provided by Lee to author, May 2016.

Notes

41. Noel Lee, electronic message to author, May 2017.

42. Daniel Kreps, "Nipple Ripples," *Rolling Stone,* January 30, 2014, http://www.rollingstone.com/culture/news/nipple-ripples-10-years-of-fallout-from-janet-jacksons-halftime-show-20140130.

43. Gil Kaufman, "P. Diddy No Longer Has Total Bad Boy Control," MTV.com, April 15, 2005, http://www.mtv.com/news/1500205/p-diddy-no-longer-has-total-bad-boy-control/.

44. Diddy, interview by author, Austin, Texas, March 2014.

45. Alex Macpherson, *Last Train to Paris* review, BBC, date unknown, http://www.bbc.co.uk/music/reviews/m98r/.

46. *Rolling Stone* staff, "The Eleven Biggest Musical Disasters of 2010," *Rolling Stone,* December 29, 2010, http://www.rollingstone.com/music/pictures/the-11-biggest-musical-disasters-of-2010-20101229/diddy-dirty-money-0817907.

47. John Biggs, "Monster Diddybeats, for All Your Diddy Music Needs," TechCrunch, May 24, 2010, https://techcrunch.com/2010/05/24/diddybeats-for-all-your-diddy-music-needs/.

48. Noel Lee, interview by author, New York, New York, May 2016.

49. Kenny Meiselas, telephone interview by author, February 2017.

50. Noel Lee, interview by author, New York, New York, May 2016.

51. Brian Dunn, telephone interview by author, December 2016.

52. Michael J. De La Merced, "Beats Gets Infusion of Capital from Carlyle Group," *New York Times,* September 27, 2013, http://dealbook.nytimes.com/2013/09/27/beats-secures-investment-from-carlyle-and-buys-out-htc/.

53. Christopher Ullman, electronic message to author, January 2017.

54. Noel Lee, interview by author, New York, New York, May 2016.

55. Michael J. De La Merced, "Beats Gets Infusion of Capital from Carlyle Group," *New York Times,* September 27, 2013, http://dealbook.nytimes.com/2013/09/27/beats-secures-investment-from-carlyle-and-buys-out-htc/.

56. PrivCo staff, "The True Financial Story of Beats Electronics," PrivCo, May 29, 2014, https://www.privco.com/apple-acquires-beats-electronics-for-unjustified-valuation-the-true-financial-story-of-beats-electronics.

57. Andrew Hampp, "Eminem, Dr. Dre, Diddy Headline 'Live Playlist' at Beats Music's Overcapacity Launch Party," *Billboard,* January 25, 2014, http://www.billboard.com/articles/news/5885293/eminem-dr-dre-diddy-headline-live-playlist-at-beats-musics-over-capacity.

58. Noel Lee, interview by author, New York, New York, May 2016.

59. PrivCo staff, "The True Financial Story of Beats Electronics," PrivCo, May 29, 2014, https://www.privco.com/apple-acquires-beats-electronics-for-unjustified-valuation-the-true-financial-story-of-beats-electronics.

60. Apple Inc., Form 10-K (Annual Report), EDGAR Online, October 27, 2014, http://files.shareholder.com/downloads/AAPL/3300446684x0xS1193125 -14-383437/320193/filing.pdf.

61. Troy Carter, interview by author, Los Angeles, California, November 2015.

62. John Biggs, "Apple's Beats Deal Is Happening, and It's a Dre Acquihire," Tech-Crunch, May 22, 2014, https://techcrunch.com/2014/05/22/apples-beats-deal -is-happening-and-its-a-dre-acquihire/.

63. Matt Richtel and Brian X. Chen, "Tim Cook, Making Apple His Own," *New York Times,* June 15, 2014, http://www.nytimes.com/2014/06/15/technology/ tim-cook-making-apple-his-own.html.

64. Troy Carter, interview by author, Los Angeles, California, November 2015.

65. Jason Tanz, "Can Jimmy Iovine and Dr. Dre Save the Music Industry?," *Wired,* August 2015, https://www.wired.com/2015/08/can-jimmy-iovine-dr-dre-save -music-industry/.

66. Noel Lee, interview by author, New York, New York, May 2016.

67. Daniel Roberts, "Will.i.am on Apple's Beats Buy: 'It's Good for the Culture,'" *Fortune,* May 29, 2014, http://fortune.com/2014/05/29/will-i-am-on-apples-beats -buy-its-good-for-the-culture/.

68. Noel Lee, interview by author, New York, New York, May 2016.

69. Monster LLC et al. Versus Beats Electronics LLC et al., Superior Court for the State of California, Case No. CIV 531991, January 6, 2014, https://timedotcom .files.wordpress.com/2015/01/legalcomplaint.0.pdf.

70. Noel Lee, interview by author, New York, New York, May 2016.

71. Associated Press staff, "Beats Wins in Case That Accused Dr. Dre and Jimmy Iovine of Double-Crossing Investor," *Los Angeles Times,* August 30, 2016, http://www.latimes.com/business/technology/la-fi-tn-beats-apple-lawsuit -20160830-snap-story.html.

72. Noel Lee, interview by author, New York, New York, May 2016.

Chapter 9: Grape Expectations

1. Lyle Fass, interview by author, New York, New York, December 2016.

2. Author's note: Yes, wine critics are far from infallible—witness the infamous 1976 "Judgment of Paris," when France's finest judges picked cheap American reds over pricey Bordeaux wines in a blind taste test—but Fass's familiarity with the grapes present in Cîroc, D'Ussé, and Armand de Brignac made him uniquely qualified to be a guide for this chapter. Also, he is hilarious.

3. Lyle Fass, interview by author, New York, New York, December 2016.

4. Eric Schmidt, telephone interview by author, December 2016.

5. Stephen Rust, telephone interview by author, January 2017.

6. Lyle Fass, interview by author, New York, New York, December 2016.

7. Armadale staff, "Our Heritage," Armadale Vodka website, accessed December 2016, https://www.vodkaarmadale.com/our-heritage/.

8. Author's note: At press time, a pair of West Coast entrepreneurs unconnected to Roc-A-Fella were trying to revive Armadale.

9. *Economist* staff, "Bubbles and Bling," *The Economist,* May 8, 2006, http://www.economist.com/node/6905921.

10. Jay-Z, *Decoded,* Spiegel and Grau, New York (2010), p. 83.

11. Philippe Bienvenu, interview by author, Chigny-les-Roses, France, May 2010. Author's note: This quote and the next one, along with some of the insights in this section, were originally published in my Jay-Z biography, *Empire State of Mind*.

12. Yvonne Lardner, electronic message to author, August 2010.

13. Branson Belchie, interview by author, New York, New York, February 2010.

14. Steve Stoute, *The Tanning of America,* Gotham Books, New York (2011), p. 128.

15. Eric Schmidt, telephone interview by author, December 2016.

16. Anthony Rose, *Financial Times,* "Added Sparkle," December 12, 2016, https://howtospendit.ft.com/fine-living/119831-added-sparkle-prestige-champagne-cuves.

17. Author's note: The list of Armand de Brignac skeptics includes a wine store employee I met in France who likened it to "shower water."

18. Lyle Fass, interview by author, New York, New York, December 2016.

19. Gil Kaufman, "Jay-Z and President Obama: A Bromance History," MTV News, September 19, 2012, http://www.mtv.com/news/1694108/jay-z-obama-bromance/.

20. Jay-Z, interview with Steve Forbes and Warren Buffett, September 2010. Transcript: http://www.forbes.com/forbes/2010/1011/rich-list-10-omaha-warren-buffett-jay-z-steve-forbes-summit-interview.html.

21. Diddy, interview by author, Austin, Texas, March 2014.

22. Diddy, "Diddy Blog #16," YouTube, August 30, 2008, https://www.youtube.com/watch?v=thmueS0ngAs.

23. Author's note: Little notched eighteen interceptions in his career. Dick "Night Train" Lane once clocked fourteen in a single season.

24. Stephen Rust, telephone interview by author, January 2017.

25. Lynette Holloway, "Hip-Hop Sales Pop," *New York Times,* September 2, 2002, http://www.nytimes.com/2002/09/02/business/media-hip-hop-sales-pop-pass-the-courvoisier-and-count-the-cash.html.

26. Kenny Meiselas, interview by author, New York, New York, November 2016.

27. Stephen Rust, telephone interview by author, January 2017.

28. Douglas Martin, "Sidney Frank, Eighty-Six, Dies," *New York Times,* January 12, 2006, http://www.nytimes.com/2006/01/12/business/sidney-frank-86-dies -took-a-german-drink-and-a-vodka-brand-to.html.

29. Stephen Rust, telephone interview by author, January 2017.

30. Eric Schmidt, telephone interview by author, December 2016.

31. Stephen Rust, telephone interview by author, January 2017.

32. Lyle Fass, interview by author, New York, New York, December 2016.

33. Roberto Rogness, electronic message to author, January 2016.

34. Stephen Rust, telephone interview by author, January 2017.

35. Lyle Fass, interview by author, New York, New York, December 2016.

36. Eric Arnold, electronic message to author, January 2017.

37. Author's note: Biggie never praised cheese eggs and Welch's potato juice; 50 Cent didn't hawk potato-flavored Vitaminwater. Why would you want to drink vodka made from potatoes when you could drink vodka made from grapes?

38. Stephen Rust, telephone interview by author, January 2017.

39. Eric Schmidt, telephone interview by author, December 2016.

40. Stephen Rust, telephone interview by author, January 2017.

41. Jonathan Mannion, interview by author, New York, New York, February 2016.

42. Diddy, interview by author, Austin, Texas, March 2014.

43. Eric Schmidt, telephone interview by author, December 2016.

44. Stephen Rust, telephone interview by author, January 2017.

45. Timbaland, telephone interview by author, May 2012. Author's note: This quote was first published in my story "Timbaland to Launch His Own Line of Liqueur This Summer," *Forbes,* May 22, 2012, http://www.forbes.com/sites/ zackomalleygreenburg/2012/05/22/timbaland-to-launch-his-own-line -of-liqueur-this-summer/.

46. Eric Schmidt, electronic message to author, February 2017.

47. PW Licensing LLC and Pharrell Williams Versus Diageo North America, Inc., United States District Court for the Southern District of New York, No. 12-cv-8424, January 3, 2013.

48. Author's note: Another liquor that failed because it didn't match its name-sake's lifestyle: Trump Vodka, hawked by a billionaire teetotaler (discontinued stateside in 2011, it did find a small audience for a time in Israel, reportedly because the booze is made from potatoes rather than grains, thereby allowing it to be kosher for Passover).

49. Jean-Claude Biver, telephone interview by author, November 2011.

50. Sean Barnett, electronic message to author, February 2017.

51. Swizz Beatz, interview by author, Englewood, New Jersey, August 2016.

52. Charles Passy, "Is This Cognac Worthy of Jay-Z?," *Wall Street Journal,* March 2, 2013, http://blogs.wsj.com/speakeasy/2013/03/02/is-this-cognac-worthy-of-jay-z/.

53. Eric Arnold, electronic message to author, January 2017.

54. Lyle Fass, interview by author, New York, New York, December 2016.

55. Author's observation, DeLeón launch, New York, New York, November 2014.

56. Sammy Hagar, interview by author, Austin, Texas, March 2017.

57. Kenny Meiselas, interview by author, New York, New York, November 2016.

58. Brent Hocking, interview by author, Los Angeles, California, June 2016.

59. Stephen Rust, telephone interview by author, January 2017.

60. Eric Schmidt, telephone interview by author, December 2016.

61. Diddy, speech to crowd at DeLeón launch, New York, New York, November 2014.

62. Lyle Fass, interview by author, New York, New York, December 2016.

63. Author's note: Fass has a deep dislike for marzipan — which is actually made from almonds, not hazelnuts — and I've included more of his rationale, in case, for some reason, you're interested in hearing more about it. "Where I grew up, marzipan came in boxes," he says. "You had green apple, you had hot dog, you had hamburger. You had all these different things and it all tasted like fucking the same thing: marzipan…I wanted to eat Big League Chew and whatever, but my parents were like, 'You should eat marzipan.' I fucking hate marzipan."

64. Lyle Fass, interview by author, New York, New York, December 2016.

Chapter 10: Sound Investments

1. Troy Carter, interview by author, Los Angeles, California, November 2015; telephone conversation with author, May 2017.

2. Mike McSherry, electronic message to author, January 2017.

3. Peter Adderton, electronic message to author, January 2017.

4. Author's note: Diddy's team didn't have anything to add about the Boost Mobile negotiations. "I only have the vaguest memory of something possibly like that," Kenny Meiselas told me.

5. Peter Adderton, electronic message to author, January 2017.

6. Ibid.

7. Mike McSherry, electronic message to author, January 2017.

8. Darryl Cobbin, telephone interview by author, August 2016; electronic message to author, January 2017. Author's note: As part of the campaign, Boost donated a portion of the song's proceeds to the United Negro College Fund, the Ludacris Foundation, and the Chicago State University Foundation. In November 2004, *Billboard* reported that Boost had raised more than $20,000 for the organizations, not to mention a significant amount of press and goodwill.

9. Darryl Cobbin, telephone interview by author, August 2016; electronic message to author, May 2017.

10. Author's note: Meneilly did not respond to a request for comment in time to be interviewed for this book.

11. Darryl Cobbin, telephone interview by author, August 2016.

12. Mike McSherry, electronic message to author, January 2017.

13. Peter Adderton, electronic message to author, January 2017.

14. Darryl Cobbin, telephone interview by author, August 2016.

15. Matthew Perpetua, "Nas Owes the IRS Nearly $6.5 Million," *Rolling Stone,* January 26, 2011, http://www.rollingstone.com/music/news/nas-owes-the-irs -nearly-6-5-million-20110126.

16. D. A. Wallach, telephone interview by author, December 2016.

17. Ibid.

18. Anthony Saleh, telephone interview by author, November 2016.

19. Ilan Zechory, telephone interview by author, January 2017.

20. Nas, telephone interview by author, May 2012.

21. Anthony Saleh, telephone interview by author, November 2016.

22. Ben Horowitz, telephone interview by author, October 2012. Author's note: This quote was originally published in my story "Inside Andreessen Horowitz's $15 Million Investment in Rap Genius," *Forbes,* October 3, 2012, http://www.forbes .com/sites/zackomalleygreenburg/2012/10/03/inside-andreessen-horowitz -15-million-investment-in-rap-genius/.

23. Nas, telephone interview by author, May 2012.

24. Anthony Saleh, telephone interview by author, October 2016.

25. Anthony Saleh, telephone interview by author, November 2016.

26. Ilan Zechory, telephone interview by author, January 2017.

27. Author's note: Defining "startup" turns out to be pretty tough. Is Facebook a startup? It was. But now its market cap is twice the size of Walmart's. Does a company have to be tech-focused to be considered a startup? Probably not. Though they both function through apps, Uber and Airbnb are touted as two of the most successful startups of the decade, and they revolve around cabs and

hotels. In the same vein, Warby Parker sells eyeglasses and Palantir focuses on data analysis, yet they have been considered startups. What about Aquahydrate? It's listed in startup finance database CrunchBase, so I figure that's close enough.

28. Diddy, telephone interview by author, January 2015.

29. Mark Wahlberg, telephone interview by author, January 2015. Author's note: This quote, as well as a few others in this section, originally appeared in my story "Liquid Asset," *Forbes,* February 4, 2015, http://www.forbes.com/sites/ zackomalleygreenburg/2015/02/04/liquid-asset-inside-mark-wahlberg-diddy -and-ron-burkles-aquahydrate/.

30. Diddy, telephone interview by author, January 2015.

31. Katherine Zeratsky, "Is Alkaline Water Better for You Than Plain Water?," Mayo Clinic website, April 4, 2015, http://www.mayoclinic.org/healthy-lifestyle/ nutrition-and-healthy-eating/expert-answers/alkaline-water/faq-20058029.

32. Diddy, telephone interview by author, January 2015.

33. Mark Wahlberg, telephone interview by author, January 2015.

34. Diddy, telephone interview by author, January 2015.

35. Mark Wahlberg, telephone interview by author, January 2015.

36. Diddy, telephone interview by author, January 2015.

37. Steven Davidoff Solomon, "Sprinkling a Little Celebrity Stardust on Silicon Valley," *New York Times,* May 5, 2015, https://www.nytimes.com/2015/05/06/ business/sprinkling-a-little-celebrity-stardust-on-silicon-valley.html.

38. Ilan Zechory, telephone interview by author, January 2017.

39. Doyle Murphy, "L'Oréal USA Buys Brooklyn Beauty Brand Carol's Daughter," *New York Daily News,* October 26, 2014, http://www.nydailynews.com/ new-york/brooklyn/oreal-usa-buys-brooklyn-beauty-brand-carol-daughter -article-1.1986483.

40. James Covert, "Jay-Z Can't Stop Investing in Private Jet Companies," *New York Post,* December 13, 2016, http://nypost.com/2016/12/13/jay-z-cant-stop-investing -in-private-jet-companies/.

41. Catherine Curan, "Jay-Z's 99 Problems," *New York Post,* May 16, 2010, http:// nypost.com/2010/05/16/jay-zs-99-problems/.

42. Frank DiGiacomo, "Hip-Hop Mogul Jay-Z Upset…," *New York Daily News,* July 28, 2010, http://www.nydailynews.com/entertainment/gossip/hip-hop-mogul -jay-z-upset-newly-minted-miami-heat-player-lebron-james-didn-consult -article-1.468536.

43. David M. Halbfinger, "With Arena, Rapper Rewrites Celebrity Investors' Playbook," *New York Times,* August 15, 2012, http://www.nytimes.com/2012/08/16/ nyregion/with-the-nets-jay-z-rewrites-the-celebrity-investors-playbook.html.

44. Ibid.

45. Author's note: The Ebbets Field Faithful know this, but others may not: Branch Rickey was the Brooklyn Dodgers' general manager responsible for signing Jackie Robinson. Rickey is up there with Indiana Jones, Han Solo, and President James "Get Off My Plane" Marshall in terms of overall awesomeness for various reasons, including the fact that Harrison Ford played all four of them in major movies.

46. Pollstar Pro, "Artist Tour History Report," 2007 to 2017, courtesy of Gary Bongiovanni.

47. Kurt Badenhausen, "Billion-Dollar Knicks and Lakers Top List of NBA's Most Valuable Teams," *Forbes,* January 23, 2013, http://www.forbes.com/sites/ kurtbadenhausen/2013/01/23/billion-dollar-knicks-and-lakers-top-list-of -nbas-most-valuable-teams/.

48. Mike Ozanian, "Jay-Z Set to Get $1.5 Million for His Barclays Center Stake," *Forbes,* September 17, 2013, http://www.forbes.com/sites/mikeozanian/2013/09/17/ jay-z-set-to-get-1-5-millon-for-his-barclays-center-stake/.

49. Ilan Zechory, telephone interview by author, January 2017.

50. Randy Phillips, interview by author, Los Angeles, California, December 2016.

51. Jacob Ganz, "How That Tupac Hologram at Coachella Worked," NPR Music, April 17, 2012, http://www.npr.org/sections/therecord/2012/04/17/150820261/ how-that-tupac-hologram-at-coachella-worked.

52. Kendrick Lamar, interview by author, Los Angeles, California, November 2015.

53. Dave Free, interview by author, Los Angeles, California, November 2015.

54. Randy Phillips, interview by author, Los Angeles, California, December 2016.

55. Troy Carter, interview by author, Los Angeles, California, November 2015.

Chapter II: Ice in the Winter

1. Jay-Z, Twitter post, September 29, 2015, https://twitter.com/S_C_/status/ 648891212317921280.

2. Author's observation, Tidal X concert, Brooklyn, New York, October 2015.

3. Jay-Z, Tidal X concert, Brooklyn, New York, October 2015.

4. Jason Aldean, interview by author, Hartford, Connecticut, May 2015. Author's note: A portion of this quote originally appeared in my story "How Jason Aldean Cashed In on the Changing Landscape of Country," *Forbes,* July 29, 2015, http:// www.forbes.com/sites/zackomalleygreenburg/2015/07/29/how-jason -aldean-cashed-in-on-the-changing-landscape-of-country/.

Notes

5. Author's note: It is incredibly cheap to visit Norway in January. (This does not come as a surprise to most Oslo residents.)

6. Aspiro staff, "Year-End Report," January to December 2014, p. 4.

7. Tommy Tee, interview by author, Oslo, Norway, January 2017.

8. Author's note: We discussed MC Solaar (she felt that he was no longer relevant) and acts like IAM and NTM (she liked them better).

9. Author's note: The name sounded like "Louise," though it could have been Luis or Lewis, but probably not, say, Horatio.

10. D. A. Wallach, telephone interview by author, December 2016.

11. Author's note: Pharrell is a *Star Trek* nerd. He named his first child Rocket.

12. D. A. Wallach, telephone interview by author, December 2016.

13. Steven Bertoni, "Spotify's Daniel Ek: The Most Important Man in Music," *Forbes,* January 4, 2012, http://www.forbes.com/sites/stevenbertoni/2012/01/04/spotifys-daniel-ek-the-most-important-man-in-music/.

14. D. A. Wallach, telephone interview by author, December 2016.

15. Ryan Faughnder, "Spotify Raises $1 Billion in New Debt Financing," *Los Angeles Times,* March 30, 2016, http://www.latimes.com/entertainment/envelope/cotown/la-et-ct-spotify-raises-1-billion-in-new-debt-financing-20160330-story.html.

16. D. A. Wallach, telephone interview by author, December 2016.

17. Miles Raymer, "Why Apple Is Really Shutting Down Beats Music," *Esquire,* November 16, 2015, http://www.esquire.com/entertainment/music/a39741/apple-shuts-down-beats-music/.

18. Gunnar Sellaeg, interview by author, Oslo, Norway, January 2017.

19. Author's note: Though Tidal's parent was founded by Swedes, the company has historically been based in Malmö, Stockholm, and Oslo; lately, it's been based in the latter. This has led to some confusion over whether Tidal should be referred to as a Norwegian or a Swedish entity. When in doubt, just call it Scandinavian.

20. Gunnar Sellaeg, interview by author, Oslo, Norway, January 2017.

21. Tommy Tee, interview by author, Oslo, Norway, January 2017.

22. Gunnar Sellaeg, interview by author, Oslo, Norway, January 2017.

23. Kjetil Saeter, interview by author, Oslo, Norway, January 2017.

24. Author's note: As the musician John Oates told me, "That's the story of the music business…'Give him a bottle of wine and take all his publishing.'" For more on this outrageous situation, read the magazine story I cowrote with Nick Messitte, "Revenge of the Record Labels," *Forbes,* April 15, 2015, http://www.forbes.com/sites/zackomalleygreenburg/2015/04/15/revenge-of-the-record-labels-how-the-majors-renewed-their-grip-on-music/.

25. Aspiro staff, "Year-End Report," January to December 2014, p. 7.

26. Kjetil Saeter, interview by author, Oslo, Norway, January 2017.

27. Aspiro staff, "Year-End Report," January to December 2014, p. 3.

28. Gunnar Sellaeg, interview by author, Oslo, Norway, January 2017.

29. Jason Aldean, interview by author, Hartford, Connecticut, May 2015.

30. Joe Coscarelli, "Four Hundred Million Streams Later, Kanye West's *Pablo* Gets a Wider Release," *New York Times,* March 31, 2016, https://www.nytimes .com/2016/04/02/arts/music/kanye-west-life-pablo-tidal-streams.html.

31. Colin Stutz, "Tidal Posts $28 Million Net Loss in 2015," *Billboard,* September 13, 2016, http://www.billboard.com/articles/news/7510245/tidal-posts-28-million-net -loss-2015-jay-z.

32. Kjetil Saeter and Markus Tobiassen, "Project Panther," *Dagens Naeringsliv,* January 21, 2017, subscription only; interview with Saeter, Oslo, Norway, January 2017.

33. Teri Thompson et al., "Alex Rodriguez Was Set to Quit Baseball," *New York Daily News,* May 18, 2014, http://www.nydailynews.com/sports/i-team/babe -ruthless-rod-shady-lady-article-1.1796578.

34. Janko Roettgers, "Jay-Z Threatens to Sue Former Tidal Owners over Inflated Subscriber Numbers," *Variety,* March 31, 2016, http://variety.com/2016/digital/ news/jay-z-tidal-subscriber-numbers-lawsuit-1201742945/.

35. Gunnar Sellaeg, interview by author, Oslo, Norway, January 2017.

36. Dan Rys, "Sprint Purchases 33 Percent Stake in Tidal," *Billboard,* January 23, 2017, http://www.billboard.com/articles/business/7662653/sprint-jay-z-tidal-33 -percent-stake-purchase.

37. Jay-Z, Tidal X concert, Brooklyn, New York, October 2015.

38. Steven J. Horowitz, "Jay-Z, Beyoncé, and Nicki Minaj Rock Barclays Center for Tidal X Spectacular," *Billboard,* October 21, 2015, http://www.billboard.com/ articles/columns/the-juice/6737436/tidal-x-concert-jay-z-beyonce-nicki -minaj-barclays-center.

Chapter 12: State of the Art

1. Swizz Beatz, interview by author, Englewood, New Jersey, August 2016.

2. Mike Dolan, telephone interview by author, August 2016.

3. Swizz Beatz, interview by author, Englewood, New Jersey, August 2016.

4. Cilvaringz, electronic messages to author, October to December 2013.

5. RZA, telephone conversation with author, March 2014. Author's note: This quote, and some of the themes in this section, originally appeared in my story "Why Wu-Tang Will Release Just One Copy of Its Secret Album," *Forbes,* March

26, 2014, http://www.forbes.com/sites/zackomalleygreenburg/2014/03/26/why-wu
-tang-will-release-just-one-copy-of-its-secret-album/.

6. Author's note: You can find my full coverage of Wu-Tang Clan's secret album,
including the minidocumentary of my visit to Morocco to hear *Once Upon a
Time in Shaolin*—filmed and edited by filmmaker extraordinaire Dikenta
Dike—at the unlikely URL forbes.com/wu-tang.

7. Yahya, interview by author, Marrakech, Morocco, April 2014.

8. Cilvaringz, interview by author, Marrakech, Morocco, April 2014. Author's note:
This quote and the one above originally appeared in my story "Unlocking the
Wu-Tang Clan's Secret Album in Morocco," *Forbes,* May 6, 2014, http://www
.forbes.com/sites/zackomalleygreenburg/2014/05/06/unlocking-the-wu-tang-clans
-secret-album-in-morocco/.

9. Author's note: Why eighty-eight? The Wu-Tang Clan is obsessed with numerology. Eight is considered to be a lucky number associated with wealth in
many Asian cultures. The number is in the name Paddle8, the auction house
tapped to sell *Once Upon a Time in Shaolin*. And RZA has an eight-toed cat.
Okay, I made up that last one. Don't think too hard about numerology.

10. Justin Hunte, "Martin Shkreli Plans to Bail Out Bobby Shmurda," HipHopDX,
December 16, 2015, http://hiphopdx.com/interviews/id.2825/title.martin-shkreli
-plans-to-bail-out-bobby-shmurda.

11. Diddy, telephone interview by author, June 2013.

12. Tiesha LeShore, interview by author, Los Angeles, California, April 2014.
Author's note: This quote originally appeared in my story "I Want to Work for
Diddy," *Forbes,* April 16, 2014, http://www.forbes.com/sites/zackomalleygreen
burg/2014/04/16/i-want-to-work-for-diddy-meet-sean-combs-real-revolt
-recruits/#1544799e71eb.

13. Diddy, telephone interview by author, June 2013.

14. Randy Lewis, "Dr. Dre, Jimmy Iovine Give $70 Million to Create New USC
Academy," *Los Angeles Times,* May 14, 2013, http://articles.latimes.com/2013/
may/14/entertainment/la-et-ms-dr-dre-jimmy-iovine-usc-gift-donate-70
-million-20130514.

15. *Rolling Stone* staff, "N.W.A. Tell All," *Rolling Stone,* August 12, 2015, http://
www.rollingstone.com/music/news/n-w-a-tell-all-inside-the-original-gangstas
-rolling-stone-cover-story-20150812.

16. Jay Balfour, *Compton* review, Pitchfork, August 11, 2015, http://pitchfork.com/
reviews/albums/20935-compton.

17. Peter Travers, *Straight Outta Compton* review, *Rolling Stone,* August 13, 2015,
http://www.rollingstone.com/movies/reviews/straight-outta-compton
-20150813.

Notes

18. Jonathan Mannion, interview by author, New York, New York, February 2016.

19. Jerry Crasnick, "Baseball's Fascinating New Rivalry," ESPN.com, November 7, 2013, http://www.espn.com/mlb/hotstove13/story/_/id/9936513/the-growing-rivalry-scott-boras-jay-z.

20. Eben Novy-Williams and Erik Matuszewski, "Robinson Cano Leaves Yankees for $240 Million Mariners Offer," Bloomberg, December 7, 2013, https://www.bloomberg.com/news/articles/2013-12-06/cano-said-to-join-mariners-with-10-year-240-million-contract.

21. Rick Maese, "Inside Roc Nation Sports, Jay-Z's High-End Boutique Athlete Agency," *Washington Post,* May 26, 2016, https://www.washingtonpost.com/sports/inside-roc-nation-sports-jay-zs-high-end-boutique-athlete-agency/2016/05/26/42287430-2372-11e6-8690-f14ca9de2972_story.html.

22. Iconix Brand Group, Inc., Form 10-K (Annual Report), United States Securities and Exchange Commission, December 31, 2014, https://www.sec.gov/Archives/edgar/data/857737/000119312515071602/d858337d10k.htm.

23. Jay-Z, interview with Steve Forbes and Warren Buffett, September 2010. Transcript: http://www.forbes.com/forbes/2010/1011/rich-list-10-omaha-warren-buffett-jay-z-steve-forbes-summit-interview.html.

24. Kevin Liles, interview by author, New York, New York, October 2015.

25. Russell Simmons, interview by author, New York, New York, April 2016.

26. Cameron "Wiz Khalifa" Thomaz, interview by author, New York, New York, December 2012. Author's note: Part of this quote first appeared in my story "All-Time High," *Forbes,* December 18, 2012, http://www.forbes.com/sites/zackomalleygreenburg/2012/12/18/all-time-high-wiz-khalifas-next-big-step/.

27. Lovebug Starski, interview by author, New York, New York, January 2016.

28. David Gest, telephone interview by author, January 2017.

29. Rocky Bucano, interview by author, Brooklyn, New York, January 2017.

30. Grandwizzard Theodore, interview by author, Bronx, New York, August 2016.

31. Grandmaster Caz, interview by author, Bronx, New York, August 2016.

32. Kurtis Blow, interview by author, Brooklyn, New York, January 2017.

33. Grandmaster Caz, interview by author, Bronx, New York, August 2016.

34. Grandwizzard Theodore, electronic message to author; interview by author, Bronx, New York, August 2016.

35. Fab 5 Freddy, interview by author, New York, New York, January 2016.

36. Cathleen McGuigan, "New Art, New Money," *New York Times,* February 10, 1985, http://www.nytimes.com/books/98/08/09/specials/basquiat-mag.html.

37. Robin Pogrebin and Scott Reyburn, "A Basquiat Sells for 'Mind-Blowing' $110.5 Million at Auction," *New York Times,* May 18, 2017, https://www.nytimes.com/2017/05/18/arts/jean-michel-basquiat-painting-is-sold-for-110-million-at-auction.html.

38. Swizz Beatz, interview by author, Englewood, New Jersey, August 2016.

39. TVC Group, "Swizz Beatz and A$AP Rocky Take Us on a Tour of the Bronx," August 3, 2016, https://www.youtube.com/watch?v=3MoTc6fx_qg.

40. Mike Dolan, telephone interview by author, August 2016.

41. Swizz Beatz, interview by author, Englewood, New Jersey, August 2016.

Afterword: Kings, Queens, Presidents, and Precedents

1. Kendrick Lamar, interview by author, Boston, Massachusetts, October 2017.

2. Tim Funk and Jim Morrill, "Donald Trump Promises 'A New Deal for Black America,'" *Charlotte Observer,* October 26, 2016, http://www.charlotteobserver.com/news/politics-government/election/article110546817.html.

3. Christopher Mele and Patrick Healy, "'Hamilton' Had Some Unscripted Lines for Pence," *New York Times,* November 19, 2016, https://www.nytimes.com/2016/11/19/us/mike-pence-hamilton.html.

4. Okieriete Onaodowan, interview with author, Boston, Massachusetts, October 2017.

5. Little Simz, interview with author, Jerusalem, Israel, April 2016.

Index

Abbatiello, Sal, 8, 28–29, 47

Above the Rim (film), 99

"Above the Rim" (motion picture soundtrack; Death Row), 87

Accel Partners, 207, 223

Adderton, Peter, 202–3

Adenuga, Julie, 224

Adidas, 54, 127

Adidas-Salomon, 152

AEG (company), 168

Aerosmith, 54

Africa, 15, 18–19

Aftermath (label), 110, 135, 144, 215

Ahearn, Charlie, 41–42

Ahlerich, Milt, 52–53

Aldean, Jason, 219–20, 228

Ali, Muhammad, 14

All Eyez on Me (album; Tupac), 90, 99

"All the Way Up" (song; Jay-Z), 243

American Gangster (album; Jay-Z), 166

American Gangster (film), 21, 60, 166

"Amityville (the House on the Hill)" (song; Starski), 35

Anderson, Orlando, 100, 276n52

Andreessen Horowitz (company), 207

Animal Ambition (album; 50 Cent), 159

Anti (album; Rihanna), 228

Apple (company), 3, 6, 176–79, 216–17, 233

Apple Music, 217, 220, 224–25, 229

Aquahydrate, 208–11, 290n27

Arcade Fire (band), 219–20, 228

Argyleculture (company), 125, 140

Arista (label), 76–78, 107–8

Armadale Vodka, 182–83, 287n8

Armand de Brignac, 184–86, 194, 231, 286n2, 287n17

Armstrong, Louis, 15

Arnold, Eric, 190, 194

Arrive (company), 213

Artest, Ron (Metta World Peace), 156

art world, 37–40, 42, 237–39

A$AP Rocky (Rakim Mayers), 139, 247

Aspiro (company), 225–28

Atom Factory (company), 199, 206

"Atomic Dog" (song; Clinton), 273n43

Azzougarh, Tarik "Cilvaringz," 236–37

Bacardí, 192–93, 235–36, 246–47

Backpack Rap (subgenre), 158

Bad Boy Records, 67–68, 76–78, 107–8, 118, 130–31, 146, 173–74

Bambaataa, Afrika, 14–15, 18–20, 34, 38, 42–43, 47, 77, 150, 244

Barclays Center, 212, 218–20, 241

Barnes, Dee, 71

Barrow, Jamal "Shyne," 121–22

Basquiat, Jean-Michel, 8, 37–38, 41, 154, 234, 246

Beastie Boys, 43, 55, 225

Beats (headphones), 132, 159, 163–66, 170–79, 213–14, 248

  Apple and, 3, 6, 176–79, 216–17, 224

Beats Music, 172–73, 175–76, 216–17, 224

"Been Around the World" (song; Diddy), 107

"Been There, Done That" (song; Dre), 111–12

Belchie, Branson "Branson B," 60–61, 64, 69, 80–82, 183–85

Index

Berrin, Michael "MC Serch," 45, 55, 136, 172

Beyoncé. *See* Knowles, Beyoncé

Bieber, Justin, 170, 206, 208, 223

Bienvenu, Philippe, 184

Big Daddy Kane. *See* Hardy, Antonio

Biggie. *See* Wallace, Christopher "Notorious B.I.G."

Biggie and Tupac (documentary), 100

Biggs, Briant "B-High," 118

Big Payback, The (Charnas), 20

"Big Poppa" (song; Biggie), 77

"Billie Jean" (song; Michael Jackson), 55

Biver, Jean-Claude, 193

Black Album, The (Jay-Z), 155, 158

"Black Republicans" (song; Nas and Jay-Z), 158

Blackstreet (group), 111

Blavatnik, Len, 172

Bleek, Memphis, 135

Blige, Mary J., 62, 67, 79, 134, 225

Blondie, 40, 41

Blueprint, The (album; Jay-Z), 136–37

Blueprint 3, The (album; Jay-Z), 169

Bongiovanni, Gary, 65–66, 168

Bono (Paul David Hewson), 7, 154, 177

Boost Mobile, 201–5, 233, 289n4, 290n8

Boras, Scott, 241–42

"Bouge de Là" (song; MC Solaar), 9

"Boyz-n-the Hood" (song; Eazy), 51

Branson, Richard, 7

Brathwaite, Fred "Fab 5 Freddy," 5, 8, 37–43, 58–59, 63, 92, 95–96, 102, 145–46, 269n4

  Dre and, 73–76

  grafitti art of, 37, 39–41, 246

  Jay-Z and, 154, 155–57

  "Rapper's Delight" and, 9, 15, 25, 245

  Yo! MTV Raps and, 37, 56, 74

Braun, Scooter, 223

break dancing, 17–20

"Breaks, The" (song; Kurtis Blow), 42

Broadus, Calvin "Snoop Doggy Dogg," 72–75, 87, 100, 113, 133–34, 158, 169, 182, 213, 244, 273n43

"Brooklyn (Go Hard)" (song; Jay-Z), 212, 292n45

Bryant, Dez, 241

Buffett, Warren, 186

Burke, Kareem "Biggs," 78, 158

Burkle, Ron, 132, 209–10

Burks, Jonathan "Jaz-O," 28, 44–45, 154

business, hip-hop, 3, 9–11, 46–49, 58–59, 137, 140, 293n24

  marketing and, 17, 77, 117, 148–50, 155, 166, 186–91, 204, 210, 288n37

  startups and, 65, 106, 200–216, 290n27

  See also financial success; *particular artists and businesses*

Busta Rhymes (Trevor George Smith Jr.), 187

Busy Bee (David Parker), 88

CAA-GBG Global Brand Management Group, 139

"California Love" (song; Tupac), 89–90

"California Vacation" (song; Xzibit), 158

Campbell, Cindy, 16–17, 245

Campbell, Clive "DJ Kool Herc," 14, 15–19, 30, 34–36, 38, 43, 244–45

Campbell, Naomi, 122, 145, 194

Canal Digital, 226–27, 229

"Can I Get Open" (song; Original Flavor), 64

Canó, Robinson, 241–42

"Can't C Me" (song; Tupac), 273n43

"Can't Nobody Hold Me Down" (song; Diddy and Mase), 107

Carlyle Group, 175–76, 179

Caro, Robert, 16

Carraby, Antoine "DJ Yella," 50–51

Carter, Shawn "Jay-Z," 9–10, 13, 43–46, 92, 109, 117–20, 143, 151–59, 201, 204–5, 265n2

  background of, 5, 10, 26–28, 44–46, 50, 64, 281n28

  Beyoncé and, 156–57, 167, 169, 186, 278n8

  businesses of, 4, 6, 151–52, 154–57, 166–70, 179, 181–86, 192–94, 211–13, 218–22, 227–31, 241–43

  as businessman, 7, 80, 198

  Diddy and, 107, 117–19, 156, 158, 174

  Dre and, 129, 133

  Fab and, 154, 155–57

  Kanye and, 136–37, 158, 169, 192–93, 212, 219, 228–29

  lifestyle of, 118–19, 154, 192–93

  music and, 45–46, 64–65, 118, 166, 169

Carter, Shawn "Jay-Z," *(cont.)*
  Nas rivalry and, 135–37, 158, 280n5
  N.W.A. and, 50–53
  personality of, 4, 79, 169–70
  songs and albums of, 28, 78–80, 118–19,
    129, 135–37, 153–56, 158, 166, 169, 174,
    183–84, 186, 192–93, 212, 219, 231, 241,
    243, 246, 273n43, 278n8, 280n5, 292n45
  Swizz and, 234, 247–48
  violence and, 10, 99, 107, 129–30
  wealth of, 3, 120, 169, 248
  See also Def Jam Recordings; Roc-A-Fella
    Records; Rocawear; Roc Nation
Carter, Terry, 102
Carter, Troy, 8, 199–201, 206–7, 216–17, 224
Cauley-Stein, Willie, 242
Caz. *See* Fisher, Curtis
Céspedes, Yoenis, 241–42
Champagne Cattier, 184–85, 197
Charnas, Dan, 20
Cheeba. *See* Sturgis, Edward
Chen, Andy, 227
Chester French (band), 222–23
"Christmas Rappin'" (song; Kurtis Blow), 30
Chronic, The (album; Dre), 72–73, 75
Chrysler, 171–72
"Cîroc Star" (song; Chester French), 223
Cîroc vodka, 7, 175, 181–82, 186–93,
    195–97, 236, 286n2, 288n37
Clinton, Bill, 200
Clinton, George, 273n43
Clinton, Hillary, 238
Cobbin, Darryl, 147–50, 203–5, 290n8
Cohen, Lyor, 55, 119–20, 157
Cold Crush Brothers, 25, 39, 246
Coldplay (band), 228
Combs, Janice, 21–22
Combs, Melvin, 20
Combs, Sean "Diddy," 56–58, 61–63,
    76–78, 105–10, 112–24, 128, 145–47,
    151, 176, 246, 265n2, 273n46
  ambition of, 117, 120–21, 131–32
  background of, 5, 10, 20–22, 85
  businesses of, 4–6, 62–63, 174–75, 179,
    194–96, 208–11, 222–24, 239–40,
    290n27
  as businessman, 7, 68–69, 131, 198, 210,
    288n37
  Troy Carter and, 200–201

Cobbin and, 204–5
Dre and, 112, 174–75
Jay-Z and, 107, 117–19, 156, 158, 174
lifestyle of, 81, 114–18, 188, 191
music and, 115, 173–74, 191, 273n43
Obama blog of, 186–87
personality of, 4–5, 57, 81, 103–4, 105,
    122, 170, 240
rap wars and, 87–90, 93, 100–101
songs and albums of, 13, 77, 86, 107, 115,
    121, 145, 173–74
Swizz and, 234, 236, 247–48
television and film and, 10, 145–46, 173
at Uptown, 57–58, 61–62, 67–68, 76
violence and, 10, 88–89, 121–22
wealth of, 3, 191
See also Bad Boy Records; Cîroc vodka;
    Sean John clothing
Comcast, 106
"Coming Home" (song; Diddy–Dirty
    Money feat. Skylar Grey), 174
Common (Lonnie Rashid Lynn Jr.), 158–59
Compton (album; Dre), 240–41
Conjure cognac, 191–92
Conscious Rap (subgenre), 158
Contes, Salvador, 92
Conzo, Joe, 39
Cook, Tim, 176, 216
Crawford, Jamal, 155
"Crazy in Love" (song; Jay-Z and Beyoncé),
    156
Cristal champagne, 183–86, 236
Crocker, Frankie, 14
Crosby, Bing, 88
"Crown" (song; Jay-Z), 241
culture, hip-hop, 51–52, 56–58, 109–10, 127,
    134, 137, 183
Curry, Tracy "D.O.C.," 70–72

Daft Punk (music duo), 219–20, 228
Danity Kane (group), 146, 174
Darden, Ebro, 224
Dash, Damon, 64–65, 78–80, 128, 138,
    154–55, 158
David, Donald, 85
Davis, Clive, 76
"Day the Niggaz Took Over, The" (song;
    Dre), 72
"Dead Presidents" (song; Jay-Z), 158

Index

Dean, Kasseem "Swizz Beatz," 8, 119, 162, 174, 194, 234–36, 246–48

Death Row (label), 6, 71, 87–90, 94, 96–97, 99, 111

Decoded (autobiography; Jay-Z), 7

Defiant Ones, The (documentary), 176

Def Jam Recordings, 30, 49, 55, 65, 205
Jay-Z and, 80, 119–20, 155, 157–58, 166–68

DeLeón tequila, 194–96

Detox (album; Dre), 214

Diageo, 182, 187–88, 192–95

Diddy. *See* Combs, Sean

Diddybeats, 174–75

Diggs, Robert "RZA," 237

"Dirt off Your Shoulder" (song; Jay-Z), 186

DJ Khaled (Khaled Mohamed Khaled), 225, 243

DJ Premier. *See* Martin, Christopher

D.O.C. *See* Curry, Tracy

Doggystyle (album; Snoop), 73, 75, 273n43

Dolan, Mike, 235–36, 247

Dole, Bob, 98–99

"Downtown" (song; Macklemore), 245

Drake (Aubrey Drake Graham), 174, 176, 225

Dr. Dre Presents…the Aftermath (album), 110

Dre. *See* Young, Andre Romell

Dr. Jay's (business), 127, 137

Dropbox, 199, 207

drug trade, 30, 44–46, 50, 64, 93, 142, 238

Dunn, Brian, 165–66, 171, 175

Dupri, Jermaine, 222–23

Durant, Kevin, 241

D'Ussé cognac, 181, 193–94, 197, 219, 286n2

"East Coast/West Coast Killas" (song; Dre and others), 111

Easy Mo Bee (Osten Harvey Jr.), 93

Eazy. *See* Wright, Eric

EMI (label), 68–69

Eminem. *See* Mathers, Marshall

Eminem Show, The (album; Eminem), 144

Empire (TV show), 10, 243

Empire State of Mind (Greenburg), 7, 45, 183, 185

"Empire State of Mind" (song; Jay-Z), 169, 232

"Ether" (song; Nas), 136

Europe, 9, 35, 42, 107, 150

Evans, Faith, 107

Fab 5 Freddy. *See* Brathwaite, Fred

Fahey, William, 179

fashion, hip-hop, 125–33, 137–40, 171, 174

Fass, Lyle, 180–82, 185, 189, 194, 196–98, 286n2, 289n63

Fatback Band, 14

Fat Boys (group), 48–49

Fat Joe (Joseph Antonio Cartagena), 156–57, 243

FBI (Federal Bureau of Investigation), 52–53, 100–101

50 Cent. *See* Jackson, Curtis

financial success, 3–4, 54–56, 64, 70, 77, 97–98, 110, 119–20, 135, 158–59, 191
See also business, hip-hop

Fisher, Curtis "Grandmaster Caz," 9, 17, 19, 23, 25–26, 39, 42–43, 244–45

Flaaten, Tommy "Tommy Tee," 9–10, 149–50, 220–21, 226

Flash. *See* Saddler, Joseph

Flowers, Jonathon Cameron "Grandmaster Flowers," 14, 38

Forbes, Malcolm, 56

Forbes, Steve, 28, 186

Forever (album; Diddy), 115, 121

40/40 Club, 155–56, 212, 218

4:44 (album; Jay-Z), 231

Frank, Sidney, 188

Franklin, Rodolfo "DJ Clark Kent," 64–65, 79, 87

Free, Dave, 215

Freeze (label), 78, 80

Fresh, Doug E., 56–57, 273n43

Frigo (company), 159, 160

Furious Five, 29–30, 39, 43, 107, 268n54
See also Saddler, Joseph

Game, The (Jayceon Terrell Taylor), 158, 203

gangsta rap, 50, 58

Genius (company), 206–7

Get Down, The (Netflix miniseries), 244–45

Get Him to the Greek (film), 146

Get Rich or Die Tryin' (album; 50 Cent), 141, 144–45

G-funk (subgenre), 72

Gibson, Tyrese, 3

Gilbert, Dan, 208

Glacéau (company), 152–53, 201

Glover, Melvin "Melle Mel," 17–18, 43, 245

Index

Good Kid, M.A.A.D. City (album; Lamar), 215

Gore, Tipper, 70

graffiti street art, 18–19, 20, 37, 234

Grandwizzard Theodore. *See* Livingston, Theodore

Gray, F. Gary, 96

Grey Goose vodka, 182, 188, 193, 236

Griffin, Verna, 31, 132–33

Griffin, Warren "Warren G," 32

Griffin, William, 32

G-Unit (label), 151

Hagar, Sammy, 140, 195

Haggerty, Benjamin "Macklemore," 245

Hamadeh, Sam, 176

Hamilton (Broadway show), 10, 20–21

Hamilton, Alexander, 20–21

Hardy, Antonio "Big Daddy Kane," 45, 63, 88, 92–93

Haring, Keith, 8, 37

Harrell, Andre, 55, 57, 62, 67–68, 88, 109, 128, 145

Harris, Calvin, 219–20

Harry, Debbie, 41, 269n4

Heavy D. *See* Myers, Dwight

Heller, Jerry, 50–51, 53, 70–71, 86

Henderson, Jocko, 14

Herc. *See* Campbell, Clive

Hilfiger, Tommy, 131, 174

hip-hop genre
  aspiration and, 9, 77, 108, 140
  as mainstream, 30–31, 42, 54, 56, 65, 244
  naming of, 14, 38, 266
  subgenres of, 72, 158, 192

Hip-Hop Is Dead (album; Nas), 205

Hirst, Damien, 234, 238

"Hit 'em Up" (song; Tupac), 90, 99

Hocking, Brent, 195

Holloway, Anthony "DJ Hollywood," 14, 15, 23–24, 28, 30

Hope, Bob, 88

Horowitz, Ben, 207

"How to Rob" (song; 50 Cent), 143

HTC (company), 171–72, 175, 178–79

Hublot (company), 192–93

Hustler's Convention (album; Nuriddin), 14

"Hypnotize" (song; Biggie), 273n43

Iceberg (company), 128

Ice Cube. *See* Jackson, O'Shea

Ice-T. *See* Morrow, Tracy

Iconix (company), 138, 242

"I Declare War" concert (Jay-Z), 158

"I Got a Story to Tell" (song; Biggie), 89

"I'll Be Missing You" (song; Diddy), 107

Illmatic (album; Nas), 65, 135, 205

"I'm Bad" (song; LL Cool J), 56

"In da Club" (song; 50 Cent), 144, 165

In My Lifetime, Vol. 1 (album; Jay-Z), 118

Interscope Records, 71, 73, 89, 97–99, 110, 135, 144, 164, 170, 174, 215

Iovine, Jimmy, 71–73, 86, 89, 111–12, 135, 174, 216–17, 240
  Beats and, 6, 163–66, 171–72, 176–78, 213–14

Irby, DeHaven, 44–45, 46

Island Def Jam (company), 157–58

"It's Like That/Sucker MCs" (single; Run-D.M.C.), 48

"It's the Hard Knock Life," 119 (song; Jay-Z)

I Want to Work for Diddy (TV show; Diddy), 146, 173

Jackson, Curtis "50 Cent," 6, 141–45, 147, 165, 213, 280n5
  businesses of, 150–53, 159–61, 171, 201, 236

Jackson, Henry "Big Bank Hank," 25, 245

Jackson, Janet, 173

Jackson, Jayson, 120–21

Jackson, Michael, 55, 111

Jackson, O'Shea "Ice Cube," 50–51, 53, 69–71, 96, 134, 176, 182, 241

Jadakiss (Jason Phillips), 77

James, LeBron, 151, 164, 170

Jay-Z. *See* Carter, Shawn

Jay-Z: Unplugged (album), 153–54

Jaz-O. *See* Burks, Jonathan

J. Cole (Jermaine Lamarr Cole), 219, 242, 244

"Jigga That Nigga" (song; Jay-Z), 273n43

Jimmy Iovine and Andre Young Academy for Arts, Technology, and the Business of Innovation, 240

Jimmy Jazz (business), 127, 137

Jobs, Steve, 7, 124, 177, 190, 216

Jodeci (group), 62–63, 67

Johnson, Magic, 106

Jonas, Nick, 219, 231

Index

Jones, Kidada, 99
Jones, Nasir "Nas," 65, 105–208, 111, 121,
    135–37, 158, 176, 205–8, 231, 280n5
Jones, Pete "DJ," 23–24, 34
Juice (film), 99
"Juicy" (song; Biggie), 13, 77, 86

Kalenna (Kalenna Harper), 174
Kallman, Craig, 6, 157
Kaws (Brian Donnelly), 235
Kelis (Kelis Rogers), 205
Kellwood (company), 137–38
Kent. *See* Franklin, Rodolfo
Keys, Alicia, 169, 219–20, 228, 234
Khezrie, James, 127–28
Kidd, Jason, 212, 218
King, Rodney, 72
Kingdom Come (album; Jay-Z), 166
Knight, Marion "Suge," 81–82, 110, 128
    rap wars and, 85–90, 93–97, 99–102
    violence of, 70–71, 81, 85–87, 94–97,
    101–2
Knopper, Steve, 168
Knowles, Beyoncé, 156–57, 167, 169, 186,
    219–20, 228–29, 231, 278n8
Kool Moe Dee (Mohandas Dewese), 88, 245
Kraftwerk, 19, 165
KRS-One. *See* Parker, Lawrence
Krush Groove (film), 49
Kurtis Blow. *See* Walker, Kurt
Kutcher, Ashton, 206
Kuti, Fela, 18, 19

"La Di Da Di" (song; Fresh and Slick
    Rick), 273n43
Lady Gaga (Stefani Joanne Angelina
    Germanotta), 170, 199, 224
LaFranco, Rob, 113–18
Lamar, Kendrick, 6, 8, 214–15
Lane, Dick "Night Train," 285n23
Last Train to Paris (album; Diddy), 173–74
"Lean Back" (song; Fat Joe), 157
Lee, Kevin, 164, 173
Lee, Noel, 6, 162–66, 170–79
Legend, John, 199, 200
Legends of the Summer tour (Jay-Z and
    Timberlake), 169
Leibovitz, Annie, 131
Lemonade (album; Beyoncé), 229

LeSutra (beverage), 191–92
Leviston, Lastonia, 160
Levy, Morris, 25
Lewis, Cara, 47–48
Lewis, Ryan, 245
Life After Death (album; Biggie), 103
Life of Pablo, The (album; West), 228–29
lifestyle, hip-hop, 4–6, 60, 81–82, 163, 171
    of Diddy, 114–18, 188, 191
    of Jay-Z, 118–19, 154, 192–93
Lightnin' Rod. *See* Nuriddin, Jalal
Lighty, Chris, 150–53, 159
Li Ka-shing, 140, 223
Liles, Kevin, 8, 10–11, 137, 157, 243
Lil Wayne (Dwayne Michael Carter Jr.),
    174, 219–20, 231
Little, Earl, 187, 287n23
Live Nation (company), 167–70, 242, 248
Livingston, Joe, 24–25
Livingston, Theodore "Grandwizzard
    Theodore," 8, 19–20, 42, 245–46
LL Cool J. *See* Smith, James
"Lodi Dodi" (song; Snoop), 273n43
Long Road Outta Compton (Verna Griffin), 31
Lopez, Jennifer, 121–22
Lovebug Starski. *See* Smith, Kevin
Lowe, Zane, 224
Lucas, Frank, 21, 23
Ludacris (Christopher Brian Bridges), 171,
    191–92, 203
Lupe Fiasco (Wasalu Muhammad Jaco), 158
luxury rap (subgenre), 192

Mack, Craig, 77
Macklemore. *See* Haggerty, Benjamin
Macy's, 131, 137–39
Madonna, 168, 219, 228
Magna Carta...Holy Grail (album; Jay-Z), 241
Making the Band (TV show; Diddy),
    145–46, 173
Mannion, Jonathan, 78–79, 118, 241
Marbury, Stephon, 156
Marcy Media LLC, 242–43
Marshall Mathers LP (album; Eminem), 133
Martin, Chris, 220
Martin, Christopher "DJ Premier," 79,
    119, 129
Martin, Kenyon, 155
Mase (Mason Durell Betha), 107, 115

Index

Mason, Anthony, 89

Mathers, Marshall "Eminem," 6, 112–13, 133–34, 137, 143–44, 176, 208, 213, 277n19

MCA Records, 99

McDaniels, Darryl "D.M.C.," 48
See also Run-D.M.C.

McGrady, Tracy, 155

MC Hammer (Stanley Kirk Burrell), 65

MC Serch. *See* Berrin, Michael

McSherry, Mike, 202

MC Solaar (Claude M'Barali), 9

Meek Mill (Robert Rihmeek Williams), 219, 231

Meiselas, Kenny, 61–62, 67–68, 76, 89, 130–31, 151, 188, 195, 289n4

Melle Mel. *See* Glover, Melvin

"Message, The" (song; Flash), 17–18, 43, 107

Miller, Percy "Master P," 203

Minaj, Nicki, 170, 191–92, 219, 231

Mizell, Jason "Jam Master Jay," 48

"Moment of Clarity" (song; Jay-Z), 155

Monster Cable, 162, 172, 178–79

Morris, Eddie "Scorpio," 43

Morrison, Dillard, Jr., 21

Morrow, Kevin, 66, 95, 134, 169

Morrow, Tracy "Ice-T," 50, 52, 56

Moses, Robert, 15–16, 18, 27, 40, 128, 241

Mosley, Timothy "Timbaland," 119, 171, 174, 191–92

Moss, Kate, 131

Motsepe, Patrice, 142

Murphy, Eddie, 234–35

Myers, Dwight "Heavy D," 57, 63, 147, 200

"My Name Is" (song; Eminem), 113, 277n19

Myx Moscato (beverage), 191–92

Nas. *See* Jones, Nasir

Nazel, Kim "Arabian Prince," 50–51

Nelly (Cornell Iral Haynes Jr.), 137

Nets (NBA team), 158, 211–13, 218, 241

Nextel, 202–4

Niggaz 4 Life (*Efil4zaggin;* album; N.W.A.), 69

Nike, 137, 151, 178

No Commission art fair, 235, 246–47

"No Diggity" (song; Blackstreet and Dre), 111

Notorious (film), 146, 212

Notorious B.I.G. *See* Wallace, Christopher

No Way Out (album; Diddy), 107, 121

Nunnely, Wayne, 85

Nuriddin, Jalal "Lightnin' Rod," 14, 38

"Nuthin' but a G Thang" (song; Dre), 73

N.W.A. (Niggaz with Attitudes; group), 5, 10, 43, 50–54, 56, 65, 69–72, 240

Oates, John, 291n24

Obama, Barack, 7, 186–87, 200

O'Brien, Guy "Master Gee," 25

Odom, Lamar, 155

O'Malley, Walter, 27

Once Upon a Time in Shaolin (album; Wu-Tang Clan), 237–39, 295n9

O'Neal, Shaquille, 8, 134–35

O'Neill, Paul, 202

On the Run tour (Jay-Z and Beyoncé), 169

Original Flavor (group), 64

"Originators, The" (song; Jaz-O and Jay-Z), 28

"Otis" (song; Jay-Z and West), 192

Outkast (hip-hop duo), 203

Oza, Rohan, 150, 152–53

Paddle8 (auction house), 238, 295n9

Parker, Lawrence "KRS-One," 11, 111

Parker, Sean, 223

"Party and Bullshit" (song; Biggie), 78

"Pass the Courvoisier, Part II" (song; Busta Rhymes), 187

Patterson, Lorenzo "MC Ren," 50–51

Perez, Desiree, 156, 229

Perez, Juan, 156

Phat Farm, 125–28, 132, 137–38

Philips, Chuck, 100–101

Phillips, Randy, 168–70, 214–15

"Picasso Baby" (song; Jay-Z), 246

Pinkett, Jada, 91

pioneers, hip-hop, 8–9, 13–20, 23–26, 28–30, 34–36, 43, 50, 244–46

Pittman, Bob, 55

"Planet Rock" (song; Bambaataa and Soulsonic Force), 42

PolyGram, 30, 42, 65, 119–20

Poole, Russell, 100, 276n52

Porter, Kim, 115

Power (TV show; 50 Cent), 160

Power Broker, The (Caro), 16

Power of the Dollar (album; 50 Cent), 143

Press Play (album; Diddy), 173

Index

Prince (Prince Rogers Nelson), 219, 232
Priority Records, 78, 80
Public Enemy, 43, 55, 65, 66–67, 246
Puff Daddy. *See* Combs, Sean
Puff Daddy and the Family tour, 108
Purpose (album; Bieber), 229
Pynchon, Thomas, 31

Qream liqueur, 191–92
QueensBridge Venture Partners, 207–8
Quiñones, Lee, 40, 42

race factors, 52, 58–59, 66–67, 134
Radio City Music Hall talent show (1983),
    47–48
Raising Hell (album; Run-D.M.C.), 54
Raisin in the Sun, A (film), 146
Rakim (William Michael Griffin), 88
Rapped in Romance (album; World Class
    Wreckin' Cru), 49–50
"Rapper's Delight" (song; Sugarhill Gang),
    9, 15, 25, 245
"Rapture" (song; Blondie), 41
rap wars, Death Row–Bad Boy (1990s), 6,
    85–104, 111, 122, 134–35, 150, 243
    Biggie and, 88–90, 93, 95, 100–103, 107,
    276n52
    Diddy and, 87–90, 93, 100–101
    Knight and, 85–90, 93–97, 99–102
    Tupac and, 87–90, 93–95, 99–103, 107,
    276n52
Ready to Die (album; Biggie), 77, 108
Reasonable Doubt (album; Jay-Z), 78–80, 118
"Recipe, The" (song; Lamar), 215
Reebok, 151–52
Reid, L. A., 158
Revolt (cable network), 106, 239–40
Reznor, Trent, 172
Rhett, Thomas, 219, 231
Richard, Dawn, 174
Rickey, Branch, 212, 292n45
Rihanna (Robyn Rihanna Fenty), 158, 219,
    228, 242
Riley, Teddy, 111
Rivera, Lance "Un," 129–30
Robinson, Jackie, 212, 292n45
Robinson, Joe, 97
Robinson, Leland, 24, 26, 97
Robinson, Sylvia, 24–25, 43, 47, 97

Roc-A-Fella Records, 78–80, 128, 135, 155,
    157–58
Rocawear (company), 126, 128–30, 132,
    137–38, 218, 231, 242
Rock, Chris, 121
Rockefeller, John D., 78, 111
Roc Nation (company), 167–68, 171, 213,
    241–43, 248
Rogers, Ian, 172
Rogness, Roberto, 189
Rosenblum, Jessica, 57–58, 62–63, 66, 80,
    92–94, 109–10, 145
Ross, Rick, 158, 160, 231
Rouzaud, Frédéric, 183
Rubin, Rick, 55
Run-D.M.C. (group), 43, 48, 50, 54–55,
    62–63, 85, 127
Run's House (TV show; Run), 146
Rust, Stephen, 7, 187–91, 195
Ruthless Records, 50–54, 70–71

Saddler, Joseph "Grandmaster Flash,"
    14–15, 17–19, 29–30, 35, 38–39, 41–43,
    107, 244–45, 268n54
Saeter, Kjetil, 221, 228, 229
Saga Continues . . . , The (album; Diddy), 145
Saleh, Anthony, 205–8
Sandberg, Sheryl, 124
Santigold (Santi White), 212, 242
Sauce Money (Todd Gaither), 64
S. Carter sneaker, 151–52, 155
Schmidt, Eric, 185, 196
Schoolly D (Jesse Bonds Weaver Jr.), 50
Scott-Heron, Gil, 14
Sean John clothing, 126, 130–32, 137–39
Seinfeld, Jerry, 117
Sellaeg, Gunnar, 225–26, 228, 230
Shafrazi, Tony, 37–38
Shakur, Afeni, 90, 103
Shakur, Tupac, 6, 43, 45, 47–48, 113,
    213–14, 244, 275n33
    rap wars and, 87–90, 93–95, 99–103, 107,
    276n52
    songs and albums of, 89–90, 99, 273n43
Sha Rock (Sharon Green), 39
Shaw, Todd "Too Short," 64, 102, 132
Shawn Carter Foundation, 193
Shea Stadium, 15–16, 241, 292n4
Shkreli, Martin, 238–39

Index

"Show Me What You Got" (song; Jay-Z), 183–84

Sigel, Beanie, 135

Silverman, Tom, 20, 42–43, 47–48, 55, 77, 97–98

Simmons, Earl "DMX," 119

Simmons, Joseph "Run," 48
   See also Run-D.M.C.

Simmons, Kimora Lee, 138

Simmons, Russell, 5–6, 8, 42, 48–49, 54–55, 80, 85, 109, 151, 243–44
   Def Jam and, 30, 49, 55, 119–20
   as designer, 125–29, 132, 137–40

Sinatra, Frank, 77, 232

Sinni brothers, 130, 132

"6 in the Mornin' " (song; Ice-T), 50

Sleek Audio, 160

Slick Rick (Richard Martin Lloyd Walters), 56, 273n43

Slim Shady LP, The (album; Eminem), 112–13

Sloan, Cle "Bone," 102

Smith, James "LL Cool J," 55–56, 151, 246, 268n49

Smith, Kevin "Lovebug Starski," 8, 13–15, 22–26, 28, 30, 34–36, 38, 43, 244, 268n54

SMS Audio, 159, 171

Snoop. *See* Broadus, Calvin

social issues, 52, 58–59, 65–67, 134

social media, 188, 205–6

"So Ghetto" (song; Jay-Z), 129, 278n8

Soulsonic Force (group), 42

South by Southwest (2014), 105–6, 122–24

Sovereign Brands, 184–85

Spotify, 199, 217, 223–24, 226, 229, 233

Sprint, 204–5, 230–33

Sprite, 147–50, 151, 205

Starski. *See* Smith, Kevin

Stein, Chris, 41

Stettler, Charles, 8, 46–49

"Still D.R.E." (song; Dre), 133

Stillmatic (album; Nas), 137

Sting, 107

Stone, Rob, 8, 68–69, 87–88, 108, 111–12, 156

Stoute, Steve, 121, 185

Straight Outta Compton (album; N.W.A.), 51–52, 75

Straight Outta Compton (film), 10, 51, 71, 96, 102, 240–41, 243

streaming services, 172–73, 216–17, 218–33, 237, 293n24
   See also particular companies

Streets Is Watching (film), 155

Sturgis, Edward "Eddie Cheeba," 24, 30

Sugarhill Gang, 9, 15, 25, 30, 245

Sugar Hill Records, 24–26, 43

Suge. *See* Knight, Marion

Suh, Ndamukong, 241

"Supa Ugly" (song; Jay-Z), 136

SV Angel (company), 207

Swizz Beatz. *See* Dean, Kasseem

"Takeover" (song; Jay-Z), 135–36

Talking Heads, 40–41

Thomaz, Cameron "Wiz Khalifa," 174, 244

Threatt, Nicole, 96

"Thrift Shop" (song; Macklemore and Lewis), 245

Tidal (streaming service), 218–22, 225–31, 243, 248, 293n19

Tidal X concert (Jay-Z), 218–19, 229, 231–32

Timbaland. *See* Mosley, Timothy

Timberlake, Justin, 169, 173, 174

Time Warner, 98–99, 106

Tobiassen, Markus, 221, 229

Tommy Boy (label), 42, 97

Tommy Tee. *See* Flaaten, Tommy

"Too Short." *See* Shaw, Todd

To Pimp a Butterfly (album; Lamar), 215

Tribe Called Quest, A, 149, 151

Trump, Donald, 109, 228, 238

Trump Vodka, 288n48

Tucker, C. DeLores, 98–99

Tupac. *See* Shakur, Tupac

Tupac: Resurrection (documentary), 91–92

2pac vs. Biggie (Weiss), 90

2001 (album; Dre), 133

Tyson, Mike, 141

Uber, 199, 211, 290n27

"U Don't Know" (song; Jay-Z), 219, 231

Universal, 157–58, 164, 167, 172, 228

Universal Hip Hop Museum, 245

Unplugged (MTV series), 153–54

Up in Smoke tour (Dre and Snoop), 169

Uptown Records, 57–58, 61–62, 67–68, 76

urban decline, 15–18, 27, 31, 127–28

Usher (Usher Raymond V), 219, 231

Index

Vanilla Ice (Robert Matthew Van Winkle), 65, 68–69, 87

V.I.M. (business), 127, 137

violence, 10, 66–67, 85–89, 99, 107, 111–13, 121–22, 143
  as lyrical theme, 51–52, 135, 137
  studio gangsters and, 85–86, 88–89, 129–30, 275n33, 278n8
  of Suge, 70–71, 81, 85–87, 94–97, 101–2
  See also rap wars, Death Row–Bad Boy

Vitaminwater, 152–53, 236

Vol. 2 . . . Hard Knock Life (album; Jay-Z), 119

Vol. 3 . . . Life and Times of S. Carter (album; Jay-Z), 129

Wahlberg, Mark, 208–10

Walker, Kurt "Kurtis Blow," 30, 33, 42, 48–49, 147, 244–45

"Walk This Way" (song; Aerosmith), 54, 56

Wallace, Christopher "Notorious B.I.G." (Biggie), 6, 8, 13, 77–79, 83–86, 106–8, 136, 200, 246
  background of, 85–86, 92–93, 281n28
  rap wars and, 88–90, 93, 95, 100–103, 107, 276n52
  songs and albums of, 77–78, 88–89, 103, 108, 273n43

Wallace, John, 155

Wallace, Voletta, 83–85, 92–93, 102–4

Wallach, D. A., 222–24

Warhol, Andy, 37, 39–41, 154, 234

Warner Music Group, 157, 228

"Watch Me" (song; Jay-Z), 129

Watch the Throne (album; Jay-Z and West), 192–93

Watch the Throne tour (Jay-Z and West), 169

Weiss, Jeff, 90, 101

West, Kanye, 47–48, 139, 203, 222–23, 234
  Jay-Z and, 136–37, 158, 169, 192–93, 212, 219, 228–29

"Where You At?" (song; West), 203

White, Jack, 219–20, 228

"Who Am I?" (song; Snoop), 73, 113, 273n43

"Who Shot Ya" (song; Biggie), 88

Wild Style (film), 37, 41–42

Wiley, Kehinde, 235, 247

Will.i.am (William James Adams), 164, 170, 177–78

Williams, Alonzo, 33, 49–50, 54

Williams, Bruce, 94, 97, 100, 144

Williams, Bryan "Birdman," 203

Williams, Pharrell, 191–92, 208, 222–23, 225, 293n11

Wilson, Chenise, 62–63, 65, 77–78, 87, 122

WiMP (company), 221–22, 226, 230

Wintour, Anna, 131, 174

Wiz Khalifa. *See* Thomaz, Cameron

World Class Wreckin' Cru (group), 33, 49–50, 269n28

Wright, Eric "Eazy-E," 50–54, 70–71, 85, 96–97

Wright, Michael "Wonder Mike," 25–26

Wu-Tang Clan (group), 137, 182, 236–39, 246, 295n9

Xzibit (Alvin Nathaniel Joiner), 158

Yetnikoff, Walter, 55

Yo! MTV Raps (TV show; Fab), 37, 56, 74

Young, Andre Romell "Dr. Dre," 49–54, 86–87, 89–90, 102, 110–13, 169, 201, 265n2, 275n41
  Apple and, 3, 177, 224–25
  background of, 5, 10, 31–34, 269n28
  business and, 3–4, 6, 161, 182
  Coachella 2012 and, 213–16
  Death Row and, 6, 71, 94, 96–97, 111
  Diddy and, 112, 174–75
  Fab and, 73–76
  50 Cent and, 143–44, 159
  Jay-Z and, 129, 133
  N.W.A. and, 50–54
  personality of, 4, 7, 33, 133, 170, 215
  as producer, 6, 74–75, 112–13, 133–35, 204, 273n43
  Snoop and, 73–75
  songs and albums of, 72–73, 75, 110–12, 133, 214, 240–41
  Swizz and, 234, 247–48
  violence and, 10, 71, 86, 111
  wealth of, 3, 6, 56, 135
  women and, 33, 71, 111
  See also Beats; Beats Music

Young, Theodore, 31

Zechory, Ilan, 206, 208, 213

About the Author

Zack O'Malley Greenburg is the senior editor of media and entertainment at *Forbes* and has authored two previous books: *Empire State of Mind* (Penguin/Portfolio, 2011), a business-focused biography of Jay-Z, and *Michael Jackson, Inc.* (Simon & Schuster/Atria, 2014), a deep dive into the king of pop's financial realm. Zack graduated from Yale in 2007 with a degree in American Studies and immediately joined the staff at *Forbes,* where his annual Hip-Hop Cash Kings packages gave the genre its first sustained, serious coverage in the mainstream business press. His work has also appeared in the *Washington Post, Billboard, Vibe, McSweeney's,* and *Sports Illustrated.* Zack has served as an expert source for outlets including NPR, BBC, MTV, and CBS's *60 Minutes*; as a speaker, he has appeared at SXSW, CES, TEDx, Harvard, Yale, and others. He lives in New York with his wife and cats. For more, follow him on social media (@zogblog) and visit his website (zogreenburg.com).